Yale Music Masterworks

Sinfonie

mit Schluss - Chor über Schillers Ode: „An die Freude"

für grosses Orchester, 4 Solo - und 4 Chor - Stimmen,

componirt und

SEINER MAJESTAET dem KÖNIG von PREUSSEN

FRIEDRICH WILHELM III.

in tiefster Ehrfurcht zugeeignet

von

Ludwig van Beethoven.

125tes Werk.

Eigenthum der Verleger.

Mainz und Paris,
bey B. Schotts Söhnen. Antwerpen, bey A. Schott?

BEETHOVEN

The Ninth Symphony

REVISED EDITION

———————————— ✃ ————————————

David Benjamin Levy

YALE UNIVERSITY PRESS
NEW HAVEN AND LONDON

Frontispiece: Title page of Beethoven's Ninth Symphony, first edition (1826). Courtesy Sibley Music Library, Eastman School of Music of the University of Rochester.

Revised edition published in 2003 by Yale University Press
Originally published in 1995 by Schirmer Books

Printed in the United States of America

Library of Congress Control Number: 2003104452
ISBN 0-300-09964-9 (pbk. : alk. paper)

A catalogue record for this book is available from the British Library.

The paper in this book meets the guidelines for permanence and durability of the Committee on Production Guidelines for Book Longevity of the Council on Library Resources.

10 9 8 7 6 5 4 3 2 1

To Kathy, Jesse, and Rebecca

Contents

Foreword

⸎

The Yale Music Masterworks series is devoted to the examination of single works, or groups of works, that have changed the course of Western music by virtue of their greatness. Some were recognized as masterpieces immediately upon creation. Others lay in obscurity for decades, to be uncovered and revered only by later generations. With the passage of time, however, all have emerged as cultural landmarks.

The Masterworks volumes are written by specialists—historians and performers—who bring to their accounts the latest discoveries of modern scholarship. They examine the political, economic, and cultural background of the works. They consider such matters as genesis, reception, influence, and performance practices. But most importantly, they explore the music itself and attempt to pinpoint the qualities that make it transcendent. The result is a series of comprehensive, engaging books that will be of interest to students, performers, scholars, and devotees alike.

It is altogether appropriate to include David Benjamin Levy's *Beethoven: The Ninth Symphony* in the first group of Masterworks volumes. Over the years, no other work has been used as frequently in an emblematic role, to christen music halls, to mark the beginning of concert seasons, or to celebrate crucial political events. Let us use it here to celebrate the beginning of a new literary project.

Even for Beethoven, the Ninth Symphony was a signal accomplishment, the most ambitious work in a series of pieces that changed forever the concept of the symphony. The Ninth required a gestation period of almost thirty years, beginning with Beethoven's initial consideration of Schiller's "An die Freude" in the 1790s, continuing with his first sketches of 1815, and ending with his completed score of 1824. Significantly, it was also the composer's last word in the realm of the symphony, since plans for the Tenth— or what seems to have been the Tenth—remained in sketch form.

In the Ninth, even more than in *Fidelio,* Beethoven set forth a visionary credo for humankind, for its "rescue from the chains of the tyrants." The work represents a forceful voice for Romantic aspirations, as expressed with such deep fervor in Schiller's famous ode. During World War II, Beethoven's Fifth Symphony was associated with "Victory" by Allied soldiers, who linked the short-short-short-long rhythm of its opening motive with the international Morse code symbol for "V," dot-dot-dot-dash. No translation from code is necessary for the Ninth: triumph is there for all to hear, in the music and the vocal exclamations of the choral finale.

The Ninth is an epic, revolutionary work. Within its extended time frame, one traverses the many plains of Beethoven's compositional landscape: demonic conflict (the opening *Allegro*), tempestuous contrasts (the scherzo), ethereal reflection (the *Adagio*), and unabashed exuberance (the finale). In the last movement, Beethoven symbolically broke not only the chains of tyrants, but those of instrumental music as well, moving out of E. T. A. Hoffmann's abstract realm of "pure expression" and into the world of the vocal symphony. The immense mixed forces of the Ninth prepared the way for the changes that took place in the symphonic repertory in the next hundred and fifty years, from Berlioz to Mahler to Berio.

Even before the Ninth had sounded, its importance was recognized by Beethoven's aristocratic followers, who petitioned the composer to keep the first performance in Vienna rather than to take it to Berlin (as he had threatened to do). From then on, it was accorded a special place in the pantheon of masterpieces, as demonstrated by Leonard Bernstein's performance to celebrate the fall of the Berlin Wall and the end of the Cold War.

But the Ninth also has a controversial side, for while it has inspired admiration it has also incurred disdain. Already at the initial performances in London in 1825 critics spoke of "crude, wild, and extraneous harmonies" and "noisy extravagance . . . and outrageous clamor." Seventy years later, Bernard Shaw wrote begrudgingly that Beethoven's finale was "at least better than an oratorio." And in our own time, the feminist music historian Susan McClary has interpreted the tonal violence of the Ninth as a male assault, the "throttling murderous rage of a rapist." The jury has not been unanimous in its verdict on Beethoven's work. After one hundred and seventy years, that jury continues to deliberate, often quite heatedly.

It is into this world of elation and contention that David Benjamin Levy takes us in his spirited, panoramic survey of the Ninth. He begins in the present, with the Ninth as established cultural icon, before leading us back in time to show how the work attained its exalted status. He scrutinizes the complex stages of the compositional process, discusses the critical events in the music, and describes the initial performances and the early reactions of Viennese and foreign audiences. He concludes by looking at the lengthy shadow that the symphony has cast on composers after Beethoven.

Levy has written an engrossing book, one that expands our view of the Ninth and helps us to appreciate the dimensions of its greatness. We see the Ninth as a work of drama and conflict, of ecstasy and hope. In Levy's account, it emerges as an extraordinary and universal music masterwork indeed.

George B. Stauffer
Series Editor

Beethoven: The Ninth Symphony

Introduction

$\mathscr{I}$clearly recall the first time I saw a score of the Ninth Symphony. At least once a week, my friends and I made a pilgrimage from New York City's High School of Music and Art to the Donnell Branch of the New York Public Library on West 53rd Street. Here we would borrow LPs of musical compositions with which we wished to become more familiar. Having selected our recording of the week, we made our way over to East 58th Street—in those days the site of the NYPL's Music Branch—in order to borrow printed music to go along with our newly acquired recording.

Being a novice at score reading, I came to learn the Beethoven symphonies through Liszt's transcriptions for piano. Even then, I sensed that the Ninth Symphony was a special case, a masterpiece *sui generis*. Upon opening the well-worn piano score, I was struck by an annotation in one of the margins inscribed by a previous (and, presumably, older and wiser) borrower. The passage in question was the explosive recapitulation of the scherzo, and the annotation read: "ALL HELL BREAKS LOOSE!" Thinking back on those days, only one question still haunts me; why the annotator didn't write the same comment at the recapitulation of the first movement.[1] Readers of the volume now lying open before you are asked to try to capture the curiosity of that eager young student and the enthusiasm of the anonymous annotator.

The issues raised by the Ninth Symphony are virtually limitless. While no single volume can address every aspect of such a major work, it can at least give the reader a good start along what ultimately is a journey of self-discovery. I am aware that people will come to the piece and this book with varying backgrounds and interests. Any chapter may be read apart from the others. A reading of the analytical chapters (3 and 4) will yield the maximum benefit with a copy of a score or transcription of the piece at hand. Even with these chapters, the reader may elect to study the movements out of order. Virtually any edition of the score will suffice, although the student should be forewarned that all editions—including the recently

published *Urtext* edition edited by Jonathan Del Mar (Bärenreiter, 1996)—
contain errors and discrepancies regarding pitches, articulations, and metronome markings (this issue will be addressed more fully in chapter 7).
Some editions (e.g., Dover) do not provide measure numbers at all, while
others do not use consecutive measure numbers for the finale, and I suggest that in these cases the reader either supply his own measure numbers
or make the appropriate adjustment. If the reader is planning to purchase a
full score, I recommend obtaining either the Del Mar edition (available in
paperback and study score formats) or the Goldmann-Schott edition, with
an excellent Introduction and Analysis (in German) by Dieter Rexroth.[2]

Chapter 1 examines Schiller's "An die Freude" and Beethoven's symphony from the perspective of the intellectual climate of the times in which
these artistic works first appeared (1785 and 1824, respectively), as well as
from some contemporary points of view. In chapter 2 the reader may trace
the compositional evolution of the Ninth through a survey of the extant
sketches, as well as assess the impact of the Choral Fantasy and *Fidelio* on
the finale's character and structure. Chapter 5 deals with issues relating to
the first performances of the Ninth, while chapter 6 traces how the Ninth
was received in subsequent years, including its impact on later composers.
Those readers who are primarily interested in performance issues may
wish to begin with chapter 7 and the discography that follows.

Many colleagues and friends have provided assistance invaluable in
preparing a book of this scope. I wish to thank George B. Stauffer and
Maribeth Anderson Payne for encouraging me to write a comprehensive
book on the Ninth Symphony. I also wish to thank William Meredith and
Patricia Elliott of the Ira F. Brilliant Center for Beethoven Studies in San
Jose, California for their cooperation and hospitality; Stewart A. Carter,
Aubrey S. Garlington Jr., Ken Fradin, and Christopher Gibbs for their care-
ful reading of early drafts of many chapters and their encouragement;
J. Alfred Martin and Jeff Kinlaw for their advice on theological issues; Jeff
Snedeker, Charles Waddell, and William Shaeffer for information about the
horn in Beethoven's Vienna; and Jurgen Thym and Ralph Locke, whose
support of my research dates to my earliest scholarly involvement with the
Ninth Symphony. Aspects of my research and the preparation of the discography were assisted by a grant from Wake Forest's Research and Creative Arts Fund (RECREAC), and I thank Julie B. Cole, former Director of
the Office of Research and Sponsored Programs at Wake Forest for her
enthusiastic support. Thanks also to the staff of Wake Forest's Z. Smith

Reynolds Library for their help and patience, and to the Music Division of
the Staatsbibliothek zu Berlin–Preußischer Kulturbesitz, Alessandra Comini, and the Sibley Music Library (Rochester, N.Y.) for assistance with pho-
tographic materials. A special acknowledgement also is due to my students, on whom I tested my analysis of the finale of the Ninth Symphony,
and who in return offered valuable suggestions.

George Stauffer's advice to me that there is no such thing as a "last
word" on a great work of art certainly has rung true in the years since I first
wrote my study of the Ninth Symphony. Several scholars (Nicholas Cook,
Esteban Buch, Andreas Eichhorn, James Parsons, Michael Tusa, and Stephen Hinton) have made useful contributions to our understanding of the
work in the form of monographs and articles. New recordings, both on
period and modern instruments, have appeared. Indeed, thanks to the generosity of Wake Forest University's "Year of the Arts," I was privileged to
conduct a performance of the Ninth on March 2, 1977, as part of a symposium and festival I organized entitled "Joy's Legacy." I thank my Wake
Forest colleagues, students, and fellow Beethoven scholars William Meredith, Ora Frischberg Saloman, and Owen Jander who helped make this
event a success and an ongoing part of my Ninth Symphony journey.

Audiences have sought to transcend the tragic events of September 11,
2001, through attendance at commemorative performances of the Ninth—a
continuation of a long-standing tradition associated with this work. As
mentioned above, an important—if problematic—new *Urtext* edition has
been published and widely adopted by conductors. Readers will find my
references to many of these recent contributions throughout the Yale edition (the *Urtext* edition of the Ninth is discussed at greatest length in chapter 7). I offer my thanks again to George Stauffer, in this instance for encouraging me to rejuvenate my book. The intervening years have given me
an opportunity to rethink several issues surrounding the Ninth Symphony.
While I find that I stand by most of what I wrote, I am grateful to Harry
Haskell and the staff of Yale University Press for the opportunity to revise
and expand my text and to correct errors that inevitably find their way into
print. Should any such infelicities—new or old—be discovered in these
pages, the author accepts complete responsibility for them. In addition to
those already mentioned, I wish to thank Dr. Johanna Cobb Biermann of
the Beethoven-Haus Archiv, Bonn, for information regarding early transcriptions, as well as her colleague, Dr. Beate Angelika Kraus, for sharing
much information growing out of her continuing work on her forthcoming

critical edition of the Ninth Symphony. I also am grateful to James Parsons and Mark Evan Bonds for their collegiality and advice.

Readers familiar with the original edition of this book will find the bibliography much expanded and updated.

My final—and deepest—expression of gratitude belongs to my family. My mother, Dorothy, and brother, Stephen could not have been more supportive. The memory of my late father, Marvin—the man who first introduced me to the majesty of Beethoven and his Ninth Symphony—served as a perpetual source of inspiration. My wife, Kathy, and my children, Jesse and Rebecca, all deserve the highest praise for weathering the *Sturm und Drang* that attends a spouse and father engaged in the writing of a book. It was— more than they will ever know—their love and support that saw me through to the end of this project.

Chapter 1

FROM "RESCUE FROM THE CHAINS OF TYRANTS" TO "ALL MEN BECOME BROTHERS": THE WORLD OF THE NINTH

Rettung von Tirannenketten,	Rescue from the chains of tyrants,
Großmut auch dem Bösewicht,	Compassion e'en for the evil sort,
Hoffnung auf den Sterbebetten,	Hope to those who lie on death's bed,
Gnade auf dem Hochgericht!	Mercy from the highest court!

—Friedrich Schiller, original version of "An die Freude" (1785)

The utopian ideals expressed in Schiller's "An die Freude" and in the finale of Beethoven's Ninth Symphony remain unfulfilled, but the hope engendered by these ideals is still very much alive. The end of the Cold War, symbolized by the razing of the Berlin Wall, has raised humanity's collective expectations of a brighter future. On Christmas Day, 1989, the Wall's fall was celebrated in historic fashion, when Leonard Bernstein led a performance of the Ninth Symphony in the Schauspielhaus of what was formerly East Berlin. Bringing together an orchestra, a chorus, and soloists from both sides of the defunct Iron Curtain, Bernstein decided that the occasion was a "heaven-sent moment," one that justified the substitution of the word "freedom" ("Freiheit") for the "joy" ("Freude") of Schiller's poem. The solemn yet jubilant concert was broadcast worldwide via television and radio, with subsequent distribution via videotape and recording.

It is unlikely that Bernstein realized some of the ironies surrounding his alteration of Schiller's poem. Just six months earlier, for example, the following report had come across the wires from Beijing:

> Soldiers advanced down Changan Avenue . . . but tens of thousands of students and others poured out into the street to stop them in front of the Beijing Hotel, several hundred yards east of [Tiananmen] Square. The middle of the square remained calm, with the "Ode to Joy" from Beethoven's Ninth Symphony blaring over the students' loudspeakers.[1]

The students in China no doubt believed that they, too, had experienced a "heaven-sent moment." The arrival of the army the next day, however, was a cruel reminder that even the joyous finale of the Ninth Symphony begins with a fierce dissonance.

Some politicians have proclaimed that a "new world order" has been established in the wake of the events of 1989 and the subsequent dissolution of the Soviet Union. But since then the world has witnessed savage ethnic warfare in Eastern Europe and horrific tribal bloodshed in Africa. Nationalistic xenophobia has found a new lease on life in Germany, even as memories of the Holocaust remain vivid in the minds and bodies of so many of its victims. Racial tension in the United States continues to run high, and a truly color-blind society remains a distant dream. Even as Europe has moved closer toward economic unification and eastward expansion, the tragedy of September 11, 2001, and subsequent events have reminded us that the world as a whole still has far to go if the idealized goal of the brotherhood of mankind is to be realized. *Alle Menschen werden Brüder*—expressed so forcefully in Schiller's poem and Beethoven's finale— remains a remote dream. If anything, people are seeking justification for a host of sins behind the façade of a narrow-minded allegiance to a given and particularized faith system. Balkanization, not universalism, is the theme of the day. But no politician, terrorist, army, or spiritual leader has relieved the tension that holds the world in its grip, and no work of art has yet appeared to supercede the Ninth Symphony's lofty vision.

Surely the most strikingly symbolic performance of the Ninth Symphony since the fall of the Berlin Wall in 1989 took place at the Mauthausen Concentration Camp in Austria on the evening of May 7, 2000 (the 177th anniversary of the work's premiere). On this occasion Simon Rattle led the

Vienna Philharmonic Orchestra before an invited audience (members of the Schwartz-Blau coalition, including Chancellor Wolfgang Schüssel and Freedom Party leader Jörg Haider, were pointedly not invited). The event was televised nationally on ORF. This gesture of reconciliation and atonement achieved its most poignant moment not during the playing of the music, but in the moment that immediately followed. As the final joyful notes reverberated throughout that horrible monument to fanaticism and death, the television camera panned out on an audience seated in total and deafening silence, each member bearing a lit candle. The effect was stunning. The multiple irony of this moment was almost too obvious.

Deep divisions also exist in the artistic arena. For example, when the pop singer Michael Jackson included a sixty-seven-second segment from the finale of the Ninth Symphony in "Will You Be There" on his album, *Dangerous,* the consequence was not universal approbation but a multi-million-dollar lawsuit filed on behalf of the Cleveland Orchestra, whose "unique" interpretation under George Szell had been used without permission. Never has the gulf between popular and art culture seemed wider.

It is unreasonable to expect that a mere piece of music could have the power to bring redemption to a troubled world, although the Ninth Symphony probably has come as close to reaching this goal as any work ever composed. But has this anthem of universal brotherhood at the same time fostered an unrealistic, unattainable, and perhaps even undesirable illusion? Has the Ninth Symphony lost its capacity to inspire people in a world that is so filled with violence and hatred that people's senses have become dulled? Has it been trivialized by overexposure (one recalls, for instance, the use of the scherzo as the theme for the Huntley-Brinkley evening newscast on NBC) and the forces of the commercial marketplace?

When one encounters a performance of Beethoven's *Sinfonie Nr. 9 mit Schlußchor über Schillers Lied "An die Freude" für Orchester, vier Solostimmen und Chor, op. 125* (to give the work its full citation), the enthusiastic response it continues to elicit argues eloquently for its ongoing power and relevance. And the cheers it evokes have not been limited to those of Western audiences. The opening of Tokyo's Kokugikan Hall, a Sumo wrestling palace, in 1985 was marked not with an athletic event, but with a performance of *Daiku*—"The Big Nine"—with two symphony orchestras and a chorus of more than five thousand voices. Indeed, no fewer than one hundred and sixty-two performances of the Ninth Symphony were given throughout Japan during the month of December 1991! *Daiku* has become for the Japanese at year's end what Handel's *Messiah* has become in the West during the Christmas and Easter seasons.

A reason for the Ninth's universal appeal, one suspects, is that an individual need not profess allegiance to "one true faith" or nation in order to be embraced by its message. The lofty, but nonspecific religiosity present in Schiller's poem, enhanced by Beethoven's even loftier music, embraces the "millions" of the world without the slightest hint of exclusivity. The popular cast of the "Freude" tune itself is a self-conscious affirmation of this universality. The Ninth Symphony, consequently, is a welcome guest everywhere, and it has become the ideal symbol for international, interfaith, and interracial events. A further example of such usage has been the ongoing performance of the "Ode to Joy" at Olympic Games, none, perhaps, more vivid than the televised transcontinental simulcast under the direction of Seiji Ozawa at the 1998 Winter Games in Nagano.[2] Only the most cynical of listeners can walk away from a performance of the Ninth Symphony without sensing that all *could* be well with the world, *if* only the world wished it so.

How did this symphony rise to its exalted status? The road that led to the Ninth's eventual triumph was not an easy one, as later chapters will reveal. In one sense, its honored place was almost literally carved in stone in 1872 when Richard Wagner performed it at the ceremony for the laying the foundation of the Festspielhaus in Bayreuth. The opening of the Vienna Secession Exhibition of 1902 with Max Klinger's famous statue and the frieze by Gustav Klimt (Plate 1–1), accompanied by a performance of Mahler's arrangement of the choral finale, was another ritualistic event that helped to magnify the Ninth Symphony's fame. As the following chapters will demonstrate, both the Beethoven myth and the legend of the Ninth Symphony loom large in our collective imagination. As is the case with all myths and legends, the lore surrounding the Ninth Symphony has its roots in shared human experience.

SCHILLER'S POEM AND BEETHOVEN'S SYMPHONY

"An die Freude," written in 1785 and published the following year, was Schiller's enthusiastic expression of elation on joining the friendly circle

Plate 1–1. Gustav Klimt, *Beethoven Frieze,* detail from Panel III: "The Longing for Happiness Finds Surcease in Poetry." This panel was inspired by the passage, "Seid umschlungen, Millionen!" Courtesy Alessandra Comini.

of the jurist Christian Gottfried Körner in Dresden after having spent a frustrating, if productive, year in Mannheim as a theater poet. Although Schiller had completed *Kabale und Liebe, Fiesko,* and much of *Don Carlos,* he was relieved to escape from the politics that accompanied the Mannheim theater. Despite the popularity that "An die Freude" has achieved, history has judged it to be one of Schiller's poorer creations.[3] Even Schiller himself, later in life, reached a point where he no longer was able to identify with it, as is clear from his letter to Körner of October 21, 1800:

> "Die Freude" is . . . I now feel, entirely flawed. Even though it occasionally impresses by dint of a certain fire of expression, it still remains a bad poem and represents a stage of my development that I since have left behind in order to produce something respectable. But because it corresponded with the flawed taste of its time, it has achieved an honor tantamount to a folk poem.[4]

"An die Freude" is an example of a *geselliges Lied,* or social song, an eighteenth-century category of poetry that lent itself to musical setting.[5] The author of a *geselliges Lied* expected the poem to be sung by a company of friends with glasses in hand, hence its mood of intoxication as well as its structural division into stanzas and choruses. Two versions of "An die Freude" were published during Schiller's lifetime. The original version was published in the second volume of Schiller's journal, *Thalia,* in 1786. A slightly revised and shortened version of the poem was issued in 1803. Figure 1–1 presents the entire text of the 1803 revision, the version of "An die Freude" upon which Beethoven based his finale. Beethoven, whose interest in "An die Freude" dates from at least as early as 1792, knew both versions of the poem, as also evidenced by his choice of "run" (*laufet*) from the original version instead of "travel" (*wandelt*) found in the revised version. Words given in brackets in Figure 1–1 denote the original version of "An die Freude." Alterations in spelling or other changes in orthography are not indicated.

One can understand how the mature Schiller might have been embarrassed by some of the excessive imagery in "An die Freude." It is important to bear in mind, however, that the poem is an Enlightenment document, filled with the hopes and expectations of an era that had yet to suffer the disappointment and disillusionment of the French Revolution, the Reign of Terror, and the Napoleonic era. The fact that its "certain fire of expression"

FIGURE 1–1
"AN DIE FREUDE" (1803 REVISION)

Freude, schöner Götterfunken,	Joy, beauteous spark of divinity,
Tochter aus Elysium,	Daughter of Elysium,
Wir betreten feuertrunken,	We enter drunk with fire,
Himmlische, dein Heiligtum!	Heavenly one, your sanctuary!
Deine Zauber binden wieder,	Your magic power reunites
Was die Mode streng [der	All that custom has rudely
Mode Schwerd] getheilt;	[custom's sword has] divided;
Alle Menschen werden Brüder	All men become brothers
[Bettler werden Fürstenbrüder,]	[Beggars become brothers of princes,]
Wo dein sanfter Flügel weilt.	Where your gentle wing abides.

Chor	Chorus
Seid umschlungen Millionen!	Be embraced you millions!
Diesen Kuß der ganzen Welt!	This kiss is for the entire world!
Brüder—überm Sternenzelt	Brothers—over the starry canopy
Muß ein lieber Vater wohnen.	A beloved father must dwell.

Wem der große Wurf gelungen,	Whoever has been fortunate enough
Eines Freundes Freund zu sein,	To be the friend of a friend,
Wer ein holdes Weib errungen,	He who has won a lovely wife,
Mische seinen Jubel ein!	Add his jubilation!
Ja—wer auch nur eine Seele	Yes—whoever even one soul
Sein nennt auf dem Erdenrund!	Can call his own in the earthly round!

Und wer's nie gekonnt, der stehle	And he who never could, should steal
Weinend sich aus diesem Bund!	Weeping from this fellowship!

Chor	Chorus
Was den großen Ring bewohnet	Let those who reside within the great ring
Huldige der Sympathie!	Give honor to Sympathy!
Zu den Sternen leitet sie,	She leads to the stars,
Wo der Unbekannte thronet.	Where the Unknown is enthroned.

Freude trinken alle Wesen	All beings drink joy
An den Brüsten der Natur,	At the breasts of Nature,

Alle Guten, Alle Bösen	All things good, all things evil
Folgen ihrer Rosenspur.	Follow her rosy trail.
Küße gab sie uns und Reben,	Kisses she gave us and wine,
Einen Freund, geprüft im Tod;	A friend, proven even in death;
Wollust ward dem Wurm gegeben,	Ecstasy was granted even to the worm,
Und der Cherub steht vor Gott.	And the cherub stands before God.

Chor	Chorus
Ihr stürzt nieder Millionen?	Do you prostrate yourselves you millions?
Ahndest du den Schöpfer, Welt?	Do you sense the Creator, world?
Such ihn überm Sternenzelt	Seek him beyond the starry canopy!
Über Sternen muß er wohnen.	Beyond the stars he surely must dwell!

Freude heißt die starke Feder	Joy is named the strong watchspring
In der ewigen Natur.	In the eternal Nature.
Freude, Freude treibt die Räder	Joy, joy drives the wheels
In der großen Weltenuhr.	In the universal clockwork.
Blumen lockt sie aus den Keimen,	Flowers she lures from their seeds,
Sonnen aus dem Firmament,	Suns from the firmament,
Sphären rollt sie in den Räumen	Spheres she rolls in the expanses
Die des Sehers Rohr nicht kennt.	Unknown to the viewer's glass.

Chor	Chorus
Froh, wie seine Sonnen fliegen	Happily, as his suns fly
Durch des Himmels prächtgen Plan,	Through Heaven's splendid firmament,
Wandelt [Laufet] Brüder, eure Bahn,	Travel [Run], Brothers, your course,
Freudig, wie ein Held zum siegen.	Joyfully, like a hero towards victory.

Aus der Wahrheit Feuerspiegel	From the fiery mirror of truth
Lächelt sie den Forscher an.	She smiles at the seeker.
Zu der Tugend steilem Hügel	To Virtue's steep hill
Leitet sie des Dulders Bahn.	She guides the sufferer's path.
Auf des Glaubens Sonnenberge	High atop belief's sunny mountain

Sieht man ihre Fahnen wehn,
Durch den Riß gesprengter Särge
Sie im Chor der Engel stehn.

One sees her banners wave,
Through the rent of coffins burst open
One sees her standing in the choir
of angels.

Chor
Duldet muthig Millionen!
Duldet für die beßre Welt!
Droben überm Sternenzelt
Wird ein großer Gott belohnen.

Chorus
Endure bravely you Millions!
Endure for the better word!
There above the starry canopy
A great God shall reward you.

Göttern kann man nicht vergelten,
schön ist's ihnen gleich zu sein.
Gram und Armuth soll sich melden,
mit den Frohnen sich erfreun.
Groll und Rache sei vergessen,

One can never repay Gods,
Lovely is it to be like them!
Sorrow and want should enlist,
With the happy to be joyful.
Let anger and vengeance be
forgotten,

Unserm Todfeind sei verziehn,
Keine Thräne soll ihn pressen,
Keine Reue nage ihn.

Our deadly enemy forgiven,
No tears shall oppress him,
No regrets torment the soul.

Chor
Unser Schuldbuch sei vernichtet!
Ausgesöhnt die ganze Welt!
Brüder—überm Sternenzelt
Richtet Gott, wie wir gerichtet.

Chorus
Let our book of sin be negated!
Atonement for the entire world!
Brothers—over the starry canopy
God judges, as we would judge.

Freude sprudelt in Pokalen,
In der Traube goldnem Blut
Trinken Sanftmut Kannibalen,
die Verzeiflung Heldenmut.
Brüder fliegt von euren Sitzen,
Wenn der volle Römer kreist,
Laßt den Schaum zum Himmel
sprützen:
Dieses Glas dem guten Geist!

Joy sparkles in goblets,
In the golden blood of grapes
Cannibals drink gentleness,
Despair takes on heroic pluck.
Brothers up from your places,
When the full glass goes around,
Let the foam now spray to heaven:

This glass to the good spirit!

Chor
Den der Sterne Wirbel loben,
Den des Seraphs Hymne preist,

Chorus
Him the stars' warblings praise,
Him the hymn of the Seraph lauds,

Dieses Glas dem guten Geist,	This glass to the good spirit,
Überm Sternenzelt dort oben!	Beyond the starry canopy above!
Festen Mut in schwerem Leiden,	Certain spirit in heavy sorrows,
Hülfe, wo die Unschuld weint,	Help, where innocence weeps,
Ewigkeit geschwornen Eiden,	Oaths sworn to eternity,
Wahrheit gegen Freund und Feind,	Truth toward friend and foe,
Männerstolz vor Königsthronen,	Manly pride before kingly thrones,
Brüder, gält es Gut und Blut!	Brothers, should it cost life and property!
Dem Verdienste seine Kronen,	To merit its crown,
Untergang der Lügenbrut!	To perfidy its downfall!

Chor	Chorus
Schließt den heilgen Zirkel dichter,	Bring the holy circle closer,
Schwört bei diesem goldnen Wein,	Swear by this golden wine:
Dem Gelübde treu zu sein,	Faithfulness to the vow,
Schwört es bei dem Sternenrichter!	Swear it by the judge of stars!
[Rettung von Tirannenketten,	[Rescue from the chains of tyrants,
Großmut auch dem Bösewicht,	Compassion e'en for the evil sort,
Hoffnung auf den Sterbebetten,	Hope to those who lie on death's bed,
Gnade auf dem Hochgericht!	Mercy from the highest court!
Auch die Todten sollen leben!	Life be granted to those parted!
Brüder trinkt und stimmet ein,	Brothers drink to this accord,
Allen Sündern soll vergeben,	To the sinners grant forgiveness,
Und die Hölle nicht mehr seyn.	And an end to Hell's reward.

Chor	Chorus
Eine heitre Abschiedsstunde!	A most serene departing hour!
Süßen Schlaf im Leichentuch!	Sweet repose in death's own shroud!
Brüder—einen sanften Spruch	Brothers—here's a gentle promise
Aus des Todtenrichters Munde!]	From the eternal judge's mouth!]

—translation by DBL

continued to inspire many—most notably Beethoven—well after its author had abandoned its style is telling.[6] "An die Freude," for all its flaws, gives impassioned expression to an utopian ideal. The content of the poem is consistent with Schiller's belief, articulated in *On the Aesthetic Education of Man* (1795), that a rational and a moral life is attainable only after first achieving the proper aesthetic condition. As Reginald Snell has explained in the introduction to his translation of *On the Aesthetic Education of Man:*

> The aesthetic condition itself has no significance—all it does is to re-store Man to himself, so that he can make of himself what he wills. He is a cipher; but he is capable of becoming anything (Schiller here treats art much as Kant did religion). Sensuous Man, then, must be-come aesthetic Man before he can be moral Man.[7]

"An die Freude" offers a vision of the elements that contribute toward the moral life. Joy, a gift of nature *and* God, is the agency through which the Elysium of antiquity and the heaven of modern man may be reconciled. Joy begins in sensuality (*Küße, Reben, Wollust*), but then becomes a metaphor for the mainspring (*starke Feder*) of a Newtonian mechanistic clockwork universe (*großen Weltenuhr*) that rolls the heavenly spheres in their orbits. Joy in turn evolves into a creative (aesthetic) force that brings forth flowers from their seeds (*Blumen lockt sie aus den Keimen*). Joy's goal, of course, is the state of moral freedom, presided over by a "loving father" (*ein lieber Vater*) whose throne lies beyond the starry canopy (*überm Sternenzelt*). Despite its obvious imperfections and a less-than-subtle political agenda (one notes the lines "Rescue from the chains of tyrants" and "Beggars become the brothers of princes" in the earlier version of the poem), "An die Freude" is not devoid of structure. Its eighteenth-century readers under-stood full well that the idea of freedom, if not synonymous with joy itself, forms the poem's larger subtext. Freedom, of course, could be interpreted in a purely political sense, especially when one considers the earlier ver-sion of "An die Freude." But according to Schiller's philosophy, articulated more clearly in the less politicized revision of "An die Freude," freedom of any kind must by definition be rooted in morality.

Beethoven, as those familiar with the Ninth Symphony are aware, selected only a small portion of "An die Freude" for use in the work's finale—verses and choruses that concentrate on the sacred and secular manifestations of joy. Freedom that is strongly rooted in morality, however, also was close to the composer's heart. Beethoven's commitment to these ideals is exhibited, for example, in his overture and incidental music for Goethe's *Egmont*, as well as in the opera, *Fidelio*. Beethoven was well read in Schiller, and he also was familiar with the writings of Immanuel Kant. While engaged in the composition of the *Missa solemnis* in 1820, Beethoven jotted down a paraphrase derived from the great German philosopher in his conversation book—a quotation that links Kant with Schiller: "the moral law within us, and the starry heaven above us."[8] Beethoven, indifferent as he may have been throughout his life toward organized religion, and disillusioned as he may have been by the repressive and immoral Austrian politics of the post-Napoleonic era, continued nevertheless to harbor a belief in humankind's moral perfectibility.

Subsequent generations have been more skeptical. In our own time, for example, Schiller's poem and Beethoven's symphony have become the testing ground for curiously divergent, even provocative, theories. Maynard Solomon, for example, has suggested that Schiller's poem and Beethoven's finale are laden with a multitude of hidden meanings:

> With blinding simultaneity, Beethoven's music and Schiller's text offer promise of a variety of extreme states, states that cloak regressive longings in feelings of magical omnipotence: blissful symbiosis with a nurturing preoedipal mother ("All creatures drink joy from Nature's breasts"); oedipal yielding to a forgiving (or punishing) father who must be both sought ("Brothers, above the vault of the stars, there surely dwells a loving Father!") and placated ("Prostrate yourselves, ye multitudes"); a thrusting drive for erotic union ("Drunk with rapture we enter thy sanctuary"); a spartan-heroic homoeroticism ("Hasten, Brothers, on your way, joyfully, like a hero on to victory"); and an undifferentiated, polymorphous love that precipitously erases all distinctions of gender ("Embrace, ye multitudes!/Let this kiss be for all the world!"). Beethoven and Schiller's ecstatic communality here finds its most profoundly compressed image: the band of brothers, God, Elysium's daughter Freude, and the nameless multitudes are all dissolved in a single embrace. Humanity has transcended its differences in a wholesale coalescence. Individuality appears to be at serious risk of annihilation.[9]

It is difficult to escape the sense that Solomon, a psychologist and one of today's most influential Beethoven scholars, is raising issues that might never have occurred to Schiller or Beethoven. His assertion, moreover, that Schiller's deity demands placation changes the poem's interrogative ("Do you prostrate yourselves, you Millions?") to the imperative ("Bow down, you Millions!")—a serious misreading of the text. Schiller's God does not demand that humanity bury its face in humble submission. If, the poet suggests, one truly wishes to sense the presence of his creator, he must raise his sights. This is no literal mapping of the geography of heaven, but rather a metaphor for the direction that will lead human beings to a moral life. In this sense, "An die Freude" is a lesson in aesthetic and moral education. Solomon is correct, however, in noting that Schiller and Beethoven invoke a wide range of imagery and musical styles to symbolize the far-reaching power of joy.[10]

It is also a sign of our own time that Solomon raises the issue of gender distinction. In a recent book, the feminist musicologist Susan McClary has identified Beethoven's music in general, and the Ninth Symphony in particular, as exemplars of the male-oriented and male-dominated culture of Western society.[11] Indeed, the very principles of tension and release inherent in Western harmonic practices and the terms used by theorists (among others, Heinrich Schenker and Arnold Schoenberg) and historians to describe them stand accused by McClary of being rooted in masculine libidinal impulses. In her view, the recapitulation of the first movement of the Ninth Symphony is a "horrifyingly violent" moment, "pockmarked with explosions" and "murderous rage" brought about in part by a deliberate postponement of the resolution of the tonal tensions inherent in the earlier stages of the movement. This "rage" also drives the rest of the symphony, except for the "dialogic" nature and "seductive lure" of the *Adagio,* which McClary characterizes as a "feminine zone" that the opening of the last movement violently rejects. Referring to Adrienne Rich's "The Ninth Symphony of Beethoven Understood at Last as a Sexual Message"—a poem that describes the creator of the Ninth as "A man in terror of impotence / or infertility, not knowing the difference"—McClary has sought to place the Ninth Symphony into the center of a modern polemic about music and gender.[12]

Interestingly enough, McClary raises no objection to the most obvious gender bias of all in Schiller's poem and the Ninth Symphony—the reference to "brothers" and a "loving father" in the finale. That this bias has not gone entirely unnoticed by others, however, is demonstrated by the sexually perverse and misogynistic behavior of the character Alex in *A Clockwork Orange* by Anthony Burgess (a male author!).[13] Alex and his fellow "droogs" may not literally "drink joy at nature's breasts," but the breast-shaped tap at the Korova Milkbar certainly is a source of nourishment for their violent lifestyle. Burgess's Alex, who constantly refers to his companions as "my brothers," takes special delight in the music of Bach, Mozart, and, above all, his favorite "Ludwig van." The finale of the Ninth, in one episode, excites Alex's libido as he "educates" (i.e., rapes) two young girls:

> Then I pulled the lovely Ninth out of its sleeve, so that Ludwig Van [sic] was now nagoy [naked] too, and I set the needle hissing on to the last movement, which was all bliss. There it was then, the bass strings like govoreeting [speaking] away from under my bed at the rest of the orchestra, and then the lovely blissful tune all about Joy being a glorious spark like of heaven, and then I felt the old tigers leap in me and then I leapt on these two young ptitsas ["chicks"]. This time they thought nothing fun and stopped creeching with high mirth, and had to submit to the strange and weird desires of Alexander the Large which, what with the Ninth and the hypo jab, were choodessny [wonderful] and zammechat [remarkable] and very demanding, O my brothers . . .
>
> When the last movement had gone round for the second time with all the banging and creeching about Joy Joy Joy Joy, then these two young ptitsas were not acting the big lady sophisto no more. They were like waking up to what was being done to their malenky [tiny] persons and saying that they wanted to go home and like I was a wild beast.[14]

There is no question that Burgess, a composer as well as a writer, sought to shock the reader by using the Ninth Symphony as the catalyst for such unspeakably horrific behavior. But horror and beauty are subject to the laws of perspective. During Alex's rehabilitation, he is shown a film of Nazis performing atrocities, accompanied by the strains of Beethoven's Fifth Symphony (the Turkish March from the finale of the Ninth Symphony was used in Stanley Kubrick's film of the book). Unable to recognize his own behavior in this, Alex is nauseated by what he sees and hears. " 'That,' I said, very sick. 'Using Ludwig van like that. He did no harm to anyone.

Beethoven just wrote music.'"[15] But therein lies the heart of the problem. Could Wilhelm Furtwängler have similarly deceived himself into thinking that the Ninth Symphony was "just music" as he led a performance of the work at Adolf Hitler's Birthday Concert in Berlin on April 19, 1942?[16] "All things good, all things evil / Follow her rosy trail" wrote Schiller. "Sexual ecstasy is granted even to the worm," Burgess might justifiably chime in. Shocked as one may be by Burgess's, McClary's, or Adrienne Rich's interpretation of Schiller and Beethoven, these readings can no longer be ignored. History has shown all too clearly and often that great art, taken out of context and removed from the intention of its creator, can be used for ill as well as for good. As Alex's doctor tells his patient, "Delimitation is always difficult. The world is one, life is one. The sweetest and most heavenly of activities partake in some measure of violence—the act of love, for instance; music, for instance. You must take your chance, boy. The choice has been all yours."[17]

Great works such as the Ninth Symphony cannot be protected from those who would abuse its immense power. The *Böse* may always be present, but it need not prevail. Power and violence may be related, but they are not synonymous. Furthermore, if the Ninth Symphony is reduced to nothing more than a metaphor for sexuality or political agendas, if "custom" once again is permitted to "rudely divide" what *Freude*'s "magic power reunites," then the work is trivialized into nothing more profound than "Wellington's Victory." When understood and perceived in the spirit of the ennobling forces that motivated its composer, however, the Ninth Symphony has proved itself capable of speaking to the highest aspirations of humanity, of wielding power for the good. Whether or not it will continue to do so in the future remains to be seen. "Heaven-sent moments" come rarely, but they do come.

Chapter 2

THE GENESIS OF THE NINTH

The compositional history of the Ninth Symphony is different from that of any other Beethoven work. Setting it apart, certainly, is the exceptionally long period of time—some thirty-two years—that elapsed between the composer's first tentative ideas for a setting of Schiller's "An die Freude" in 1792 and the eventual fulfillment of that plan in 1824 in a context that even he did not anticipate. The work as we know it represents a synthesis of at least two separate projects: the composition of a symphony in D minor (begun in earnest in 1817 in response to the Philharmonic Society of London's interest in commissioning and premiering new symphonies by Beethoven), and the composer's desire to set "An die Freude" to music. The merging of these two projects occurred sometime in the late months of 1822, near the time when Beethoven reached a firm agreement with the Philharmonic Society.

Beethoven was wary about introducing a vocal component into the genre of the symphony, and he retained his reservations right up to the first performance of the Ninth. And even afterwards, as evidence that surfaced only very recently shows, Beethoven continued to effect minor changes in the work.[1] But while he may have had misgivings about the finale (see chapter 4), these were never serious enough to cause him to retreat from what he had achieved with such strenuous effort. It also is important to bear in mind that the Ninth is the only symphony to emerge from the last decade and a half of Beethoven's life. There is no reason to doubt that if circumstances had been different, Beethoven would not have permitted twelve years to elapse between the composition of his Eighth and Ninth Symphonies. Indeed, evidence shows that Beethoven's interest in the genre after 1812 (the year in which he completed the Eighth) remained keen. But several factors delayed the completion of the Ninth Symphony, and it is impossible to isolate the work from the compositional tendencies of Beethoven's "late" period, despite Maynard Solomon's suggestion that it represents a reversion to the "heroic" style.[2] This is not to say that the Ninth Symphony shares nothing with the composer's earlier works. Several of these compositions—most importantly *Fidelio* and the Choral Fantasy, op. 80—influenced the evolution of the Ninth Symphony in significant ways.

Sketches for the Ninth Symphony

Beethoven used sketchbooks throughout most of his career to jot down fleeting ideas for musical projects as well as for the working out of compositions in greater detail. The pioneer in the study of Beethoven's sketches was Gustav Nottebohm (1817–1882).[3] While Nottebohm was one of the first scholars to show the significance of Beethoven's sketchbooks, more recent scholarship has been devoted to the systematic investigation, restoration, and analysis of these important sources. Thanks to the work of many devoted scholars, a reliable inventory of the extant sketches now exists which has enabled scholars to trace more precisely the compositional histories of most of Beethoven's works.[4]

The precise interpretation of the sketches has proven to be a hazardous branch of research, however. After the composer's death, many of his desk and pocket sketchbooks were lost, sold, or given away as mementos. In certain cases, individual leaves were removed from their original sources, which has made the establishment of reliable chronologies of the sketchbooks extremely difficult. Scholars, therefore, have had to become expert in the identification of ink types, watermarks, stitching patterns, rastrology (the measurement of the staff lines drawn on blank paper with a five-pronged device called a rastrum), and page gatherings, simply to restore these sources to some semblance of their original state. But even with successful reconstruction, the sheer illegibility of many of the sketches has made an accurate transcription a forbidding task. To further complicate matters, it is often difficult—especially in the case of preliminary sketches—to determine just which composition Beethoven may have had in mind when he jotted down seemingly random ideas. The result has often been variant and even contradictory readings for the same sketches. Finally, the overarching question of the ways in which sketches can, and should, be used, continues to be a point of disagreement among some of the scholars who have been most active in investigating these sources.[5] Despite these problems, the sketches provide a fascinating glimpse into the composer's workshop, and it is often as interesting to ponder ideas that Beethoven rejected as it is to watch the progress of the ones that survived his severe critical judgment. As illuminating as it may be to witness Beethoven's mind at work, the sketches cannot fully explain how he arrived at a finished composition.

Studies by Sieghard Brandenburg, Robert Winter, and Jenny L. Kallick have added greatly to our understanding of the Ninth Symphony's evolution.[6] Kallick's dissertation includes a useful chronological survey of the sketch sources for the entire symphony. Table 2–1 summarizes the known sketches of the Ninth.[7] Research on these documents is an ongoing process, however, and this account must be viewed as provisional, at best.

As Table 2–1 indicates, the earliest sketches that bear any relation to the Ninth Symphony are those drafted by Beethoven as early as 1792 in contemplation of setting Schiller's "An die Freude" to music. Had Beethoven fulfilled the plan to set the poem "strophe by strophe," if we are to trust Fischenich's testimony, he would not have been the only composer to have done so. The popular *geselliges Lied* was published in 1786 by Schiller's friend, Christian Gottfried Körner, the jurist and musician for whom the poem was written. Indeed, no fewer than forty settings of "An die Freude" that predate Beethoven's finale have been identified, including ones by Karl Friedrich Zelter (publ. 1792), Johann Dalberg (publ. 1799), Johann Rudolph Zumsteeg (1796), and Franz Schubert (1815).[8] Beethoven's early ideas for a setting of "An die Freude," however, bear no resemblance whatsoever to the final product, as demonstrated by the sketch found in Grasnick 1 (1798–99) shown in Ex. 2–1.[9]

No more recognizable are the entries from the Petter Sketchbook of 1811–12, where one finds among Beethoven's work on the Seventh and Eighth Symphonies the indication "Freude schöner Götterfunken Tochter/ Overture ausarbeiten" along with the notations of Ex. 2–2. These musical

TABLE 2-1
SKETCHES OF THE NINTH SYMPHONY

I. Preliminary Sketches for Setting Schiller's "An die Freude"

1792–93	Bartolomäus Fischenich reports that Beethoven is planning to set "An die Freude" (Fischenich's letter of January 26, 1793, to Charlotte Schiller; Thayer/Forbes, pp. 120–121).
1798–99	First known notations for a setting of "An die Freude," in C Major (Grasnick I, fol. 13r; Winter, pp. 177–178).
1811–12	References to Schiller appear amidst sketches to "Zur Namensfeier" Overture, op. 115 (Grasnick 20a, fol. 1v and Mh 59 [Petter] fols. 42 and 43).

II. Early Sketches (Concept Drafts)

1815–16	Notation of the scherzo theme intended as a fugue subject for a string quintet; possible ideas for other movements (Bonn BSk 12 and BSk7 [SBH 704 and 709] which may originally have been leaves P and Q of the Scheide Sketchbook).
June 9, 1817	Ferdinand Ries writes on behalf of the London Philharmonic requesting two new symphonies. Brandenburg believes that this request launched serious work on the Ninth Symphony (and the incipient Tenth Symphony as well).
1816–18	Early work on the first movement. (Autograph 11/1, which may have overlapped with the lost Boldrini Sketchbook. This source included a single leaf, identified by Brandenburg as "Weimar," and an additional leaf in Schott archives in Mainz. Also Paris, BN Ms. 103 and Ms. 78; Mus. Ms. Autogr. Beethoven Mendelssohn-Stiftung 2 located in Biblioteka Jagiellonska, Kraków).
1817–18	Plan for an "Adagio Cantique" and vocal finale. Also sketches for opening measures of first movement. (Boldrini Sketchbook [SV 71] lost since 1890's; Vienna, A45 and A44; B Sk 8 [BH, Bonn] and fragment now in private hands in the United States, formerly in the possession of Pablo Casals; Brandenburg, p. 103).

[1819–1823: work on last three piano sonatas, *Missa solemnis,* and "Diabelli" Variations]

TABLE 2–1
CONTINUED

1819–20	Sketches for "Abendlied unterm gestirnten Himmel," WoO 150 and a projected "Todten Marsch" (BSk 1 = Wittgenstein Sketchbook, Grasnick 20b, fols. 1–6)

[Two and a half years lapse before the sketching of the Ninth resumes]

Oct. 1822	Early sketches for all movements (Artaria 201, pp. 111, 116–123; Nottebohm, 164–168 and Brandenburg, 106–115).

[1822–23; work on "Diabelli" Variations]

III. Advanced Sketches (Concept and Continuity Drafts)

ca. Feb./Mar. 1823	Detailed sketches for first movement and ideas—mostly rejected—for other movements (Engelmann Sketchbook [BSk 21 and Grasnick 20b, fol. 20]; Brandenburg, pp. 115–120 and Winter, pp. 209–210).
ca. April 1823	Advanced work on exposition of first movement, preliminary work on development, recapitulation, and coda. Preliminary work on trio of scherzo and third movement (Landsberg 8/1 [originally part of Engelmann?] with Ms. 96, p. 5 and Ms. 57/2; Brandenburg, pp. 115–120 and Winter, p. 210).
April/May 1823	Work on first, second, and third movements. (Artaria 205/5, representing parallel work to what is found in Landsberg 8/1 and 2, and the preparation of the autograph).
May 1823–June 1824	Final sketches for second, third, and fourth movements (Landsberg 8/2, Landsberg 12, A50, and SBH 676, Rolland [pocket sketchbook now housed in BH], Aut. 8/1 and Aut. 8/2 [pocket sketchbooks in BJ, Kraków], Artaria 205/4, pp. 37–44; Brandenburg, pp. 122–129, Winter, pp. 210–211, facsimile in Schindler-McArdle, pp. 265–268).

muss ein   lieb - er Vat - er   wohn -   en

[muss ein   lieb - er   Vat - er   wohn -   en]

Example 2–1. Grasnick 1, fol. 13ʳ (from Winter, p. 178)

themes associated with Schiller's poem in the Petter Sketchbook never made their way into the Ninth Symphony. Instead they proved useful for the "Zur Namensfeier" Overture, op. 115.

The earliest sketch of material that actually was used in the Ninth Symphony dates from 1815. Here one finds a hint of what will become the principal theme of the scherzo (Ex. 2–3), although at this point the idea seems to have been intended for a projected string quintet rather than a symphony. According to Brandenburg, other fragmentary ideas found in the Scheide Sketchbook also may be linked to the Ninth Symphony; the most significant outlines the pitch sequence D-B♭-A that is found in all four movements of the piece. Further exploration of this pitch sequence (Ex. 2–4) also may be seen in the Boldrini Sketchbook (now lost), a source that had been investigated by Nottebohm. Another significant entry in the Scheide Sketchbook is a verbal instruction on page 51: "Symphony, first opening in four voices only—2 violins, viola, bass. Between them, in the other voices forte and, if possible, have all other instruments enter one by one."[10] With these words, one can perceive the seed of the plan for the opening of the first movement.

Further progress on the first and second movements took place during 1817–18, as witnessed in the concept sketches of Autograph 11/1, in single leaves of sketches located in Weimar and Mainz, and in the Boldrini Sketchbook material transcribed by Nottebohm. The ideas notated in these sources for the opening of the first movement are particularly intriguing as they show that by this date Beethoven had already arrived at a fully developed version of its principal theme (Ex. 2–5). The distinctive murmur based on the interval of the fifth and compression of motivic fragments that coalesce into the theme also are present (Ex. 2–6), although Beethoven was still far from certain as to how these ideas should proceed.

Example 2–2. Petter (from Rexroth, p. 322)

One idea in the Boldrini Sketchbook (Ex. 2–7) shows Beethoven—for a moment, at least—contemplating beginning the first movement in a rather traditional, and far less idiosyncratic, fashion. Other sketches in Boldrini and Mendelssohn 2 indicate that Beethoven was also looking ahead to later stages of the movement. In Ex. 2–8 we can recognize passage work that found its way into mm. 63–64 of the exposition, as well as the D-major horn

Example 2–3. Scheide, p. 51 (from Nottebohm, p. 157)

Example 2–4. Boldrini (from Brandenburg, p. 94)

Example 2–5. Weimar (from Brandenburg, p. 96)

episode from the coda (mm. 469–472). The coupling of the descending
arpeggio idea with dotted rhythms seen in Ex. 2–9 show that Beethoven
was still struggling to give his opening theme its proper contour. The
Boldrini Sketchbook shows that Beethoven also was beginning to conceive
a "a 2nd movement, with 4 horns, 2 in basso and 2 in high Bb." This may
have been the earliest concept for what would eventually become the
Adagio third movement of the Ninth.

Plans for the Ninth Symphony at this point still remained rather tentative. Brandenburg has noted that Beethoven was deeply involved in advanced work on the Piano Sonata, op. 106 ("Hammerklavier"), and was still
thinking along the lines of two symphonies for London. A sketch shown by
Nottebohm demonstrates that Beethoven was still uncertain about the
rhythmic value of the murmur as sextuplets ("nur 6tel und im Stück 16tel").
Even more important is the following indication:

Example 2–6. Mainz, Schott Archive (from Brandenburg, p. 97)

Example 2–7. Boldrini (from Nottebohm, p. 160)

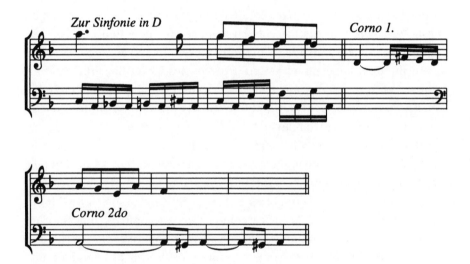

Example 2–8. Boldrini (from Nottebohm, p. 159)

Example 2–9. Mendelssohn 2, p. 94 (from Brandenburg, p. 102)

Adagio Cantique—

Solemn song in a symphony in the old modes—Lord God we praise
you—alleluja—either as an independent piece or an introduction to a
fugue. Perhaps the entire second symphony will be characterized in
this manner, whereby singing voices will enter in the finale, or even in
the Adagio. The violins, etc. in the orchestra will be increased tenfold
in the finale. Or the Adagio will in a distinct way be repeated in the
finale, with the singing voices introduced one by one. In the Adagio
text, a Greek myth, the text of an ecclesiastical song—in the Allegro, a
celebration of Bacchus.[11]

Beethoven may not have had Schiller's "An die Freude" in mind when he
wrote this plan, but it is the earliest evidence to show that he was contemplating the introduction of human voices into a symphony. Furthermore, the dual concepts of an *Allegro* "celebration of Bacchus" and an
Adagio "ecclesiastical song" rooted in Greek mythology are significant,
since both these elements are not only clearly present in Schiller's poem,
but were eventually given musical expression in the finale.

Sketch fragments for the Ninth Symphony in the Wittgenstein Sketchbook of 1819–20 include a quotation of a "Funeral March" from Handel's
oratorio *Saul.* Brandenburg relates this sketch to the reports that reached
Vienna in March 1820 of the funeral rites in England associated with the
death of King George III. These ceremonies were accompanied by the *Saul*
march, as well as by another Handelian score, a funeral cantata written to
commemorate the death of Princess Caroline. According to an entry in one
of his Conversation Books, Beethoven contemplated writing a set of variations on Handel's "Funeral March" in which voices would appear toward
the end (Ex. 2–10). Again it is noteworthy that the composer is linking
a vocal element to an instrumental work. The dotted-note figure accom-
panying the word "Gott" also bears a fascinating similarity to that found
throughout the Ninth Symphony's first movement.

A gap of some two and a half years separates the entries in the Wittgenstein Sketchbook and the next visible work on the Ninth Symphony. Beethoven was hardly idle in this intervening period (1820 to October 1822), having completed the *Missa solemnis;* the Bagatelles, op. 119; the "Diabelli"
Variations, op. 120; his final three Piano Sonatas (opp. 109, 110, 111); the
"Consecration of the House" Overture, op. 124; and a chorus, WoO 98. The
last two works were written for the opening of the Josephstadt Theater on

Example 2–10. Wittgenstein, fol. 2ᵛ (from Brandenburg, p. 105)

October 3, 1822. Renewed activity on a symphony may have been spurred by renewed contact with the Philharmonic Society of London. On April 6, 1822, Beethoven wrote his former pupil Ferdinand Ries in London, asking how much the Philharmonic Society would offer for a symphony. Seven months later, in a letter dated November 15, Ries informed Beethoven that five days earlier the Directors of the Society resolved to offer £50 for such a work. On December 20, Beethoven accepted the offer, albeit with reservations:

> My dear Ries!
> I have been overwhelmingly occupied, and only now find time to an-
> swer your letter of November 15.—I accept with pleasure the offer to
> write a new symphony for the Philharmonic Society, even if the hono-
> rarium from England cannot bear comparison with those of other
> nations. If only I were not that poor Beethoven, I would compose for
> Europe's greatest artists for free. If only I were in London, I would
> compose everything for the Philharmonic Society! But even if nothing
> else in the world is granted him, Beethoven can, thank God, compose. If
> God were to restore my health, which at least has improved a little bit, I
> can then make good on the offers from all parts of Europe, indeed even
> from North America, and thus acquire yet another laurel wreath.[12]

Sketches in Artaria 201 coincide with the letter to Ries, although they appear to have been written before Beethoven had formally received the commission from London. Beethoven may have considered holding an academy concert in Vienna either toward the end of 1822 or in the early months of 1823. If this were so, it might have been appropriate for him to present a new symphony on this occasion. Viewed in this context, the correspondence with London may have served less as a primary cause than as an additional incentive for Beethoven to return to a symphony project.

Nottebohm believed that Beethoven was still thinking in terms of two distinct symphonies at this stage—one with a vocal finale and the other, seemingly for England, with an instrumental finale. His theory was based partly on Beethoven's reference to a "Sinfonie allemand," an annotation that was meant to differentiate a sketch of "An die Freude" from another nascent symphony project. Nottebohm surmised that since the Seventh and Eighth Symphonies were conceived as a pair, it was reasonable to conclude that Beethoven again was considering writing two symphonies. Supporting evidence seems to come from the secondhand testimony of Friedrich Rochlitz, who reported that during the summer of 1822, Beethoven mentioned plans for two projected symphonies. It is now known that this conversation never took place, however.[13] The conflicting evidence surrounding Nottebohms's supposition has also become part of the ongoing controversy surrounding the sketches for a Tenth Symphony—a controversy that has intensified in recent years thanks to Barry Cooper's "realization," publication, and recording of this phantom work. The issues—both musical and ethical—raised by Cooper's work are too complex to explore here. What Cooper identified as the opening *Andante* of a Tenth Symphony bears a striking resemblance to parts of the third movement of the Ninth Symphony. As suggested earlier, it is difficult to identify with certainty the exact piece for which a concept sketch was intended.[14]

Brandenburg has pointed to two factors that make the Artaria 201 sketches especially significant. First, Beethoven started to place the early ideas for the first and second movements of the Ninth into the broader plan of a four-movement symphonic cycle. Second, he introduced sketches for a setting of "An die Freude" in D major that are linked to a plan for a symphony. Brandenburg also has challenged Nottebohm's assertion that the "An die Freude" sketches are unrelated to the D minor symphony project, arguing that it was highly improbable that Beethoven would have been contemplating two symphonies in D at the same time.

Found in the pages of Artaria 201 are old and new ideas for the first movement (Ex. 2–11), as well as an unused idea (for the scherzo? Ex. 2–12)

Example 2–11. Artaria 201 (from Nottebohm, pp. 164–165)

that bears an interesting resemblance to the trio section of the third movement from the Second Symphony.

In working out the general conception of the symphony (Ex. 2–13), Beethoven moved toward placing his scherzo (marked "recht fugirt" in a rough
sketch located elsewhere in the book) as the second movement. He was as
yet unsure as to the nature of the third movement, but has hit upon a
familiar idea (untexted) for the finale. "An die Freude" is given a less familiar melody on page 119, accompanied by the remark: "German symphony
either with variation after the (?) chorus . . . as entrance or also without
variation. End of the symphony with Turkish music and chorus." With
many essential ingredients conceived, if not yet in place, Beethoven was
now ready to begin intensive work on the Ninth Symphony.

The "Advanced Sketches" in Table 2–1 represent the first period of sustained work on the individual movements. Most are continuity sketches—

Example 2–12. Artaria 201 (from Nottebohm, p. 165)

Example 2–13. Artaria 201 (from Nottebohm, p. 167)

that is, sketches that work out details such as phrase structure, harmony, modulation, motivic development, and formal articulation. Kallick has provided a thorough study of the evolution of the first movement, and Winter's article on the finale concentrates on the evolution of the "Freude" theme (identifying it as Beethoven's "triumph over the popular style"), the music for "Seid umschlungen, Millionen," and Beethoven's overall plan for the treatment of Schiller's poem.[15] The continuity sketches for the scherzo and *Adagio* have yet to receive comparable attention.

Example 2–14. Autograph 8/2 (from Nottebohm, p. 180)

Freude schö-ner Göt - ter - fun- ken

Example 2–15. Landsberg 8/1 (from Nottebohm, p. 182)

The Landsberg sketches of the spring and summer of 1823 and the pocket sketchbooks (which once belonged to Schindler) known as Autograph 8/1 and 8/2 of the fall and winter of 1823 and 1824 are of particular interest because they show that even though Beethoven had arrived at a recognizable form of the "Freude" theme as early as October 1823, he was still reluctant to use either voices or Schiller's poem in his finale. Indeed, one finds along with continuity drafts for the first movement concept sketches for other movements. In Autograph 8/2 we find, for example, the sketch to a "Finale instromentale" in D minor that eventually became the principal theme of the finale of the String Quartet in A Minor, op. 132 (Ex. 2–14). Also found in Landsberg 8/1 are drafts for the two themes from the third movement, as well as a dance-like idea for the finale (Ex. 2–15).

Landsberg 8/2, a document of some forty leaves, contains evidence of progress on all movements. As Exs. 2–16 and 2–17 show, Beethoven was making substantial headway firming up the profile of both themes from the third movement, including the distinctive echoes that are so characteristic of the *Adagio* theme. The indication, "alla Menuetto" for the *Andante*

Example 2–16. Landsberg 8/2 (from Nottebohm, p. 178)

theme in Ex. 2–17 is of particular interest for conductors, as it may provide a clue to the style, if not tempo, in which this theme should be performed.[16]

The sketches for the "Freude" theme in Autograph 8/1 demonstrate that arriving at the proper balance of folksiness and sophistication was no simple matter. Exs. 2–18 and 2–19 demonstrate how Beethoven struggled with the melodic and rhythmic contours of the theme, the definitive version of which was so near, yet still so far, from his grasp.

Autograph 8/1 also shows Beethoven exploring the contrapuntal compatibility of the "Freude" and "Seid umschlungen" tunes, which are combined in a climactic union starting in m. 655 in the finished work. As can be seen in Ex. 2–20, the sketch concentrates not merely on pitch and rhythm, but also text underlay.

Surely the most fascinating entry in Landsberg 8/2 is the sketch pertaining to the fanfare and recitative passage in the finale (Ex. 2–21). In viewing this somewhat absurd sketch with its rough text underlay, one would do well to bear in mind Nottebohm's caveat not to mock it, since Beethoven never expected others to see it. The sketch begins with a reference to the fanfare. The recitative passage that follows exhorts a celebration with "song" (and, according to Deiters' transcription in Thayer-Forbes, possibly

Example 2–17. Landsberg 8/2 (from Nottebohm, p. 175)

Example 2–18. Autograph 8/1 (from Nottebohm, p. 183)

Example 2-19. Autograph 8/1 (from Nottebohm, pp. 183-184)

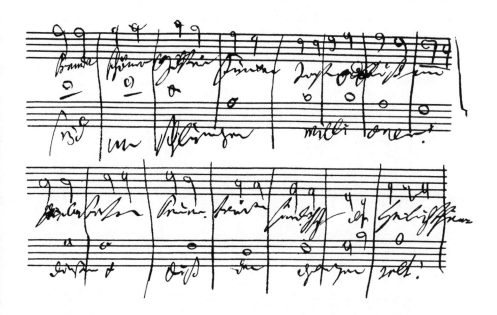

Example 2–20. Autograph 8/1 (from Schindler-McArdle, *Beethoven as I Knew Him*, p. 266)

"Tanz" or "Scherz," both of which qualities certainly are found in the finale). A quotation from the first movement follows, but is rejected as not "pleasing." A fragment from the second movement appears, but is dismissed as "but sport" (not shown by Nottebohm). The *Adagio* theme likewise is rejected because it is "too tender." The recitant, demanding something more lively, then offers to intone something myself," and proceeds to invoke the "Freude" melody.

Example 2–21 reveals Beethoven's first attempt at working out the most critical passage of the entire Ninth Symphony. Here is the climactic moment when all the components of the work—the first three movements, recitative, Schiller's poem, and the "Freude" theme—arrive at their confluence. Once Beethoven was able to successfully bridge the gap between the instrumental and vocal worlds, the task of sketching was at an end. The completion of the manuscript score and parts now took priority.

Example 2–21. Landsberg 8/2 (from Nottebohm, pp. 190–191)

THE AUTOGRAPH MANUSCRIPT AND OTHER PRIMARY SOURCES

It is difficult to say exactly when the Ninth Symphony was completed. The last sketchbook entries (devoted to the finale) may be found in Artaria 205/4. After the sketching was over, Beethoven's continuing work on the Ninth was devoted almost exclusively to the preparation of the autograph manuscript of the score. An incomplete facsimile of the autograph manuscript was published in 1924 by Kistner and Siegel. Another facsimile—of poorer quality, but more complete than the 1924 one—was published by Peters in 1975. The autograph manuscript, while the single most important document, is not the only primary source for the transmission of the text of the Ninth Symphony.[17]

Thanks to the two facsimiles, people with access to good music research libraries may examine the autograph manuscript for themselves, except for mm. 650–654 of the finale (the end of the *Andante maestoso*), which are lost. But for these missing measures, one can follow along a performance of the Ninth from the Peters facsimile. The reader of the facsimile will discern that the autograph contains certain discrepancies from published editions of the work. One also will notice that even at this late stage in the genesis of the work, Beethoven was still unsettled about certain tempos, pitches, meters, and orchestrations. Beethoven resolved these issues by the time the other primary sources were prepared, although several inconsistencies may be found when comparing the various sources. Many of these problems will be examined in chapters 3, 4, and 7.

The autograph manuscript score of the Ninth Symphony was divided after Beethoven's death with parts of it for a long time being housed in several different libraries. The first three movements and part of the finale (mm. 331–594) resided in the Deutsche Staatsbibliothek (DSB), Berlin [Mus. ms. autogr. Beethoven 2, Sammlung Schindler]. Additional parts of the finale (mm. 1–330, 595–698) also were the property of the same library [Artaria 204, 1, 2, 3a]. The autograph of additional parts of the finale (mm. 699–940) were housed in the Staatsbibliothek Preußischer Kulturbesitz (SPK) [Artaria 204, 3b, 4].[18] An autograph contrabassoon part and an insert for mm. 255–258 of first movement [Artaria 204 (6)], previously believed to have been a sketch (see Kallick, pp. 231–232) may also be found there. An insert for the coda of the second movement (mm. 531–559) is housed in the

Beethovenhaus in Bonn (BH) [Sammlung H. C. Bodmer, SBH Nr. 569]. This fragment had been presented to H. Phillips of London by Ignaz Moscheles in 1846. The Bibliothèque Nationale (BN) in Paris [Ms. 43] possesses an insert for the instrumental introduction to the Turkish March in the finale (mm. 343–374).

Next in importance as a source for the text of the Ninth Symphony is the publisher's copy (*Stichvorlage*). This source was used for the engraving of the first edition and was, until its recent auction, housed in the archives of B. Schott Söhne in Mainz. It was prepared during the latter half of 1824 by no fewer than five copyists who worked under Beethoven's supervision (see Anderson nos. 1275 and 1285). Beethoven offered the Ninth Symphony to several publishers—Probst, Schlesinger, and Schott—but in a letter dated January 22, 1825, he formally sold it to Schott (see Anderson nos. 1267, 1269, 1270, 1291, 1299, 1305, 1345).

The first edition score of the Ninth Symphony was not issued until the end of August 1826 (B. Schott Söhne, Mainz; Plate Number 2322), and it was marketed as Beethoven's "125tes Werk" on a subscription basis along with the score of the *Missa solemnis,* op. 123 and the "Consecretion of the House" Overture, op. 124. Beethoven promised the Philharmonic Society of London that he would not publish the Ninth until after it had been performed in London. A revised edition, including the metronome indications that the composer sent to Schott on October 13, 1826, was issued in 1827. Schott also issued a set of twenty-six orchestral and four vocal parts with a replication of the cover title page found in the printed score.

One of the first performances of the Ninth Symphony after its premiere in Vienna took place at the Niederrheinische Musikfest in Aachen on May 23, 1825 under the direction of Ferdinand Ries.[19] The Aachen performance omitted the scherzo and a portion of the third movement, as well as using an altered version of the text of the finale's vocal recitative (mm. 216–236). Beethoven sent Ries a copy of the full score for movements 1–3 and a piano score and parts for the finale (minus the contrabassoon part). A letter from Beethoven to Ries (Anderson no. 1358) calls attention to a small correction to the oboe part in m. 258 (the letter says m. 242) of the first movement. These materials reveal many small discrepancies—mostly regarding articulation and dynamics—when compared with the autograph manuscript and other primary materials. The Aachen documents now reside in that city's Bibliothek des städtischen Konzerthauses.

Another source for the text of the Ninth is the dedication copy (*Wid-*

mungsexemplar) of the score that was presented to its dedicatee, King Friedrich Wilhelm III of Prussia. The principal feature of this document is its title page in Beethoven's hand bearing the dedication: *Sinfonie / mit Schluß-chor über Schillers ode: "an die Freude" / für großes Orchester, 4 Solo und 4 chor-stimmen, / componirt und / Seiner Majestät dem König von Preußen/ Friedrich Wilhelm III / in tiefster Ehrfurcht zugeeignet / Von / Ludwig van Beethoven. / 125tes Werk.* The dedication copy of the score is located in the Staatsbibliothek zu Berlin–Preußischer Kulturbesitz.

Beethoven's copyists prepared an additional manuscript score for the Philharmonic Society in London (British Library, Loan 4 MS. 21) which was used for the first London performance of the Ninth Symphony on March 21, 1825. This score contains a title page (*"Geschrieben für die Philharmonische Gesellschaft in London"*) and movement titles in Beethoven's hand. Although the score itself is not in Beethoven's hand (at least two copyists were involved in its preparation), it does contain certain corrections and additions that may have been his own.[20] Additional changes and annotations in this score were made by conductors in London such as Sir George Smart and Ignaz Moscheles.

A two-folio autograph manuscript surfaced on May 5–6, 1988 at an auction at Sotheby's in London (Lot 304). This hitherto unknown source, which probably dates from after the first performance on May 7, 1824, contains significant changes in the first, second, and last movements. Many of these corrections, written mainly in the hand of Wolanek (one of the copyists who worked on the Ninth Symphony), were forwarded to Charles Neate in London on January 20, 1825. The Sotheby manuscript seems to have been the original source from which Wolanek made his copy. The corrections found in this source also were incorporated in the *Stichvorlage* and first edition of the score.

A summary of the primary sources for the text of the Ninth must also include the surviving parts used in the first performances in Vienna on May 7 and 23, 1824. The parts, which are housed in the library of the Gesellschaft der Musikfreunde (GdMf) in Vienna, have as yet not been subjected to careful musicological study.[21]

With so many primary sources, it is clear that a definitive score of the Ninth Symphony is not possible. Given the many changes in the work during its early stages of transmission, editors will be hard pressed even to produce an authoritative critical edition. Some of the more important variant readings will be discussed in chapters 3, and 4, while chapter 7 will focus on performance issues raised by discrepancies among the various sources.

The Finale from *Fidelio* and the Choral Fantasy

The choral portion of the Ninth Symphony bears certain characteristics of an operatic finale, and it is likely that in composing the music, Beethoven recalled an earlier use he had made of at least part of Schiller's "An die Freude"—albeit in a slightly paraphrased form—in *Fidelio:*

"An die Freude," 2nd strophe:

Wer ein holdes Weib errungen,	He who has obtained a dear wife,
Mische seinem Jubel ein!	Add his jubilation!

Fidelio (Act II, Finale):

Wer ein holdes Weib errungen,	He who has obtained a dear wife,
Stimm in unsern Jubel ein!	join in our rejoicing!

The paraphrase also occurs in the original version of the opera, *Leonore,* composed in 1805. The similarities between the opera and the symphony, however, are by no means limited to this one likeness. Consider, for example, the words sung by Don Fernando, the minister of the king, whose arrival signals Florestan's rescue:

Tyrannenstrenge sei mir fern.	May tyrant's rule stay far from me.
Es sucht der Bruder seiner Brüder,	A brother seeks his brothers,
Und kann er helfen, hilft er gern.	And if he can help, he helps gladly.

As discussed in chapter 1, Schiller's concept of *Freude* cannot be separated from the parallel concept of *Freiheit.* The common currents of Enlightenment philosophy—political, aesthetic, and moral freedom; the pursuit of happiness—were inextricably bound in Schiller's poem, which itself owed much to other writers.[22] Seen in this context, the finale of Act II of *Fidelio* (along with Beethoven's music for Goethe's *Egmont*) comes nearest

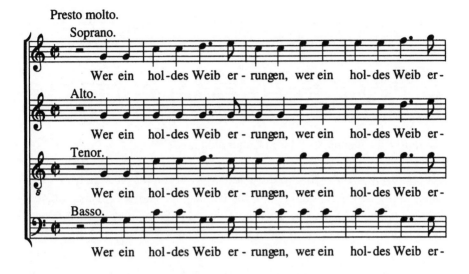

Example 2–22. Beethoven, *Fidelio;* finale, Act II

in expression to the sentiment and mood of the finale of the Ninth Symphony and may be considered an additional compositional model for it.
Musically speaking, the vigorous and jubilant setting of "Wer ein holdes
Weib errungen" in *Fidelio* also has a direct bearing on the choral writing in
the Ninth Symphony. Indeed, all that seems missing from the *Fidelio* finale
are the Turkish instruments, as illustrated by Ex. 2–22.

Example 2–23. Beethoven: Choral Fantasy, theme

Beethoven was the first to draw attention to the parallels between the finale of the Ninth Symphony and his Fantasy for Piano, Chorus, and Orchestra, op. 80: in letters to potential publishers he identified the finale of the symphony as being on a "grander" and "larger" scale than the earlier work. The Choral Fantasy was composed as the closing piece for Beethoven's *Academie* of December 22, 1808. This four-hour-long concert offered its patient audience an embarrassment of riches that included the premiere of the "Pastoral" Symphony, the concert aria, *Ah! Perfido,* the Gloria from the Mass in C, the premiere of the Fourth Piano Concerto, the premiere of the Fifth Symphony, and an improvisation at the piano by the composer (possibly the Fantasia, op. 77, published in 1809). An advertisement for the concert announced that the program would conclude with a "Fantasia for the piano which ends as a finale with the gradual entrance of the entire orchestra and finally the introduction of choruses."

The Choral Fantasy begins with an extended solo for the piano in the style of a free improvisation that leads without break to the "finale." This section is introduced by the contrabasses and cellos (note the instrumentation in comparison with the Ninth) who steal in mysteriously, interrupted by phrases for the piano in recitative style. The exchange between the soloist and strings has been characterized as the artist communicating with his muse. After a series of signals from the horns and oboes (marked "Hört ihr wohl" in the sketches), the pianist initiates the principal melody in C major (Ex. 2–23), a tune borrowed from Beethoven's own song, "Requited Love" ("Gegenliebe"), composed in 1795, and whose likeness to the "Freude" theme of the Ninth is self evident. Another link to the Ninth is the way in which Beethoven treats the tune in a series of characteristic instrumental variations (in the case of op. 80, featuring in succession a solo flute, a pair of oboes, clarinets and bassoon, string quartet, and full orchestra). A brief coda leads to a furious variation for piano and orchestra in C minor, followed then by a dreamy barcarolle-like variation in A major. A hint of the horn and oboe signal (in dotted rhythm) ushers in a *Marcia assai vivace,* which eventually dissolves into a free solo for the piano, accompanied by a scurrying pizzicato strings. Dramatic arpeggios in the piano and a return of the mysterious string figure (all of which may be likened to the second "horror fanfare" of the Ninth's finale) set the stage for a last appearance of the oboe and horn signal, which this time is resplendently joined by the piano and strings.

The solo and choral voices now enter singing the following poem, whose authorship is uncertain (it may have been written by Christoph Kuffner), again to music based on the "Gegenliebe" tune:

Schmeichelnd hold und lieblich klingen
unsers Lebens Harmonien,
und dem Schönheitssinn entschwingen
Blumen sich, die ewig blühn.

Coaxing, fair, lovely is the sound
of harmony in our life,
and sense of beauty generates
flowers that bloom for ever.

Fried' und Freude gleiten freundlich
wie der Wellen Wechselspiel;
was sich drängte rauh und feindlich,
ordnet sich zu Hochgefühl.

Peace and joy flow as kindly
as the tide of waves.
Rough, hostile pressures
are transformed to lofty emotion.

Wenn der Töne Zauber walten
und des Wortes Weihe spricht,
muß sich Herrliches gestalten,
Nacht und Stürme werden Licht.

When magical sound is in command
and words convey devotion,
wonders must take shape;
night and tempest turn to light.

Äuß're Ruhe, inn're Wonne
herrschen für den Glücklichen.
Doch der Künste Frühlingssonne
lässt aus beiden Licht entstehn.

Quietness without, bliss within
are the happy man's rulers.
But the spring sun of the arts
gives us light from them both.

Großes, das in's Herz gedrungen,
blüht dann neu und schön empor,
hat ein Geist sich aufgeschwungen,
hall't ihm stets ein Geisterchor.

Grandeur impressed in the heart
then shoots anew and fair on high.
When the spirit leaps up,
a choir of spirits resounds eternal.

Nehmt denn hin, ihr schönen Seelen,   So, lovely spirits, accept
froh die Gaben schöner Kunst.   the gifts of fair art gladly.
Wenn sich Lieb' und Kraft vermählen,   When love and strength are wedded,
lohnt dem Menschen Göttergunst.   divine grace is man's reward.[23]

The parallels between the finales of the Choral Fantasy and the Ninth Symphony run deeper than the obvious kinship of the tunes themselves. The introductory gesture of instrumental recitative is no less significant than the selection of a theme in the popular style. Also striking, of course, is the presence of both instrumental and vocal variations. As is the case in the finale of Act II of *Fidelio,* the Choral Fantasy has a *Presto* coda that brings the piece to an exhilarating conclusion.

More often than not, comparisons of the Choral Fantasy with the finale of the Ninth Symphony deem the earlier work to be decidedly inferior. It is unfortunate that such an attitude persists even today. Had Beethoven never composed a Ninth Symphony with its imposing choral finale, the Choral Fantasy would undoubtedly be acknowledged by all to be a charming and inspired work instead of a poor relative, or—even more inaccurately—a "study" for the Ninth. It should, at very least, be appreciated as a work that was as an important—indeed necessary—stage along Beethoven's compositional journey, a journey that would pass through still richer realms some sixteen years later.

Chapter 3

THE NINTH: MOVEMENTS I–III

I. ALLEGRO MA NON TROPPO, UN POCO MAESTOSO SONATA FORM, 2/4 METER

EXPOSITION
    1st KEY AREA (D MINOR)—mm. 1–70
    TRANSITION—mm. 70–79
    2nd KEY AREA (B♭ MAJOR)—mm. 80–149
    CLOSING SECTION—mm. 150–160

*I*t would be no exaggeration to state that the mysterious beginning of the first movement of the Ninth Symphony is the work's most striking feature. The murmuring sextuplets of the second violins and cellos and open fifth (A–E) of the horns of the first two measures are couched in a soft dynamic that obscures any clear sense of time, space, or tonality. The sextuplet figure, however, articulates a precisely-measured subdivision of each beat, and one could argue that the listener ought to be able to hear those subdivisions distinctly. Others have maintained that the sextuplet murmur is meant to suggest an unmeasured tremolo, and that it ought to be performed without the slightest hint of accentuation. A true unmeasured tremolo was a notational gesture that did not exist in Beethoven's time, however, and if this is the effect that he actually wanted, would it not have been more logical for him to use thirty-second notes—values that would have resulted in a faster murmur more in keeping with the

49

Example 3–1. Ninth Symphony/I, mm. 1–5

2/4 meter in which the movement is cast?[1] Beethoven heightens the mys-
tique of his opening by introducing, *sotto voce,* a rhythmic motive that
begins to bring order and shape to the amorphous murmur of sound
(Ex. 3–1).

The issue of how to play the sextuplets is neither unimportant nor purely
academic. A performance of the Ninth Symphony cannot have it both ways.
The sextuplets must be played either distinctly or indistinctly. Elaborate
metaphysical theories have been offered to explain this astounding opening. On one extreme, cosmologists liken it to the beginning of Genesis, a
reenactment of the creation of the universe out of the void of nothingness
(*creatio ex nihilo*). This interpretation would favor an indistinct rendering
of the sextuplets. Others, preferring a less speculative interpretation, view
the opening gesture as the quiet humming of an engine that had been
running before the piece began. From the standpoint of structure, mm. 1–
16 have been labeled by some analysts as an introduction. But if mm. 1–16
form an introduction, how does one account for the events of mm. 35–50, in
which the same gesture is repeated on a new tonal level? Is this also an
introduction? And if it is, at what point, then, does the introduction end and
the movement proper begin?

The role of mm. 1–16 is clarified, at least to some extent, by two subsequent passages. The first occurs at the onset of the development (m. 162),
and the second at the cataclysmic arrival of the recapitulation (m. 301). The
latter passage in particular undermines the interpretation of mm. 1–16 as
an introduction. Introductions normally have no role to play in the re-

capitulation of sonata-form movements, of which the first movement of the Ninth Symphony is a clear example.[2] An analysis of a piece of music certainly is free to label musical gestures in light of subsequent events, i.e., from a retrospective position. But the listener must make a provisional judgment about each gesture *as it occurs*. One cannot be certain, especially on a first hearing, that mm. 1–16 form an introduction. Tovey, who also was suspicious of analyses that relied too much on hindsight, wrote of these measures that "it is impossible to imagine anything that more definitely plunges us into the midst of things."[3] He also cautioned against too specific an explanation of the bare fifth that opens the movement:

> Half the musical miseducation in the world comes from people who know that the Ninth Symphony begins on the dominant of D minor, when the fact is that its opening bare fifth may mean anything within D major, D minor, A major, A minor, E major, E minor, C sharp minor, G major, C major, and F major, until the bass descends to D and settles most (but not all) of the question. A true analysis takes the standpoint of a listener who knows nothing beforehand, but hears and remembers everything.[4]

Nearly all analyses of the first movement of the Ninth Symphony do agree upon at least two essential points; (1) that the *quality* of expression found in its opening is unprecedented, even for Beethoven, and (2) that its cumulative effect projects an immense time scale. Beethoven realized, far better than his contemporaries or successors, that immensity is better achieved by a process of compression, than by expansion, and although he was no scientist, an atomic physicist could not produce a clearer example of nuclear fusion than the accelerated gathering of power leading to the statement of the opening theme (Ex. 3–2).

The first movement of the Ninth Symphony *is* immense, but it is not *longer* than that of the "Eroica," regardless of whether one measures things by numbers of bars or by actual time. The drama that Beethoven will play out in the Ninth Symphony, however, is a different one from the Third, more nearly entering into the spirit of the Fifth Symphony—a work that also uses tightly compacted means to achieve its aesthetic goal. The comparison is unavoidable, since the Ninth is Beethoven's only other symphony with a first movement in a minor key, and like the Fifth Symphony, the Ninth ends

Example 3–2. Ninth Symphony/I, mm. 11–22

in the blinding light of a triumphant major. But throughout Beethoven's career, it had always been his habit to move on to new challenges once he believed that he had solved a particular compositional problem. For all their surface similarities, the Fifth and Ninth Symphonies are vastly different works that address different aesthetic, philosophical, and compositional issues.

Many of the crucial harmonic events in the first movement of the Ninth Symphony occur on unexpected beats of the measure, and the first hint of D minor is provided by the bassoons, who descend to D on the second eighth-note beat of m. 15. This change is anticipated by a corresponding abandonment of E by the other instruments on the fourth eighth-note beat of the previous measure. The effect of these changes is strangely disorienting, the tension heightened by the eradication any clear sense of strong and weak beats. Only the announcement of the principal theme, *fortissimo*, permits the listener to gain a metrical (and tonal) bearing. Other such moments of disorientation permeate the movement, the next one occurring in m. 24, when the cellos and basses leap from the subdominant (iv) chord to ♭II (E♭) on the second eighth-note beat, sustaining this surprising harmony through the next two measures (Ex. 3–3).

This harmonic digression is short-lived, and its full meaning is deferred until the finale. But its agogic stress here momentarily undermines the supremacy of the tonic, an effect that Beethoven continues to foster by deliberately avoiding any root-position tonic chords. These gestures give

Example 3–3. Ninth Symphony/I, mm. 24–27

the music a strangely unsettled feeling, and for the moment at least, the listener is at a loss to know why the composer has chosen to destabilize the home key at such an early stage of the movement. Further metrical displacements resume in m. 31 with vehement Beethovenian sforzandos on the normally weaker second beats. The overlapping of tonic and dominant harmonies also adds to a sense of confusion (Ex. 3–4).

As the first violins and violas literally sweep away the remains of what has just transpired with a scalar rush of thirty-second notes, the second violins and cellos resume the sextuplet murmur and bare fifth, but this time on the pitches D and A. The events of mm. 1–16 are reenacted in mm. 35–50 on a new tonal level. If the first sixteen measures of the movement were a Beethovenian creation myth, how is one supposed to interpret the events that now unfold? Is the world being created anew? Did something go wrong the first time?

If the listener were to use mm. 1–16 as a gauge, it would be logical to expect this renewed sequence of events to arrive at a climax in G minor. Unexpectedly, however, the counter-statement of the principal theme in m. 51 is in B♭ major (the relative major of the anticipated key). But as soon as B♭ is established, a sequential dialogue between winds and strings leads the music to the dominant of D minor—that is, A major—in m. 63. Even

Example 3–4. Ninth Symphony/I, mm. 31–35

though the relationship of B♭ and A in this passage (a phenomenon that theorists identify as a "Neapolitan" relationship) forms a parallel to that of E♭ and D described above, the unfolding of events in the first key area of this movement has been anything but predictable.

The appearance of D♭ and G♭ in mm. 71 and 73 weakens the autonomy of D minor, and the old key yields to the dominant of B♭ major in m. 74. A new theme in the winds in m. 74 (and a change of key signature in m. 80)

Example 3-5. Ninth Symphony/I, mm. 74–79

confirms the new tonality, but it is worth noting that Beethoven carefully avoids a root-position tonic triad in the new key until the arriving at the closing section in m. 150. The composer once again has chosen to destabilize a region where stability would be expected.

Every diligent music student knows that the normal second key area for sonata-form movements in minor keys is the relative major (III), which in this movement ought to be F major. The fact that Beethoven selected B♭ major (VI) instead of F major was a choice governed by the overall design not only of this movement, but of the entire symphony.[5] The listener, however, is more aware that the mood of the music has changed, and not that the tonal level is "wrong." Wagner and others have identified the brief *dolce* woodwind theme that begins in m. 74 as a prefiguration of the "Joy" theme from the finale (Ex. 3-5). This reading cannot be dismissed, since the

Example 3–6. Ninth Symphony/I, mm. 80–84

Example 3–7. Ninth Symphony/I, mm. 102–103

chronology of Beethoven's sketches reveal that Beethoven had drafted the "Joy" theme before he had worked out the details of the other movements (see chapter 2).

A new four-measure woodwind theme, delicately accompanied by sixteenth notes in the strings, begins in m. 80 (Ex. 3–6) and is repeated immediately in a syncopated and ornamented form. Measure 81 of the autograph manuscript clearly shows that Beethoven had written D—not B♭—as the fourth note of this new theme. The parallel passage in the recapitulation (m. 346), however, suggests that the manuscript may be in error and that the B♭ normally heard (and found in most editions of the score) is the correct note. Scalar figures in contrary motion (based on Ex. 3–3, but with an expressive chromatic passing tone) ensue, leading to a new figure in m. 102 (Ex. 3–7, itself based on the dotted rhythm heard in the first key area). A restatement of this new theme in m. 106 deflects the G downward to G♭, leading magically into the fresh and unexpected region of C♭ major (enharmonically respelled as B major)—a reinforcement of the semitone relationship discussed above.

Example 3–8. Ninth Symphony/I, mm. 116–119

Example 3–9. Ninth Symphony/I, mm. 120–123

A four-measure paragraph in the new key ensues, accompanied by the
dotted figure in the violas and cellos. The melody comprises two rising
fourths—F# to B, and C# to F#. A wonderfully mysterious passage begins in
m. 114 as a descent from F# wends its way down through the B major scale
until it overshoots its mark by a half step on the second half of m. 115. The
scalar descent is reciprocated by a rising sequence in the strings in the next
measure (Ex. 3–8), punctuated by expressive eighth notes in the winds that
emphasize the half-step/whole-step inflections that have been important
throughout the entire exposition. The bittersweet tension of this passage is
heightened in mm. 120–129 as G and Gb vie for supremacy (Ex. 3–9).

Metrical displacement once again dominates as the woodwinds begin a
strained conversation in m. 138. This passage is filled with interesting details and complexities, brought on in large part by octave displacements in
the flute and oboe. According to Wagner, the elaborate and broken writing
for the woodwinds here presented considerable difficulties in early performances of the Ninth (Wagner's "solution" to this problem will be discussed in chapter 7). Metrical regularity is restored only when the *tutti*
orchestra arrives to begin the closing section in m. 150. As mentioned earlier, this also is the point where the key of Bb major is fully confirmed by a
root position tonic triad. Having reestablished tonal and metrical stability,

Example 3–10. Ninth Symphony/I, mm. 179–183

Beethoven boldly parades the B♭ major arpeggio as he brings the exposition to a close.

DEVELOPMENT
    PART 1—mm. 160–217
    PART 2—mm. 218–252
    PART 3—mm. 253–300

As the pitch sinks from B♭ to A in mm. 159–160, the listener is left uncertain as to where the music is heading. Anyone familiar with the precedents of sonata-form first movements in symphonies—including all of Beethoven's—would expect a repeat of the exposition at this point. Only the "miseducated" listener would be aware that the Ninth Symphony is the exception to the rule. The foreboding drop from B♭ to A, the resumption of the sextuplets in m. 160, and the addition of the fifth in the next measure, all suggest that the repeat of the exposition is beginning. The gentle punctuations of timpani and trumpet on the second beat of mm. 160 and 166 hint that something else may be afoot, but even these additions would not have been out of place in a first ending intended to lead back to the beginning of the movement. In point of fact, then, the listener has no idea whether or not the music is returning to the beginning until the second half of m. 170, when Beethoven introduces (for the first time in this movement) a D major chord, albeit one with the third of the chord (F♯) in the bass.[6]

Example 3–11. Ninth Symphony/I, mm. 192–197

The effect of this chord—a first inversion major triad—is both exhilarating and ominous, and its inherent instability is fraught with anxiety.
When Beethoven resolves the chord to G minor at m. 178, he at last has
introduced the tonality that one expected to encounter in the exposition at
m. 51. The development now unfolds as the winds engage in an imitative
passage based on the principal theme of the movement (Ex. 3–10). A cadential formula in the winds based on the tail of the same theme is introduced in m. 192 (Ex. 3–11).[7] The violins and violas continue in m. 198, answered in imitation by the clarinet and bassoon. The addition in m. 201 of a
downwardly-inflected upper neighbor (A♭) serves as a poignant reminder

Example 3–12. Ninth Symphony/I, mm. 216–217

of these same inflections encountered in the exposition. The key shifts toward C minor, and a reprise of the cadential formula begins in m. 210, this time extended by two additional measures. An especially pungent harmonic clash occurs on the first beat of m. 217 (Ex. 3–12), an event that has led some to conclude that the notes found in either the oboe or viola parts are incorrect.[8]

The next major division of the development section begins with the workmanlike triple counterpoint at m. 218 (Ex. 3–13). Each of the three subjects is derived from the opening theme (Ex. 3–2). Beethoven takes this triple counterpoint through four episodic stages, starting in C minor (m. 218), passing through G minor (m. 224), and leading to B♭ major

Example 3–13. Ninth Symphony/I, mm. 218–222

(m. 232 and m. 236). The fourth stage of this section places the syncopated
metrical displacement in the foreground, with an added level of confusion
created by the rhythm in the trumpets and timpani (Ex. 3–14). Beethoven
turns the screw a notch tighter in m. 240 with a reintroduction of the sextuplet rhythm from the movement's opening measures.

Once the storm has passed, the music temporarily settles on the level of
A minor to begin the third and final division of the development section.
Beethoven continues to work with the same thematic material, but without
the relentless metrical displacement that had marked the previous division. In m. 275 he turns his attention to the theme from the second key area
of the exposition (Ex. 3–6), shifting to F major (the first appearance of the
tonality one expected to encounter in the second key area of the exposition). For a brief moment, turbulence has given place to relative calm and
serenity.

An indication that a new and more terrible storm is coming, however, is
hinted at by the cellos. An ostinato based on the tail of the principal theme
(mm. 19–20) starts to insinuate itself, gently at first, but growing ever more

Example 3–14. Ninth Symphony/I, mm. 236–239

sinister as its low C is inflected upward to C# in m. 295, accompanied by a violent crescendo. The course has been set for a return to D minor, hammered angrily by *forte* accents on each beat. Even though it is clear that something momentous is about to occur, nothing in the music literature, not even the other works from Beethoven's own pen, could adequately prepare the listener for the catastrophe that is about to take place.

> RECAPITULATION
>   1st KEY AREA—mm. 301–336
>   TRANSITION—mm. 337–344
>   2nd KEY AREA—mm. 345–418
>   CLOSING SECTION—mm. 419–426

The recapitulation of this first movement is as unexpected as it is astonishing. Recapitulations normally represent an area of affirmation and stability after the turbulence and tonal meandering of the developing section. Never before had a composer destabilized this critical formal juncture as does Beethoven with his first-inversion D major triad. And never before had a major chord sounded so apocalyptic! A sense of arrival is unequivocal, but the effect is, at the same time, profoundly disturbing. The F#'s in the cellos and basses range over two octaves, straining to be heard over the relentlessly thundering Ds in the kettledrum. Evidence that the composer was concerned that the F# would be overshadowed by the D in the timpani may be found in the autograph manuscript of the score, where one sees an alternative contrabass part in dotted rhythms (Plate 3–1).[9]

The dotted rhythm certainly would draw attention to the F#, and Beethoven may also have been contemplating forging a direct link to mm. 517–525 of the finale (Ex. 3–15). He must have concluded, however, that such an active bass line would overshadow the return of the fragments of the

Plate 3–1. Ninth Symphony/I, mm. 301–304 (autograph manuscript). Courtesy Staatsbibliothek zu Berlin–Preußischer Kulturbesitz, Musikabteilung mit Mendelssohn-Archiv.

Example 3–15. Ninth Symphony/IV, mm. 517–522

principal theme. The alternative figuration, consequently, never found its way into published editions.[10] The ranging of F# over two octaves creates a perfect foil for the two-octave descent of the principal theme itself (Ex. 3–16), and the resulting contrary motion lends additional power to this awe-inspiring moment.

An examination of the autograph manuscript also reveals what may be an error that is found in all editions of the Ninth Symphony, including the first edition, which was supervised by the composer himself. This discrepancy is in the cello and bass line in m. 312, the critical moment when the F# finally yields to F♮. Ex. 3–17 shows how this measure appears in published editions, with the octave descent occurring *on* the second beat. Plate 3–2, however, clearly shows that Beethoven originally wanted the change of octave to occur on the *second half of the first beat* (a reading that is confirmed in the alternative bass line shown in Plate 3–2). The version

Example 3–16. Ninth Symphony/I, mm. 301–304

Example 3–17. Ninth Symphony/I, m. 312

found in the manuscript is consistent with Beethoven's tendency throughout this movement to place harmonic shifts on the weaker beats of the
measure.[11]

As decisive a moment of arrival as the recapitulation may be, it is abun-
dantly clear that Beethoven does not intend for the listener to interpret its
harmony as the resolution of a minor-major tension. The reversion from
F# to F♮ that occurs on the last half of the second beat in m. 312 does,
however, serve to drive the music back to D minor (the "proper" key for the
recapitulation). The principal theme returns in m. 315, its texture thick-
ened by counterpoint in the cellos and basses. After a canonic dialogue
between strings and winds over a pedal D in the cellos, basses, and timpani,
the storm comes to rest on the dominant of D major, preparing the way for a
reprise of the themes from the second key area, now couched in that key.
But just as in the analogous passage in the exposition, it is only with the
return of the arpeggiated dotted-rhythmic figure in mm. 419–427 that D
minor is unequivocally affirmed.

CODA
     PART 1—mm. 427–468
     PART 2—mm. 469–512
     PART 3—mm. 513–547

Plate 3–2. Ninth Symphony/I, m. 312 (autograph manuscript). Courtesy Staats-bibliothek zu Berlin–Preußischer Kulturbesitz, Musikabteilung mit Mendels-sohn-Archiv.

Example 3–18. Ninth Symphony/I, mm. 427–430

Beethoven's codas, even more than his recapitulations, are segments in which the conflicts posed by the exposition section are resolved. Beethoven begins this coda by expanding the principal theme into broad four-measure phrases (Ex. 3–18), lending the melody a regularity of phrasing only hinted at in the development section. The passage arrives at its *fortissimo* climax at m. 453 with a return of the contrary-motion scalar work

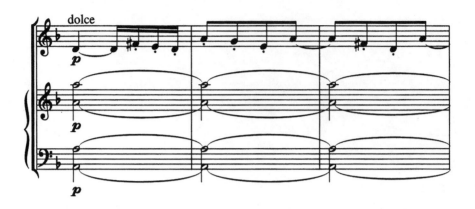

Example 3–19. Ninth Symphony/I, mm. 469–471

from the exposition, followed by a strenuous sequence based upon the dotted rhythmic figure.

A window of light opens at m. 469 with the arrival, for one last time in this movement, of D major. Its appearance this time is in a relatively stable second inversion, with the fifth of the chord (A) not only in the bass, but sounded throughout four octaves. The first horn sings the subject derived from the tail end of the principal theme (Ex. 3–19). The oboe picks up this subject in the next measure, followed later by the bassoon and the flute. The four-octave-deep A in the strings lends a pastoral serenity to the passage, but it soon becomes apparent that once again this is only a lull between storms. The music in m. 477 takes a sinister turn back to the minor mode, and a struggle for dominance ensues between the syncopation in the strings and the perpetual sixteenth notes in the winds (Ex. 3–20). This passage has been cited by some as an example of poor orchestration caused by Beethoven's deafness. But surely this is not the case. It is true that the solo wind instruments cannot cut through the texture of the *tutti* strings, but Beethoven's obscuring of the winds (and the barline) seems quite deliberate. He allows the syncopated string ostinato to dominate the texture (abetted by the crescendo that begins in m. 481), effectively eclipsing the sixteenth notes in the winds. The climax of this passage is reached in m. 490, followed by a diminuendo that, like the passing of an eclipse, allows the winds once again to become audible. The syncopated strings, however, have so upset the metrical equilibrium, that not even the return of the scalar passages in m. 495 (cleverly begun just a little too soon) can fully

Example 3–20. Ninth Symphony/I, mm. 477–484

restore it. Only the return of the cadential formula in m. 505 is able to reestablish the autonomy of the downbeat. The cadential formula appears two times, with its second statement punctuated by limpid afterbeats in the flute, a gesture that produces a profound sense of resignation.[12]

What occurs next is one of the most celebrated perorations in the entire history of music. The bassoons, violas, cellos, and basses begin an ostinato that wends its way down chromatically from D to A, followed by a return to D. In the Baroque era, this figuration was used to express lamentation (in "Dido's Lament" from Purcell's *Dido and Aeneas,* for instance), and there is no reason to doubt that this is precisely the affect that Beethoven sought to

Example 3–21. Ninth Symphony/I, mm. 513–516

Example 3–22. Ninth Symphony/I, mm. 530–534

evoke at this moment. The mood is set by the low instruments as the brass and winds intone a funereal march above it (Ex. 3–21). The *pianissimo* dynamic with which the march begins adds to its sense of dread, and one is almost relieved when Beethoven introduces a crescendo in m. 521. The sense of fear that this moment instills in the listener intensifies into a terror of truly alarming proportions in m. 531 when the harmony takes an unexpected turn. The collapse of the C# to C♮ in the strings produces a shattering effect, as does the dramatic harmony that follows (Ex. 3–22). Even here at the end, the harmonic conflicts of the first movement seem to defy final resolution. Only by means of a final reprise of the principal theme, thundered *fortissimo* throughout the entire orchestra in m. 539, does D minor achieve a temporary victory as Beethoven quickly brings down the curtain on this remarkable opening movement.

II. Molto vivace—Presto—Molto vivace Scherzo and Trio, 3/4 meter

Scherzo (mm. 1–411; Sonata form)

EXPOSITION
  1st KEY AREA (D MINOR)—mm. 1–56
  TRANSITION—mm. 57–92
  2nd KEY AREA (C MAJOR)—mm. 93–150

The Ninth is the only one of Beethoven's symphonies to place the scherzo as the second movement. Precedents may be found for this placement: Haydn's String Quartets, op. 33 ("Gli scherzi"), Mozart's String Quartet in G Major, K. 387, and Beethoven's String Quartet, op. 59, no. 1, and Piano Sonatas, opp. 101 and 106, to name a few examples. Even the earliest critics who wrote about the work took note of the unusual positioning, not so much to complain, as to point out that Beethoven had deviated (again) from an expected norm.

Maynard Solomon has characterized the scherzo of the Ninth Symphony as the tragedy of the first movement transformed into "farce."[13] *Scherzo* is the Italian word for joke (the German word for joke or tease, *Scherz*, derives from the same root), and as grim and demonic as this scherzo may be, one

Example 3–23. Ninth Symphony/II, mm. 1–8

would do well to remember this meaning. Perhaps the first of its many
jokes is its unorthodox placement within the scheme of the entire work.

If the *raison d'être* of a scherzo is to make jokes, then Beethoven's kettledrums are comedians *par excellence*. The opening of the scherzo (Ex. 3–
23)—a descending D minor arpeggio—is an unambiguous reference back
to the principal theme of the first movement (Ex. 3–2). Tovey observed that
this opening gesture also forms a regular eight-measure period, the first
phrase (measure-rest-measure-rest) of which is complemented in the second phrase by a compression of the first (measure-measure-rest-rest).
Once again Beethoven uses compression to project a large time-scale. If the
opening of the first movement sounded ambiguous due to the lack of either
a major or minor third, the kettledrums in m. 5—tuned in a most unorthodox way to octave Fs—leave no doubt that the present movement is in
D minor. This tuning—the same Beethoven used in the finale of his Eighth
Symphony—is as unexpected as it is audacious.[14]

After the opening gambit, the exposition of this scherzo evolves into a
fugal texture, a "learned" procedure that demonstrates that this jokester is
well-schooled. The finales of Mozart's "Jupiter" Symphony and String Quartet, K. 387, as well as the finale of Beethoven's String Quartet, op. 59, no. 3 all
are fine precedents for the use of fugal techniques in sonata form exposi-
tions. The head of the fugue subject in the scherzo of the Ninth is derived
from the dotted rhythmic figure and characteristic octave leap of the first
eight measures, now followed by staccato quarter notes in conjunct motion
(Ex. 3–24). The tonal answer in the violas is on the level of A minor (v),
which in itself is not particularly remarkable except for the fact that Beethoven, as in the first movement, once again leads the music into the "wrong"
tonality—this time C major—for his second key area. The level of A minor,
therefore, provides a perfect conduit to that distant and unexpected key.[15]

Example 3–24. Ninth Symphony/II, mm. 9–12

Example 3–25. Ninth Symphony/II, mm. 93–100

The dynamic level remains pianissimo until a crescendo begins in m. 45. The phrase structure leading up to the climax of the crescendo at m. 57 has been in predictable four-measure groupings (In another context, Beethoven might have written *ritmo di quattro batutte* [rhythm of four beats] in the score). A piquant moment occurs in the measure immediately preceding the climax of this crescendo, where the regular four-measure grouping is interrupted by an early appearance of the octave leap of the subject.[16]

The *fortissimo* statement of the fugue in m. 57 denotes the onset of a transition to C major. Beethoven teases the listener momentarily by feigning a move toward C minor, but this only makes the subsequent confirmation of C major in m. 93 all the more satisfactory. The arrival at C major is greeted by a new theme in the winds, jubilantly accompanied by the octave-leap motive of the principal theme (Ex. 3–25). Beethoven's choice of C major for this second key area, however, poses an interesting compositional dilemma.

C major and D minor, despite the close proximity of their tonics, are rather far removed from each other in terms of the hierarchy that governs modulations. Convention demands that the exposition of the scherzo should be repeated at this juncture, and Beethoven is obliged to find an efficient way to return to D minor. He does this in mm. 143–146 by means of a tidy sequence built upon descending thirds in the bass line that lands the harmony squarely on the D minor triad. The sequence is punctuated by a three-measure rest, after which the reversion to m. 9 for the reprise of the exposition sounds both logical and inevitable.

DEVELOPMENT AND RECAPITULATION

After the repeat of the exposition, Beethoven enters into a transitional passage designed to lead to the development section. The sequence that took the music from C to D now passes through Eb, F, Gb, Ab (= G#), A, and A#, to B, an arrival punctuated by a fermata. The onset of the development section is marked by a change in the key signature from one flat to one sharp. The entrance of the wind instruments, led by the droll bassoons, gives the impression that Beethoven has again resumed the fugal texture from the exposition, but this time it is merely an illusion, as the oboe and clarinet answer the bassoon on the same pitch level. The phrasing now shifts from four-beat units to three-beat groups (*Ritmo di tre batutte* [rhythm of three beats]), as shown in Ex. 3–26.

The entrance of the flute and oboe in m. 186 shifts the tonal level from E to A minor, but the kettledrums rudely insist that the music follow a much different tonal trajectory. The timpani strokes cajole the other instruments toward the "forgotten" tonality of F major, and the winds (as well as the key signature) obediently follow suit. The timpanist hammers the Fs four times, each time followed by two measures of woodwind response, thus maintaining the *ritmo di tre battute* units, as well as perpetuating a succession of regular phrase lengths (4 × 3). But Beethoven is determined to keep things off balance in this scherzo. The following succession of three-measure phrases introduces a dialogue between winds and strings, and the timpani (replaced in the next three phrases by horns and trumpets), having accomplished its task, enters sluggishly on the second measure of the next phrase. Three three-measure phrases follow, again led by the leaping octave motto. Having cleverly misled the ear, Beethoven returns to a four-measure phrase structure in m. 234 (indicated as *ritmo di quattro battute*).

Example 3–26. Ninth Symphony/II, mm. 177–182

The return to the four-beats units, as well as to D minor, comes as a relief after all this confusing banter. But the relief is short-lived. The harmony takes an unexpected shift to E♭ major (a reminder of events from the first movement), followed by a fateful crescendo that prepares the way for a dramatic return to the home key.

The recapitulation abandons the fugal texture and quiet banter of the exposition in favor of a *fortissimo* explosion by the full orchestra. After a modified transition, the material from the second key area returns in D major. The insistent kettledrums intrude as if to remind the rest of the orchestra that D minor is, after all, the proper key in which to close. The minor key prevails as the truncated recapitulation draws to a conclusion.

Because of the convention of repeating the second part of a scherzo, a first ending leads back to m. 159 (i.e., eighteen measures before the *ritmo di tre battute* episode).[17] After the repeat is observed, a second ending leads to a fermata analogous to the one heard immediately preceding the development section, but this time poised on the dominant of D minor. A *stringendo* passage ensues leading to an *alla breve* in m. 412 that marks the beginning of the *Presto* trio.[18]

Trio (mm. 412–530)

The opening gesture of the trio (Ex. 3–27) is fraught with referential meanings. Its octave leaps represent not only a compression of the opening of the scherzo, but the omission of its third (the notes here being only A and D) is an unmistakable reference to the opening of the first movement. The principal tune of the trio—in D major—begins in m. 414, launched by a *fortissimo* D in the bass trombone, and accompanied by staccato quarter notes in the bassoons (Ex. 3–28). This tune is of a type—Joseph Kerman labels them "doublets"—found in many works from Beethoven's later period.[19] Part of the attractiveness of this tune is the way in which it begins a half measure too soon. This anticipatory gesture is the musical equivalent of an *enjambment* in poetry, that is, the beginning of a poetic line is placed at the end of the previous one (Beethoven uses the same device in the "Freude" tune from the finale).

Analysts have made much of the ties between this tune and the "Freude" melody.[20] A first-time listener to the Ninth Symphony cannot know that such a relationship exists at this stage, but this same listener might well be familiar with other tunes of its type, such as the opening theme of the finale of Haydn's Symphony no. 104, the Russian melodies used by Beethoven in the "Razumovsky" Quartets, or the themes heard in the finale of the "Pastoral" Symphony. What these tunes have in common is a kind of studied naïveté; the "Pastoral" example, in particular, is suggestive of the serenity of nature. The trio of the Ninth Symphony is, like the "Pastoral," a musette, a designation that is confirmed by the drone of the second horn in m. 438 (Ex. 3–29). The musette, it should be pointed out, was a small rustic bagpipe. In eighteenth- and nineteenth-century music, the evocation of its sound was meant to suggest to the listener the world of nature.

The harmony of the trio seems perfectly content to remain for the most part on D major or its dominant. Such a lazy harmonic rhythm is one of the defining characteristics of musettes. A wonderful digression does occur in mm. 469–474, as the oboe phrase takes a brief and unexpected excursion

Example 3–27. Ninth Symphony/II, mm. 412–414

Example 3–28. Ninth Symphony/II, mm. 414–422

into F major (Ex. 3–30).[21] Five-octave-deep pedal Ds in mm. 491–530 lend an added measure of stability to the end of the trio, whose relaxed luminosity is disturbed only by the turn to the minor subdominant (G minor) in m. 530, a gesture that prepares the way for a reprise of the scherzo.

Reprise of the Scherzo and Coda

In a letter to Charles Neate in London, Beethoven gave a clear instruction that the reprise of the scherzo should be performed without repeats:

> I seem to have omitted in the second movement of the Symphony that at the reprise of the minor after the Presto, one should begin again at the sign, and then continue *without repeats* until the fermata; then go immediately to the Coda.[22]

Example 3–29. Ninth Symphony/II, mm. 438–446

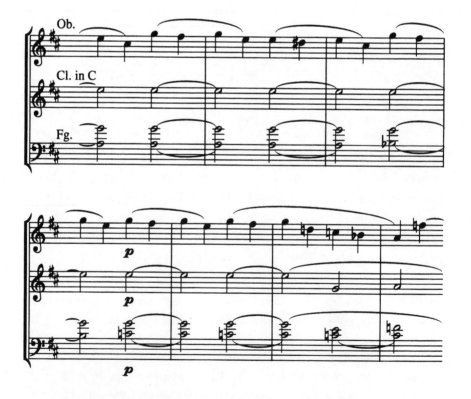

Example 3–30. Ninth Symphony/II, mm. 467–473

The autograph manuscript also contains an indication, marked "streng," that the reprise of the scherzo should omit all repetitions.

   The reprise returns the listener to the beginning of the movement and lasts until m. 395, where a *segno* indicates the start of the coda. But the listener is warned once again that this movement is a scherzo, and Beethoven is not yet finished with his jokes. One characteristic of Beethoven's music composed between 1805 and 1820 was a reprise of the trio, followed by a third playing of the scherzo, thus expanding a three-part scherzo-trio-scherzo form into a weightier five-part structure: a scherzo-trio-scherzo-trio-scherzo. The scherzos of the Fourth, Fifth, Sixth, and Seventh Symphonies all have two trio sections, as does the Piano Trio, op. 97 ("Archduke"). Contemporaries of Beethoven would have had every right to expect that the same would hold true in the Ninth Symphony as well. The events of the coda, at least up to its final three measures, give every indication that a repeat is in the offing. The *stringendo* leading into the trio returns, but the "doublet" is cut off unceremoniously after only seven measures. A *tutti fortissimo* statement of the leaping quarter notes that inaugurated the trio brings the movement to an abrupt conclusion.

III. Adagio molto e cantabile
Sonata-rondo with varied reprises, 4/4 meter

EXPOSITION—mm. 1–82
DEVELOPMENT—mm. 83–98
RECAPITULATION—mm. 99–120
CODA—mm. 121–157

The arrival of the third movement brings the Ninth back to the realm of B♭ major, the tonality that was used for the second key area of the first movement, but which here serves as the primary tonal center. Other tonal centers that have played a significant role thus far—D, G, E♭, and C♭ (B)—also are destined to play pivotal roles in this movement. Of the many examples of instrumental pieces from Beethoven's later period that exhibit what Joseph Kerman has called "voice," this *Adagio* is a prime example. Kerman also has noted that the main theme of this movement, which subsequently yields two decorative variations (variations being another signal feature of

Beethoven's late style), is the progenitor of many lyrical moments in the late quartets, most notably the *Adagio cantabile* of op. 127 (which was composed at about the same time as the Ninth Symphony) and even more directly, the cadential echoes found in the Cavatina from op. 130.

The vocal impulse of Beethoven's later style also is evident in the last movements of his Piano Sonatas, opp. 109 and 111 (Arietta)—important works that preceded the Ninth Symphony. The third and fourth movements of the Ninth, like the sonata finales, conflate these two favorite idioms of Beethoven—song and variation. The variations in the *Adagio* of the Ninth Symphony seem rather perfunctory, relying on decorative figurations more characteristic of Beethoven's earlier style, than the profounder insights one encounters in the variations of the late quartets, sonatas, and the "Diabelli" Variations, op. 120.

This is not to say that the variations of the *Adagio* of the Ninth Symphony are devoid of beauty or ingenuity. The principal difference between this movement and the ones to which it may be compared is the matter of relative weight within the work as a whole. The variation movements of opp. 109 and 111 are the finales of each respective piece—the terminus of a multi-movement work—and as such, they are meant to carry more weight. This is decidedly not the case of the *Adagio* of the Ninth, which may be seen as a lyrical station on the road toward a different goal, and, therefore, not an end in itself. It also is useful to bear in mind that chamber music and symphonic music are vastly different media, with chamber music permitting the composer greater freedom to explore adventuresome harmonic regions. Beethoven came to understand this distinction rather early in his career, having learned the lesson (consciously or not) from Haydn.[23]

Although many have identified the *Adagio* as an example of theme and variation structure, the idiosyncracies of this movement are too plentiful for such an analysis to be persuasive. Table 3–1 presents an analysis of this movement as the hybrid form known as sonata-rondo. The clearly articulated divisions of this movement strongly suggest a rondo with two themes whose reprises are varied.[24] An analysis of this movement as a sonata-rondo pays due attention to the next division of the movement, the section that begins in E♭ major and reaches its climax in C♭ major, by viewing it as a development section, rather than as an interpolated episode. The return to B♭ major for a final varied reprise of the principal theme marks the beginning of an abbreviated recapitulation, followed by an extended coda.

Looking at this movement in closer detail, one sees that its first two

TABLE 3–1

	Exposition			Development	Recapitulation	Coda
A	B	A¹	B¹	Based on A	A²	
Adagio	Andante	Adagio	Andante	Adagio	Lo stesso tempo	
1–24	25–42	43–64	65–82	83–98	99–120	121–157
B♭	D	B♭	G	E♭–C♭	B♭	E♭–B♭–D♭–B♭

measures (Ex. 3–31) are a gently opening curtain that reveal some of the movement's most important motivic and harmonic material. The first sonority heard is the woodwinds, starting with the second bassoon, followed by first bassoon, second clarinet, and finally first clarinet. This sonority foreshadows the extremely important role that the woodwinds will play throughout the movement. Each constituent note of the dominant seventh chord in these opening measures is approached by its upper neighboring tone—a motivic gesture that will also figure prominently in what follows. Also worthy of note is the highly expressive G♭ in the cellos—a chromatic inflection within an otherwise purely diatonic context that at the same moment evokes memories of previous events in the symphony, as well as holding forth a promise (or warning) of future events.

The theme that begins in m. 3 (Ex. 3–32) is one of those hymn-like tunes that Beethoven favored in his late style, but which also may be found in his early- and middle-period compositions.[25] The first two phrases of the tune

Example 3–31. Ninth Symphony/III, mm. 1–3

Example 3-32. Ninth Symphony/III, mm. 3–23

Example 3–32. (Continued)

unfold in regular four-measure groups, with each cadence punctuated by an echo in the clarinet. The C# in mm. 10 and 11 (faithfully echoed by the clarinet) alters the harmony into an augmented triad that has the effect of weakening the arrival on the tonic chord that follows. This destabilization is furthered by the placement of root-position Bb major chords on the weaker beats of mm. 12 and 14, and by shortening of the next phrase of the tune to two measures. The third phrase is a reharmonized and truncated version of the second phrase, which in turn is answered by harmonic and metrical surprises in the fourth phrase—surprises that explain why Beethoven has deliberately weakened the tonic triad. Indeed, this is one of those moments when Beethoven does what Charles Rosen calls the "seemingly impossible" (i.e., turning the most stable of chords—the tonic—into an unstable harmony without a modulation taking place).[26] Unexpectedly, the harmonic movement comes to a halt on the fourth beat of m. 15 on an Eb major (IV) harmony (accompanied by a crescendo, and the first of many arabesques for the fourth horn) and which is prolonged through the first two beats of m. 16. This brief passage turns the tonic temporarily into the dominant of Eb, while at the same time disorienting the listener because of its metrical placement. The reader may recall that Eb major harmony played an important role in the first movement (mm. 24–26). Beethoven has further plans for this tonality later in the third movement, as well as

Example 3–33. Ninth Symphony/III, mm. 25–28

in the finale. The temporary tonicization of E♭ is reiterated by the echo in mm. 20–21.

The extended echo, unlike the original statement in the strings, suppresses the resolution of the final cadence, placing the listener in a state of suspense. In a moment of pure magic, Beethoven gently inflects the harmony to a first-inversion D major sonority, while at the same time dropping the dynamic level from *piano* to *pianissimo.* The sonority of the first-inversion D major chord is by now a familiar one. Based on previous experience, however, the listener should be alert to the possibility that Beethoven may lead this chord to a resolution in any number of directions. Only when the bass moves to the root of the chord on the second half of m. 24 does one suspect that D major is the goal the composer has chosen. A shift to 3/4 meter, a change of tempo to *Andante moderato,* and a change of key signature to two sharps, greet the arrival of the second theme (Ex. 3–33).

The *Andante* tune, with its anticipations and appoggiaturas, has an unmistakable yearning quality. In an 1837 analytical essay on the Ninth Symphony, Henry John Gauntlett, an English critic and composer, identified this tune as a polacca.[27] Gauntlett's characterization was provoked, no doubt, by the theme's meter, as well as by its syncopated first beat. Whether or not this tune is truly a polonaise is open to debate, although its graceful dance-like character is often overlooked by conductors who choose a tempo for this movement that is much slower than the ♩ = 63 indicated by Beethoven.[28]

Example 3–34. Ninth Symphony/III, mm. 43–46

The *Andante* unfolds as a double period in regular four measure phrases. The final two measures of the section reverse the process that led the harmony from B♭ to D by coming to a halt on the dominant seventh of B♭ in preparation of the reprise of the *Adagio* theme. This reprise is interesting not only because it is varied, but also because the melody has clearly been affected by the *Andante* tune. The *Adagio* theme, which unfolds in animated eighth and sixteenth notes, now includes suspensions and appoggiaturas derived from the *Andante* (Ex. 3–34). The echoes of the theme's cadences—still in the winds—remain rather aloof from the increased activity of this varied reprise, retaining the purity of the melody's original rhythmic pace. The basic structure, phraseology, and harmonization of the original *Adagio* also remain the same throughout the reprise, as do the final two measures which once again lead to a first inversion D major chord. But this time, instead of remaining in D major, Beethoven uses his first inversion chord as a conduit to G major, a sonority that is reached on the final beat of m. 64.

Having established G as the new tonal center, Beethoven continues with a varied reprise of the *Andante* tune. The most significant change in this statement lies in its scoring, which now places the woodwinds in the foreground. The double-period structure of the tune is retained, but the counterpoint surrounding the second phrase is considerably more active and expressive than it had been earlier.

The final two measures of G major *Andante* take an unexpected turn toward E♭ major and prepare the way for the development section of the sonata-rondo design. The arrival on E♭ major, surprising as it is, makes sense from several perspectives. This key stands in the same relationship to G (♭ VI) as did B♭ did to D not only in the earlier part of this movement, but also in the exposition of the first movement. The reader may also recall that an E♭ sonority played an important role in mm. 24–26 of the first movement's

exposition, as well as in the retransition to D minor before the recapitulation of the scherzo. In the context of the third movement, this passage in E♭
major explains the importance of the harmonic event that we first encountered in the third phrase of the *Adagio* melody (mm. 15–16).

Standing as it does at the spiritual and temporal center of the entire
Ninth Symphony, the E♭ major passage possesses an uncanny serenity that
at first blush would seem to be at odds with labeling it a development
section. Its poetic tranquility—or tranquil poetry—transcends any theoret-
ical label, and its otherworldly beauty seems to shield the listener from all
possible harm. Virtually everyone who has written on the Ninth Symphony
has taken note of the special nature of this passage. Perhaps Robert Winter
put it best: "Beethoven seems to have retreated into a world where time has
stopped and eternity has begun."[29] Indeed, in passages from the finales of
the Piano Sonatas, opp. 109 and 111, the magician Beethoven had demonstrated how it is possible to make time stand still. Who has not at one time
or another wished, with Faust, that the beauty of these moments would last
forever?

A factor that helps create the mood of this section is its remarkable
scoring—two clarinets, a bassoon, and a horn—a combination that brings to
mind the sonority of the many serenades for winds (*Harmoniemusik*) of the
eighteenth century. Couched in a *pianissimo* dynamic, the first clarinet,
imitated two measures later by the horn, presents the opening fourths of
the *Adagio* theme, while the second clarinet and bassoon discreetly em-
broider a counterpoint derived from the rhythm of mm. 1–2 and from the
Andante theme. The pizzicato strings reinforce the rhythm, but as the harmony shifts toward E♭ minor, the eighth notes are pressed into triplets. The
horn at the same time begins an extraordinary descent to B♭ in m. 89, after
which it suddenly leaps into a higher register as the music enters into the
tonal region of C♭ major. The arrival at this goal is punctuated by the entrance of the flute in m. 91, and for the next three measures the flute and
horn lovingly sing a duet at the interval of the octave. All time and motion
cease in m. 96, at which point the unaccompanied horn plays a serene (yet
perilous for the player!) scale passage in C♭ major. The strings resume their
arpeggiation accompanied by a crescendo in m. 97, reaching a climax on
the fourth beat of m. 98, when the harmony slips magically back into B♭
major to mark the arrival of the recapitulation.

It is interesting to note that Beethoven placed the extraordinary horn
solos in this movement in the fourth horn part. There has been much

speculation about what kind of instrument he may have had in mind, as well as about why he assigned the difficult and exposed solos to the fourth-chair player. Beethoven's Conversation Books, letters, and sketches shed no light on the issue, and nothing has surfaced to confirm the theory of Sir George Grove and Tovey that the fourth hornist at the premiere of the Ninth Symphony may have owned an instrument equipped with valves. A two-valved horn was available in Vienna in Beethoven's time, but this instrument was not yet the chromatic horn found in modern orchestras. It would have been of no help in playing the Cb major scale. Recent performances and recordings demonstrate that the part can be played successfully on the natural horn with the aid of hand-stopping to inflect those pitches that do not fall within the instrument's natural scale. Indeed, Berlioz found the colors that result from the hand-stopping (*notes bouchés*) to be a desirable quality in a performance of the Cb major scale.[30] The *Adagio* calls for two pairs of horns, one pair in Bb and the other in Eb. Since the passages in question are all cast in Eb, they would have to have been performed by either the third or fourth chair player. The range of the part, which extends over more than four octaves (BBb to cb¹), as well as its many arpeggiated figures, makes it more suitable for a low horn specialist than for one who specializes in higher notes.[31]

But to return to the music: A smooth transition to the recapitulation is abetted by a shift to 12/8 meter, whose flow had been foreshadowed by the triplets of the preceding section. The flute and oboe sing the *Adagio* theme in its entirety, under which the first violins spin arabesque-like decorations in sixteenth notes (Ex. 3–35) while the clarinets resume their role as carriers of the cadential echoes. The agogic stress on the Eb major harmony now unleashes even bolder escapades in the fourth horn (mm. 111 and 117), whose arpeggiations rival the delicate embroideries of the violins.

The listener justifiably would expect a reprise of the *Andante* tune to follow at this point, but Beethoven instead moves directly to the coda, which is ushered in by a noble *tutti* fanfare, with calls answered by the first violins (Ex. 3–36). Some analysts have identified this fanfare as a new theme, but in reality it is a further compression of the eighth-note rhythms from the development section (m. 87), now shifted from their formerly subsidiary role to the foreground. The music dwells for a moment on the head motive of the *Adagio* tune, before resuming its gentle progress forward. The clarinets, bassoons, and horns broadly sing the first phrase of the tune (mm. 127–130) accompanied by the peripatetic violins and a

Example 3–35. Ninth Symphony/III, mm. 99–103

Example 3–35. (Continued)

Example 3–36. Ninth Symphony/III, mm. 121–122

crescendo that leads to a second presentation of the fanfare. The conclusion of the fanfare this time produces one of the most awe-inspiring moments in the entire Ninth Symphony. The harmony in m. 133 suddenly
plunges, *fortissimo,* into the dark realm of D♭ major, as the second violins
attempt to maintain a sense of forward movement with a continuation of
the head motive of the fanfare.[32] The music rises sequentially through the
still darker realms of E♭ and B♭ minor, until a shaft of light penetrates the
darkness, and B♭ major is restored, never again to be threatened.

The remainder of the coda seems intent on preventing this movement
from coming to an end, as again and again the music rises and falls in
expressive waves. The peaceful mood remains intact, save for the plaintive
G♭s that darken the harmony in mm. 151–153—a gesture that at once serves
as a reminder of that same expressive note first sounded by the cellos in m.
2 as well as a warning of new disturbances that lie ahead in the finale.
Indeed, the return of sixteenth-note triplets in mm. 151–154 may also be a
deliberate reference back to the murmuring sextuplets that began the entire symphony. One final crescendo sweeps away the momentary doubt,
and the movement concludes with an overriding sense of calm.

Chapter 4

THE NINTH: THE CHORAL FINALE

---- ✀ ----

GENERAL OBSERVATIONS

ew movements in the history of symphonic music have generated as diverse an array of analytical and aesthetic interpretations as the finale of the Ninth Symphony. Its structure, if not its meaning, has at times seemed ineffable. One can understand how Tovey might have concluded that it is "a law unto itself," while at the same time asserting that there "is no part of Beethoven's Choral Symphony which does not become clearer to us when we assume that the choral finale is right; and there is hardly a point that does not become difficult and obscure as soon as we fall into the habit which assumes that the choral finale is wrong."[1] More recently, Maynard Solomon, in reflecting over the entirety of the work, observed that "the Ninth Symphony is a symbol whose referents cannot be completely known and whose full effects will never be experienced."[2] But the complexities inherent in the finale have neither dissuaded analysts from plying their trade nor prevented audiences from enjoying the work in performance.

Among the referents to which Solomon alludes is a network of semiotic codes that would have been familiar to Beethoven's contemporaries, although they are no longer quite so widely known today except by specialists. Other referents are unique to Beethoven's later style and to the syntax of this particular work. Such codes (or topics, to use the term suggested by Leonard Ratner) pervade all music of the so-called Classical style, and they encompass concepts such as "ombra," "musette," "sensibility," "march,"

"pastoral," "learned style," "hunting," and "aria."[3] While an understanding
of these topics can provide considerable insights into the meaning of works
from this period, modern audiences have been able to intuit a great deal
without the benefit of knowing them. When, as is the case with the finale of
the Ninth Symphony, words are brought into play, however, the meaning
implicit in some of these codes is rendered explicit. The goal of the Ninth
Symphony, the text of the last movement teaches us, is to join Elysium and
heaven through the agent of joy. Athens and Jerusalem, so to speak, are
reconciled under joy's "gentle wing." *All* mankind—Christian, Jew, Muslim,
pagan, beggar, prince, good, and evil—(will) become brothers.[4] The idealism of the Enlightenment and the French Revolution remains alive so long
as audiences continue to be inspired by Beethoven and Schiller's vision.

    Many essayists have agreed that the first movement of the Ninth Sym-
phony plays out a scenario of heroic tragedy. The scherzo then reiterates
that same tragedy as farce (with the musette-like trio offering a pastoral
respite), while the *Adagio* dwells in the realm of serene, yet intense, lyricism. Such descriptive interpretations (known as hermeneutics) may be
helpful to the listener, although any attempt to be more specific regarding
the meaning of the music becomes too speculative to be of any real use.
Technical analyses, of which there are several examples, are useful only to
those with sufficient training to penetrate them. It is safe to say that relatively little controversy surrounds the musical forms that are operative in
the first two movements of the Ninth. The third movement has proven
somewhat more problematical. Structuralists are quick to part company,
however, where the finale is concerned. Some critics of the Ninth Symphony have faulted the finale for its seeming want of order. Others, refusing
to accept that Beethoven was capable of composing without a rigorous,
thorough, and consistent logic, have sought to either find or impose order.
Even an understanding of the most obvious precedent—the Choral Fantasy,
op. 80—offers little help in penetrating the structural mysteries of the finale.[5]

    It is impossible to do justice to all analytical points of view, but a sum-
mary of some representative analyses may be useful. No structural reading,
of course, can ever be considered definitive, and the narrative that accompanies many analyses demonstrates that the writers were aware of predecessors' work. Heinrich Schenker, in his celebrated monograph of 1912,
divides the finale into three large sections.[6] The first consists of two parts—
purely instrumental and vocal, respectively—encompassing mm. 1–207
and 208–594. The second section, which is sung by the chorus without
the vocal soloists, begins with "Seid umschlungen" at m. 595 (*Andante*

maestoso) and continues through m. 654. Schenker's third section comprises three smaller subsections: a) mm. 655–762, defined by the chorus alone and beginning the contrapuntal joining of "Seid umschlungen" with the "Freude" theme, b) mm. 763–850 (beginning with the *Allegro ma non tanto*), defined by the use of soloists and chorus, and c) mm. 851–940, beginning with the *Prestissimo* in which the soloists no longer participate.

Schenker's monograph was followed in 1930 by the important and richly detailed essay of Otto Baensch.[7] Baensch, guided by Alfred Lorenz's theories of form in Richard Wagner's operas, viewed the finale of the Ninth Symphony as an example of the venerable Bar form—A A B, or *Stollen, Stollen, Abgesang*—dating from the Middle Ages and immortalized in Wagner's *Die Meistersinger von Nürnberg*. Baensch sees the first half of the finale as two immense *Stollen*, one instrumental (mm. 1–207) and one vocal (mm. 208–330). Baensch goes on to view the remainder of the movement as a huge double *Abgesang*, the first running from m. 331 to m. 594, the second from m. 595 ("Seid umschlungen") to the end. The principal feature that unites Baensch's two *Abgesang* segments is the shift to D major in each case (from B♭ major in the first, and from G major in the second).

More recently, analyses have been offered by Ernest Sanders and Robert Winter.[8] Sanders argues that the movement essentially is a sonata-form structure with a double exposition (such as one finds in concertos, according to some analysts). The first exposition (mm. 1–207) is incomplete. The second, which comprises mm. 208–431, parallels the first one insofar as it includes an introduction, a main theme (with three statements instead of four), and a bridge. In Sanders's view, the secondary theme is the "Turkish" music that begins in m. 331 in the contrasting tonality of B♭ major. The development section encompasses mm. 431–542 and the recapitulation, defined by a return to D major, begins in m. 543. Within the recapitulation, the bridge section is the "Seid umschlungen" music in the subdominant key of G major (mm. 591–654), and the double fugue in compound meter (mm. 655–729) represents the concluding section. After a transition (mm. 730–762), the movement concludes with a tripartite coda.

Robert Winter's analysis, which owes much to Sanders, can be set forth as follows:[9]

Opening Ritornello (mm. 1–207)
   Horror Fanfare/Recitative
   Recollection: Movements 1, 2, and 3
   Joy Theme: Statements 1, 2, 3, and 4

Exposition (mm. 208–431)
   Horror Fanfare/Recitative
   Primary Area (Joy) 1, 2, and 3
   Secondary Area (Turkish)
Development (mm. 432–542)
   Retransition
Recapitulation (mm. 543–654)
   Joy Theme
   Awe Theme
Coda (mm. 655–940)
   Episode 1: Joy and Awe
   Episode 2: Joy
   Episode 3: Awe and Joy

The techniques of variation, concerto, and sonata form invoked in the various analyses seem plausible, but leave important questions either unanswered or poorly explained. If, for example, the return of the chorus (mm. 543 ff.) after the instrumental double fugue marks the recapitulation within a sonata-form design (Sanders and Winter), how is one to explain the appearance of a new tempo, theme, and tonality for "Seid umschlungen, Millionen!" (m. 595ff.)? Schenker's tripartite division, on the other hand, places this same passage in the center of the movement, but without accounting for its insistent G-major tonality—an axiom of Sanders's and Winter's analyses (although not rigorously pursued in either). Baensch, heavily influenced by Lorenz, seems inclined to make the music fit the Bar form, whether or not this approach makes structural or dramatic sense.[10]

Charles Rosen, Leo Treitler, and more recently Michael Tusa have argued that the structure of the finale is that of a "four-movement symphonic form."[11] Rosen, for instance, writes:

The opening expository movement [of the finale] leads to a B flat major scherzo in military style with Turkish music; a slow movement in G major introduces a new theme; and a finale begins with the triumphant combination of the two themes in double counterpoint.... About the shape itself there is no question: the proportions and the feeling for climax and expansion are solely those of the classical symphony ... With the Ninth Symphony, the variation set is completely transformed into the most massive of finales, one that is itself a four-movement work in miniature.

. While I fully agree with the essentials of Rosen's analysis, I would take his argument an important step further. The finale's structure is not only the articulation of a four-movement symphony, but is a *microcosm of the entire Ninth Symphony itself,* the outline of which is as follows[12]:

"Movement" I (mm. 1–330)
    "Introduction": Fanfare, Instrumental Recitative, Recollections (mm. 1–91)
    Instrumental theme and variations (mm. 92–207)
    Fanfare, Vocal Recitative, Vocal theme and variations (mm. 208–330)
    Text = Verses 1–3
"Movement" II (mm. 331–594)
    "Scherzo" ("Turkish" music)
    Text = Chorus 4
"Movement" III (mm. 595–654)
    "Andante-Adagio"
    Text = Chorus 1 and 3
"Movement" IV (mm. 655–940)
    "Finale"
    Text = Verse 1 and Chorus 1

The more detailed analysis that follows here describes the events of the finale along this line.

"Movement I," Introduction

Presto—Allegro ma non troppo—Tempo I—Vivace—Tempo I—
Adagio cantabile—Tempo I. Allegro—Allegro assai—
Tempo I. Allegro—Allegro assai (mm. 1–91)

The full force of the *tutti* orchestra completely and rudely shatters the serene ending of the third movement. More precisely, it might be said that the conclusion of the *Adagio* hangs over into the start of the finale. Had it not been for the inconvenient necessity of re-tuning the timpani and of changing the crooks of the natural horns and trumpets, Beethoven might

Example 4–1. Beethoven: Ninth Symphony/finale, mm. 1–2

very well have indicated that the last movement should ensue in an uninterrupted *segue*. Beethoven himself had forged such a link in earlier works,
most notably in his Fifth and Sixth Symphonies, but none of these precedents result in the sheer disturbance produced by the opening measures of
the Ninth's finale.

The suggestion that a *segue* may be appropriate is based on purely musical considerations. The opening harmony of the *Presto* is a tonic D-minor
chord in first inversion (the F in the contrabassoon sounding below the A in
the timpani), over which is sounded octave B♭s in the flutes, oboes, and
clarinets (Ex. 4–1). Clearly B♭ is the source of the harmonic clash, and
while the opening of Beethoven's First Symphony demonstrated that the
composer had no compunction about beginning a piece with an *unpre-
pared* dissonance, the dissonance that opens the finale of the Ninth Symphony is a *prepared* one—prepared by the B♭ tonality of the *Adagio* movement that precedes it. The B♭—resolving in normal fashion to A—may
therefore be identified as a suspension held over from the *Adagio*. Any
performance of the Ninth Symphony with modern resources (pedal timpani and valved horns and trumpets) is capable of rendering the effect of
this suspension all the more clearly by beginning the *Presto* with little or no
pause after the *Adagio*.

The downward half-step resolution of the suspension from B♭ to A is
familiar since this linear gesture, as discussed in chapter 3, has played
a prominent structural role throughout the first three movements of the
Ninth. The purpose of beginning this movement with a suspension, as well
as with the chaotic measures that follow it (Wagner referred to it as the
Schreckensfanfare—the fanfare of terror) is to disrupt the mood of the preceding *Adagio* in the rudest possible fashion. Beethoven achieves this end
by superimposing two pitches that have played a pivotal role throughout

Figure 4–1.

the piece. The principle of compression that we have been observing since the beginning of the first movement now finds its ultimate expression in the grating superimposition of these pitches. Bb major and D minor have been near neighbors all along, separated by the merest of all intervals—the semitone (Fig. 4–1). The gesture here is shattering in its effect, but it also is logical.

The logic of what follows—(1) the invocation of reminiscences from the earlier movements, and (2) the recitative for the cellos and contrabasses—is, however, less clear. Beethoven himself had created a useful model for reminiscences at least as early as in the finale of his Fifth Symphony, where the scherzo is invoked at the end of the development section of the finale. The salient difference between that movement and the finale of the Ninth is, of course, dramatic and structural placement. The unequivocal triumph of C Major over C Minor in the Fifth Symphony is assured long before the ghostly spirit of the scherzo returns toward the end of the development section. This recall of the scherzo never truly threatens the ultimate victory of C Major, but rather intensifies that victory (reaffirmed by the recapitulation) by reminding the listener of the nearly-forgotten terror that had so effectively been overcome. In the Ninth, however, the victory has yet to be achieved, despite the episodic invocation of D major in earlier movements. Another important difference lies in the fact that the finale of the Ninth conjures a reminiscence of *all* preceding movements, and not just the scherzo.

Other Beethovenian examples of thematic recall come closer in time to the composition of the Ninth Symphony and therefore may shed even more relevant light on the composer's train of thought about such matters. One such passage occurs in the last movement of the Piano Sonata in Ab, op. 110, of 1821, where the *fuga* is interrupted by a return, marked *L'istesso tempo di Arioso,* in which the earlier *Arioso dolente* (*Klagender Gesang* [Lamenting Song]) is evoked, now marked *Perdendo le forze, dolento* (*Ermattet klagend*

[Losing force, lamenting]). This poignant passage serves as a bridge between the first part of the fugue and the second, in which the subject is inverted. Martin Cooper refers to the overall design of this movement as a conflation of slow movement and finale.[13] This observation is useful with regard to the finale of the Ninth Symphony, a movement in which Beethoven creates a multitude of fusions, including the merging of instrumental and vocal elements. The process of recollection, therefore, serves as a vehicle for linking the vocal finale with the earlier instrumental movements of the work. The finale of op. 110 may thus be seen as a helpful step along the way toward resolving the single thorniest compositional issue that Beethoven faced in the finale of the Ninth Symphony, the conjoining of vocal music to that which has been purely instrumental.

Another example of thematic recall, albeit a more subtle one, comes from the "Hammerklavier" Sonata, op. 106, whose genesis also overlapped with that of the Ninth Symphony. The passage in question comes near the end of *Largo* introduction to the concluding fugue. In this case, Beethoven compels the listener to glance backward toward the main theme of the first and second movements, while at the same time providing an anticipation the subject of the fugue we are about to hear (Ex. 4–2).[14] It may be argued that the use of thematic recall in both opp. 106 and 110 is more sophisticated than what occurs in the finale of the Ninth Symphony. But it is important to bear in mind (as Beethoven himself surely did) that these genres—sonata and symphony—do not allow for the same subtlety and freedom of expression. We cannot expect a symphony to behave like chamber music any more than we should expect a sonata to have the extended timbral palette of a symphony. But all the same one may observe, as we find here, similarities between Beethoven's chamber and orchestral works throughout the course of his career.[15]

We now arrive at the famous cello and contrabass instrumental recitatives.[16] While Joseph Kerman's useful observations about Beethoven's desire in his later style to imbue his instrumental music with a vocal quality may be germane to the case at hand, further insight into the composer's decision to use instrumental recitative is provided by looking at his earlier experiments with this device. Several such examples may be cited, most notably the Sonata for Piano, op. 31, no. 2, as well as op. 106 and, again, op. 110. Jurgen Thym has pointed out that in Beethoven, the unusual gesture of instrumental receitative serves a twofold function of mimesis and gesture that may be elucidated along either structural or less specific

Example 4–2. Beethoven: Piano Sonata in B♭, op. 106 ("Hammerklavier")/ *Largo* introduction to finale

interpretive lines.[17] Thym cites as an example op. 110, where Beethoven, in his search for a mediation between larger movements of considerably different characters (the quirky duple-meter scherzo and the *Arioso dolente* mentioned earlier), uses recitative as the most effective conduit. It is useful to observe here that the movement that follows the recitative passage in op. 110 is derived from a vocal model. Such, of course, is also the case in the finale of the Ninth Symphony, where the instrumental recitatives are preceded by three purely instrumental movements and are followed by an instrumental presentation of the vocally derived "Freude" theme—a theme that will quite soon literally take voice. The introduction of instrumental recitative, then, is the first gesture employed to reconcile the multiplicity of genres that occurs in the finale.

An additional explanation for Beethoven's use of instrumental recitative is the primary harmonic function of all recitative: the facilitation of quick modulation from one tonality to another. The reminiscences from the first three movements are couched in the first-inversion dominant of D (first movement), A minor with a shift toward F major (second movement), and B♭ major (third movement). The cello and contrabass recitative, therefore, may also be seen as an efficient tool for bridging different tonal regions. From a structural standpoint, therefore, the recitative is rendered necessary by the thematic recalls that it serves to connect.

It is also interesting to note at this point that each of the thematic recollections recalls the middle of its respective movement. The evocation of the first movement is from m. 170 of its development section, where the murmuring fifth is undergirded by the third of the chord in the bass, gently, yet urgently, punctuated by the trumpets and timpani.[18] Similarly, the eight-measure recall from the scherzo is reminiscent of its development section (m. 177ff., but in the rhythm of four beats rather than three). The same may be said for the citation from the *Adagio*, where the spirit of the development, dominated by the sonority of the *Harmonie* (wind) instruments (m. 83ff.), is invoked. To these three recollections we should now add an anticipation—the brief foreshadowing of the "Freude" melody on the dominant of D major. Beethoven was free to select virtually any segment from the earlier movements that he saw fit, of course. His choices, however, seem designed to keep the listener in a state of suspense. Beethoven truly is playing the role of dramatist, and recitative is a musical dramatist's tool *par excellence.* Having hinted at the "Freude" theme in m. 77, the final recitative passage brings us to an affirmation of both the new theme and its tonality of D major by means of a decisive cadence (m. 91).

In viewing the finale of the Ninth Symphony in this manner, the gesture of presenting reminiscences of the previous three movements with an anticipation of the "Freude" tune takes on a layer of meaning in addition to a rejection of the spirit of the earlier movements. These reminiscences and anticipations in themselves are a smaller microcosmic division of the overall design of the piece—a forecast of the structure of this most unusual of finales. Having stated his premise, Beethoven proceeds to the business at hand.

"Movement I," Continued

Allegro assai (mm. 92–207)

The cellos and contrabasses immediately present the famous tune, beginning in m. 92 (Ex. 4–3). Attention to detail is a quality that separates the great composers from the merely good ones, and Beethoven's place should never be in doubt, even when he is dealing with the essence of simplicity. Detail here concerns two matters: the crescendos in mm. 103 and 111 and the enjambment that connects the phrases at the end of these same measures. Both gestures serve to keep the tune, with its *a a′ b a′ b a′* structure, from becoming too predictable in its otherwise straight-forward four-measure phraseology.[19]

Self-contained tunes of a "popular" cast may be found in the mature instrumental works of Mozart and, even more characteristically, in the music of Haydn. Often, but not always, such tunes form the basis for variations. Dénes Bartha has suggested that the famous tune "Gott erhalte Franz den Kaiser" from the second movement of Haydn's "Emperor" Quartet was the likely model for the "Freude" melody and it is not insignificant that variation procedure plays an important role in both works. While Beethoven was certainly familiar with the usefulness of "popular" tunes, he was often wary of them, as seen in his dismissal of Diabelli's waltz tune as a "cobbler's patch" (*Schusterfleck*).[20] This opinion, it should be quickly noted, did not prevent such tunes from becoming worthy grist for Beethoven's creative mill, as the "Diabelli" Variations, op. 120 so eloquently attest.

The first two instrumental variations of the "Freude" theme, with their

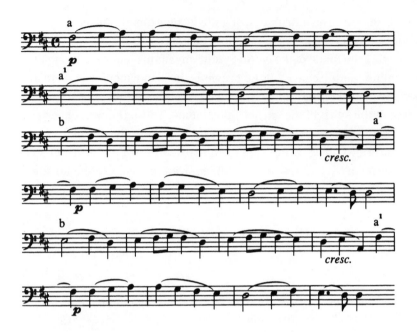

Example 4–3. Ninth Symphony/finale, "Freude" theme

respective three- and four-voice counterpoint, bring no essential alterations to the tune itself, except for the octave in which it is sounded and the
instruments that play it (two additional features the finale of the Ninth
shares with Haydn's "Emperor" Quartet, as well as with the finale of the
"Eroica" Symphony). A particularly attractive sonority is provided in these
variations by the addition of the bassoon to the luxuriant strings.[21] The in-
toxicatingly powerful *tutti* variation that follows (beginning at m. 164), with
its stirring martial character, similarly leaves the tune relatively unchanged
except for matters of scoring, dynamics, and details of articulation.

Having introduced the "Freude" theme and subjected it to three instrumental variations, Beethoven now introduces a codetta by means of a sequence (mm. 188–198) that eventually comes to rest on the dominant of the
newly triumphant D major. A new phrase is hesitantly introduced, marked
piano and *poco ritenente,* whose chromatic harmony casts a momentary
shadow on the hegemony of D major. A tentative sequence based on this
new idea traverses A major, B minor, and E♭ minor, before jolting us back
to the dominant of D with an explosive *forte* return to *Tempo I.*

"Movement I," conclusion

Presto—Recitativo—Allegro assai; Verses 1–3
of "An die Freude" (mm. 208–330)[22]

Freude, schöner Götterfunken,	Joy, beauteous spark of divinity,
Tochter aus Elysium,	Daughter of Elysium,
Wir betreten feuertrunken,	We enter drunk with fire,
Himmlische, dein Heiligtum!	Heavenly one, your sanctuary!
Deine Zauber binden wieder,	Thy magic power reunites,
Was die Mode streng getheilt;	All that custom has strictly divided;
Alle Menschen werden Brüder	All men become brothers
Wo dein sanfter Flügel weilt.	Where your gentle wing abides.
Wem der große Wurf gelungen,	Whoever has been so fortunate,
Eines Freundes Freund zu sein,	To be the friend of a friend,
Wer ein holdes Weib errungen,	He who has obtained a dear wife,
Mische seinem Jubel ein!	Add his jubilation!
Ja, wer auch nur eine Seele	Yes, whoever also one soul
Sein nennt auf dem Erdenrund!	Can call his own in the earthly round!
Und wer's nie gekönnt, der stehle	And who never could, he should steal
Weinend sich aus diesem Bund!	Weeping from this fellowship!
Freude trinken alle Wesen	All beings drink joy
An den Brüsten der Natur;	At the breasts of Nature;
Alle Guten, alle Bösen	All things good, all things evil
Folgen ihrer Rosenspur.	Follow her rosy trail.
Küße gab sie uns und Reben,	Kisses gave she us and wine,
Einen Freund, geprüft in Tod;	A friend, proven even in death;
Wollust ward dem Wurm gegeben,	Ecstasy is granted even to the worm
Und der Cherub steht vor Gott.	And the cherub stands before God.

The excursions into B and E♭ minor alert us to the possibility of a new onslaught of D minor, which is precisely what we encounter with a grating reprise of the *Schreckensfanfare*, ushered in by a superimposition of a D minor triad and a fully diminished seventh chord based on its leading tone (Ex. 4–4).

The human voice is at last ushered in, but with the tersest of all possible proclamations from the bass soloist:

Example 4–4. Ninth Symphony/finale, mm. 208–209

> O friends, not these sounds! rather let us sing more pleasant ones, and
> more full of joy.

Regardless of how familiar one is with the Ninth Symphony, this moment that introduces the human voice never fails to retain its epochal quality. It is a fateful event in the history of music. Several writers have alluded
to the assertion by Czerny that Beethoven had articulated to his friends
after the first performance of the Ninth that the vocal finale was an error
and that he should have replaced it with a purely instrumental one.[23] While
one may choose not to dispute Czerny's allegation, it is important to bear in
mind that despite any misgivings Beethoven may have had, he did not
retreat from his original plan. As we have seen in chapter 2, Schiller's "An
die Freude" had occupied Beethoven's thoughts for a long time. It may
never be possible to determine just why Beethoven chose the Ninth Symphony to be the vehicle through which he would finally fulfill his long-held
desire to bring Schiller's poem to music. We can assert, however, that many
an *ex post facto* explanation has been tendered by posterity. Perhaps the
composer saw the Ninth Symphony as his last best opportunity to deal with
"An die Freude" in a forum worthy of what he perceived to be its exalted

vision. Having recently completed a monumental vocal work with the *Missa solemnis,* it would not have been unreasonable for Beethoven to have decided to strike while the iron was still hot. Words, and how to set them to music, were very much on his mind.

We may add to this Joseph Kerman's astute observation that much of Beethoven's music in the later stages of his career searched, as it were, for "voice."[24] The time was ripe once again for the "voice" to become fully articulate through the use of words. The fact that Beethoven wrote no symphonies after the Ninth, and therefore ended his career in this genre with a vocal movement, became useful propaganda for Wagner. One can only wonder what implications a purely instrumental Tenth Symphony might have had for the master from Bayreuth.

Beethoven's introductory text refers to the *Schreckensfanfare,* and not to the "sounds" of the first three movements (as has been suggested by some writers). The music for "O friends, not these sounds" is a slightly varied version of the first phrase of the previously heard instrumental recitative, while the pitches given for "rather let us sing more pleasant ones" closely follow the second phrase.[25] Only then does the key signature revert to D major for the words "and more full of joy," as the voice invokes the sixth and final phrase of the instrumental recitative (patterned after the pickup to m. 85).

The autograph manuscript reveals that Beethoven at one point considered resolving the dominant harmony in m. 236 to the tonic, which would have produced a cadence analogous to the one heard in m. 91. The composer rejected this closure in favor of a renewed foreshadowing of the tune similar to mm. 77–80, but now punctuated by the soloist and basses of the chorus on the key word "Freude." Surely Beethoven's purpose in altering his original plan was to foster a sense of continuation that will inexorably draw the listener into Schiller's poem, which now begins to unfold in m. 241, lightly accompanied by plucked strings, oboe, and clarinet (note the small alteration on the last beat of m. 244—another one of those small details that wards off predictability!). A new element is introduced by a *forte* repetition of the last two phrases of the tune sounded by the *tutti* orchestra and chorus, a feature that Beethoven retains throughout the two variations that follow. The vocal presentation of the tune and of its first variation is followed by the codetta figure that we first encountered after the third instrumental variation, now neatly rounded off into a graceful four-measure phrase (Ex. 4–5).

Example 4–5. Ninth Symphony/finale, mm. 265–268

The choral echo of the tune (mm. 257–264) omits the soprano voice, a feature that continues through the first phrase of the first vocal variation ("Whoever has been so fortunate"). It is likely that by holding the soprano voice in reserve, Beethoven was engaging in a bit of text painting. When the soprano joins in taking up the tenor's line from the first phrase for the words "He who has obtained a dear wife / Add his jubilation," the new sonority gives the variation a real lift. The dramatically graphic diminuendo on the words "he should steal weeping from this fellowship" is no less inspired a pictorial touch. The second vocal variation ("All beings drink joy at the breasts of nature") becomes positively intoxicated with roulades of eighth notes. Here again Beethoven becomes a true *Tondichter* by beginning the strophe as a duet for bass and tenor ("All beings drink joy"), adding the alto ("All things good, all things evil"), and again reserving the soprano for the end ("Kisses gave she us and wine"). Having whipped up a Bacchanalian frenzy of rejoicing, Beethoven's chorus joins the instruments for the codetta, which this time reverts to its original open endedness, and which leads to a harmonic *coup de théâtre* in m. 330—the celebrated shift from the dominant of D major to F major— for the exalted vision of the cherub standing before the throne of God (Ex. 4–6).[26]

"Movement II," Scherzo

Allegro assai vivace. Alla Marcia; Schiller, "Chorus"
from Verse 4 (mm. 331–594)

Froh, wie seine Sonnen fliegen	Happily, flying like his suns
Durch des Himmels Prächt' gen Plan,	Through Heaven's splendid firmament,
Laufet Brüder, eure Bahn,	Run, Brothers, your course.
Freudig, wie ein Held zum Siegen.	Joyfully, like a hero towards victory.

Theorists who view the finale of the Ninth as an exemplar of sonata form consider the music at the onset of the Turkish March as the beginning of the second key area (B♭ major) of the exposition section, which leads without break to the development section (the first double fugue, beginning in m. 431). There are many reasons to support this view. The juxtaposition of D major and B♭ major presents a parallel to the sequence of keys that form the exposition of the first movement (D minor and B♭ major). Furthermore, the contrapuntal turbulence of the double fugue and its far-flung modulations behave in just the manner that we would expect from a development section. Finally, the triumphant return of the chorus singing the opening strophe of the "Freude" theme in D major (m. 543) certainly bears the fingerprint of a true recapitulation.

While in some respects the Turkish March represents a continuation of what we have encountered up to this point (i.e., a new variation of the "Freude" theme), its change of key, tempo, and meter sets it apart in many ways. Beethoven's striking treatment of "vor Gott" at the end of the previous "movement" also suggests that the new section represents a fresh beginning. Looking back toward the second movement of the work, we noted that the scherzo seemed to be a replaying of the tragedy of the first movement in the character of a farce. It would not be unreasonable, therefore, to view the Turkish March as an analogous reenactment of that past event. The metrical continuity of 6/8 time also argues for viewing mm. 331–594 as a discrete unit. One argument against seeing the segment this way, however, concerns the issue of tonality. This new "moment" begins in B♭ major, but concludes in D major (with an abrupt move to G major after the chorus is finished), whereas movements in the Classical style customarily end in the same key in which they begin. But it should be noted that we are not speaking here of discrete movements, but rather *gestures* of movements within the finale. Seen from this perspective, the issue of tonal integrity is less crucial than other factors.

One further issue needs to be explored before looking closer at the events of this section. Few writers have failed to mention the irony of Beethoven's decision to follow Schiller's vision of the cherub at the throne of God with the "vulgarity" of the "Turkish" music. It would seem at first glance that we have suddenly moved from the sublime to the ridiculous. But have we? Schiller's chorus, with its comparison of heros running their victorious course like suns flying through Heaven's firmament, may be more religiously-based than commonly believed.

Compare verses 5–7 from Psalm 19 with Schiller. The text is given here both in English and as it appears in Luther's translation (i.e., the text of the Bible that Schiller would have known):

Example 4–6. Ninth Symphony/finale, mm. 326–330

Er hat der Sonne ein Zelt am Himmel	In them hath He set a tent for the sun,
gemacht;	
sie geht heraus wie ein Bräutigam aus	Which is as a bridegroom coming out
seiner Kammer	of his chamber,
und freut sich wie ein Held,	And rejoiceth as a strong man to run
zu laufen ihre Bahn.	his course.
Sie geht auf an einem Ende	His going forth is from the end of the
des Himmels und läuft	heaven,
um bis wieder an sein Ende,	And his circuit unto the ends of it;
und nichts bleibt vor ihrer	And there is nothing hid from the heat
Glut verborgen.	thereof.

The parallel between the biblical psalm and Schiller's poetry is unmistakable.[27] In Beethoven's day, "Turkish" music could simply have been an exoticism, but it also could have been interpreted as a code for heroism. In no other case had "Turkish" music also been associated with religiosity. It may be viewed as doubly ironic, then, that Beethoven composed in a rather hymn-like style when setting the more "pagan" part of Schiller's poem, and adopted a "vulgar" style for the portion that is religiously oriented. In light of the psalm text, it would not be unreasonable to see the Turkish March also serving as a metaphoric wedding procession. Such an interpretation certainly would create a new referential meaning for this passage. When we also take into consideration Beethoven's decision to include a reprise of Schiller's first verse within the matrix of the ongoing 6/8 meter, we may view the second "movement" as a new stage along the path toward the union of "All that custom has strictly divided."

The first part of this "movement" begins with the coarse—even grotesque—sound of bass drum, bassoons, and contrabassoon (introduced for the first time in this symphony). Clarinets and horns are soon added. M. 343 then presents the "Turkish" version of the "Freude" tune in the winds (dominated by the piccolo), with the Janissary (Turkish military) battery of triangle and cymbal now joining the bass drum (Ex. 4–7). An especially charming, if droll, effect is created by the second trumpet with its tonic-dominant punctuation and the staccato strings, which are added at the cadences in mm. 358 and 376.

The entrance of the solo tenor with Schiller's "chorus" at first seems to offer nothing more than a vocal counterpoint to this farcical transformation of the "Freude" tune. But a crescendo and the addition of the men's choral

Example 4–7. Ninth Symphony/finale, mm. 343–351

Example 4–8. Ninth Symphony/finale, mm. 431–434

forces at the words "Run, Brothers, your course" shows that something truly heroic may emerge from such humble beginnings. The final cadence of the tenor and men's chorus overlaps with the onset of a double fugue in m. 431, based on two ideas from the "Freude" theme (Ex. 4–8). This breathtaking episode traverses a myriad of keys (B♭, F, G, C minor, E♭, B♭ minor, B minor) until its dramatic arrival on an F# in m. 517 (Ex. 4–9). This note is cast about wildly from octave to octave, and in chapter 3 we observed how Beethoven at one stage in the evolution of the first movement contemplated using a transformation of the F# idea in the contrabasses at

Example 4–9. Ninth Symphony/finale, mm. 517–520

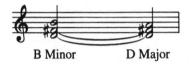

B Minor   D Major

Figure 4–2

Example 4–10. Ninth Symphony/finale, mm. 543–550

its climactic recapitulation. Here in the finale the composer uses this pitch as the suspenseful trigger for B major, B minor, and ultimately for D major (respectively, mm. 529–530, 535–536, and 541–542). Tovey especially wishes us to note the fateful descent from B to A in the bass line. One may further add that this change of pitch forms a perfect parallel to the relationship shown in Fig. 4–1, but which now is adjusted to the major mode (Fig. 4–2).

The second "movement" is rounded off by a reprise of the first verse of Schiller's poem in D major, now enthusiastically proclaimed by the full chorus and orchestra, whose strings continue to hammer out its accompaniment in the continuous eighth-note rhythm that formed one of the subjects of the instrumental double fugue (Ex. 4–10). This reprise is one of the most exhilarating moments of the entire Ninth Symphony. But our symphony in "miniature" is barely more than half over.

"Movement III"

Andante maestoso—Adagio ma non troppo, ma divoto;
Schiller, "Chorus" from Verses 1 and 3 (mm. 595–654)

Seid umschlungen, Millionen!	Be embraced, you millions!
Diesen Kuß der ganzen Welt!	This kiss is for the entire world!
Brüder! über' m Sternenzelt	Brothers! over the starry canopy
Muß ein lieber Vater wohnen!	Must a loving father dwell!
Ihr stürzt nieder, Millionen?	Do you prostrate yourselves, you millions?
Ahnest du den Schöpfer, Welt?	Do you sense the Creator, world?
Such ihn über' m Sternenzelt!	Seek him beyond the starry canopy!
Über Sternen muß er wohnen!	Beyond the stars he surely must dwell!

As stated earlier, the largest problem with a sonata form construct lies in its inability to explain the new *Andante* section in G major that now unfolds. The codetta of the second "movement" abruptly leaves us on the doorstep of this new tonality. The covertly sacred referential meaning of chorus 4 of "An die Freude" becomes unmistakably overt in the choruses from verses 1 and 3, whose text now lies before us. Beethoven's response is to present a new theme (coined the "Awe" theme by Winter) with harmonic underpinnings that deliberately evoke a flavor of antiquity (Ex. 4–11).

Example 4–11. Ninth Symphony/finale, mm. 595–602

Example 4–12. Ninth Symphony/finale, mm. 631–634

As was the case with the "Freude" theme, this new melody is first presented unharmonized by men's voices and instruments (including the bass
trombone, which last had been heard in the trio of the second movement).
A sense of grandeur is fostered by a loud dynamic, a rhythmic angularity,
and wide melodic leaps at "Millionen" and "ganzen Welt!" The use of the
trombone here is another one of those semiotic codes, as this instrument
traditionally was associated with sacred music. The splendor of Beethoven's "church" is enhanced in a repetition of the theme, now harmonized
with full chorus and orchestra. The setting of the next two lines ("Brothers! Beyond the starry canopy") is given the same essential treatment as

Example 4–13. Ninth Symphony/finale, mm. 643–646

mm. 595–610, but with new modal harmonic inflections that lead us eventually toward G minor for the *Adagio ma non troppo, ma divoto* at m. 627.

With this change of tempo, the grandeur deepens as the chorus interro-
gates the "millions" in hushed tones as to why they would prostrate themselves in order to find their creator (Ex. 4–12). The falling figuration rises
inexorably in pitch and volume, as if to show the true direction toward
which their collective prayers should be offered. The climax of this moment arrives when, on a *fortissimo* Eb major chord that places both voices
and emotions at a point of great tension, the world is assured that the seat of
God lies not in the dust, but beyond the stars (Ex. 4–13).

William Kinderman has convincingly demonstrated that in the Credo of
the *Missa solemnis* and in the Ninth Symphony, Beethoven uses this Eb
chord and its sonority as a symbol for the presence of the deity:

> As in the Credo, the sonority assumes symbolic importance in relation
> to the idea of a divine presence above the stars. The sonority is repeated
> eight times, so as to accompany every syllable of the text. The chord
> seems static and immutable, becoming in effect an audible monolithic
> symbol; even when the sonority is transmuted to a diminished-seventh
> chord in the orchestra and a minor-ninth chord moments later, the
> high G is retained.[28]

Example 4–14. Ninth Symphony/I, m. 24

Kinderman might also have added that Beethoven used the same chord
and sonority in mm. 24–25 of the first movement of the Ninth Symphony,
where the leap of the cellos and basses from G to E♭ forms a parallel to the
same leap in the altos of the chorus in the passage from the finale (Ex. 4–
14). The shimmering harmonic transmutations in mm. 647–654 described
by Kinderman mark the emotional apex of the entire finale, a moment aptly
characterized by Winter as one where with "a serene sense of both eternity
and expectation, first the orchestra, and then the chorus, hover at the edge
of the stars. Time seems to have been suspended indefinitely."[29]

"Movement IV"

Allegro energico, sempre ben marcato—Allegro ma non tanto—
Poco adagio—Tempo I— Poco adagio—Poco allegro, stringendo
il tempo, sempre più allegro—Prestissimo—Maestoso—
Prestissimo; Schiller, modified Verse I (with "Chorus")
and "Chorus" from Verse 3 (mm. 655–940)

Freude, schöner Götterfunken, etc.	Joy, beauteous spark of divinity, etc.
	combined with
Seid umschlungen, Millionen!, etc.	Be embraced, you millions!, etc.

Ihr stürzt nieder, Millionen?
Ahnest du den Schöpfer, Welt?

Such ihn über' m Sternenzelt!
Brüder! Über Sternenzelt muß ein
    lieber Vater wohnen!
Freude, Tochter aus Elysium!
Deine Zauber binden wieder,
Was die Mode streng getheilt,
Alle Menschen werden Brüder
Wo dein sanfter Flügel weilt.

Seid umschlungen, Millionen!
Diesen Kuß der ganzen Welt!
Brüder, über' m Sternenzelt
Muß ein lieber Vater wohnen.

Seid umschlungen, Millionen!
Diesen Kuß der ganzen Welt!
Freude, schöner Götterfunken,
Tochter aus Elysium,
Freude, schöner Götterfunken.

Relatively early sketches for the Ninth Symphony reveal that Beethoven had recognized that the theme for "Seid umschlungen, Millionen" was contrapuntally compatible with the "Freude" theme. The two ideas now are wed in a symbolic contrapuntal union of the sacred and the profane as the finale of the symphony moves into its denouement with a shift of tempo to *Allegro energico, sempre ben marcato* in 6/4 time (Ex. 4–15). Few have failed to see a parallel between this exhilarating passage and the instrumental double fugue in 6/8 that formed the central part of the second "movement" of the finale, although it is curious that many conductors ignore the fact that Beethoven's metronomic indications for the two episodes are analogous ($\downarrow$. = 84 and $\downarrow$. = 84, respectively).

There are several compelling reasons to identify the events starting in m. 655 as the beginning of the last "movement" of the finale. The recollections heard in mm. 1–91 referred back to the first three movements of the entire symphony. The events that unfold here produce a similar effect, although this time instead of presenting a *successive* review of previous material, Beethoven combines the theme (and key) of "Movement I," the metrical gesture of "Movement II," and the theme of "Movement III" into a

Example 4–15. Ninth Symphony/finale, mm. 655–662

simultaneous retrospective glance. Just as mm. 1–91 serve to reconcile the vocal finale with the purely instrumental movements, the events of mm. 655–762 reconcile the last "movement" of the finale with what has previously transpired, both in a musical and philosophical sense.

The last "movement" continues *pianissimo* in alla breve meter (m. 762) with rapidly moving strings which play a version of the "Freude" theme in diminution, joined by the return of the vocal soloists. The soloists express in a childlike round their happiness that the "magic" of joy has succeeded in reconciling and reuniting "all that custom has strictly divided" (Ex. 4–16). The chorus, unable to resist the enthusiasm of the soloists, joins in the round in m. 795 as part of a crescendo of celebration. So wonderful is the achievement of this goal, the chorus seizes the text "All mankind" in a fourfold repetition, the last of which melts into a gentle diminuendo and slackening of tempo (*Poco adagio*) to complete the thought of universal brotherhood (Ex. 4–17). The praise of joy's "magic" is rejuvenated in

Example 4–16. Ninth Symphony/finale, mm. 782–789

m. 814 with similar effect. But the reiteration of "All mankind" is taken over from the chorus by the soloists, whose *Poco adagio,* coupled with a striking shift to B major now turns into a more florid and extended contemplation on the sweetness of brotherhood, complete with elaborate cadenzas for each singer.

This sudden turn towards B major is, by now, no stranger to our ears. We first encountered it in the first movement at mm. 106–107, and again at the solo horn passage in the development section of the third movement (mm. 91–98). In the context of these earlier appearances, B major operated within the context of B♭ major (in the third movement, B major was written

Example 4–17. Ninth Symphony/finale, mm. 806–814

Example 4–18. Ninth Symphony/finale, mm. 841–842

out in its enharmonic equivalent of C♭ major); the secondary tonal center
for the entire symphony. Even in the finale, the glancing reference to B
major at mm. 529–530 emerged from out of the aftermath of the Turkish
March in B♭. In the present passage, however, B♭ is only a distant memory.
But having for one last time established B as tonic, Beethoven exits it in
much the same way he did earlier in the movement, i.e., by passing through
B minor with a descent from B to A in the bass in mm. 841–842 (Ex. 4–18).

The strings pick up this descent in mm. 843–850 with an infectious
crescendo and quickening of speed (*stringendo*) that leads us back to D
major for the *Prestissimo* in m. 851. Symbolic of joy's ultimate victory in
denying "custom" its power to divide, the "Turkish" instruments (piccolo,
contrabassoon, and Janissary percussion) rejoin the celebration in the service of Schiller's most overtly religious lines and a transformation of Beethoven's theme used to set them. The collective jubilation returns us once
more to the opening verse of "An die Freude" in m. 904, with a final loving
Maestoso homage to the "Daughter of Elysium, Joy the divine spark of the
Gods," the agent of reconciliation (Ex. 4–19). With a return to *Prestissimo*,
the orchestra rushes jubilantly toward the final cadence.

Much occurs within this final "movement" of the finale, not the least of
which being eight changes of tempo. Its events fairly transport the listener
on a wave of enthusiasm as Beethoven revels in the rapprochement of faith

Example 4–19. Ninth Symphony/finale, mm. 915–917

and Enlightenment idealism, of the worldly and the sacred. Joseph Kerman spoke of the "Freude" tune as "blinding in its demagogic innocence," and in placing the entire work within the context of "late" Beethoven, he correctly observes. "We live in the valley of the Ninth Symphony—that we cannot help—but we would probably breathe easier if the mountain were hidden by a perpetual cloud, by a critical smog of our own manufacture."[30]

As we have seen, and as the following chapters will show, in our collective attempt to come to terms with the Ninth Symphony, we have at times shrouded the work in "a critical smog" of either polemical language or dense analysis (and sometimes both). Some enshrine it, others attempt to tear it down. But the mountain remains, and, as is the case with revelation itself, the essential truth of the Ninth Symphony can be neither proven nor disproven. Coming to terms with the work involves a kind of leap of faith. The story of our faith, or lack thereof, follows.

Chapter 5

THE PERFORMANCES OF 1824

BEETHOVEN'S FORTUNES, 1824

*H*ad Beethoven waited for encouragement from the Viennese, he might never have finished the Ninth Symphony. The impetus for the work's final shaping and completion came not from local patrons, but from the directors of London's Philharmonic Society who had requested in 1822 that Beethoven provide them a new symphony. The Society forwarded the agreed payment of £50 with the reasonable expectation that the first performance of the new work would take place in the British capital. The directors also harbored the hope that Beethoven himself would take a hand in leading the auspicious event, just as Haydn had done at the Salomon concerts during the 1790s. A manuscript score of the Ninth bearing the dedication "Geschrieben für die Philharmonische Gesellschaft in London" was handed to Kirchhoffer, the Society's agent, on April 27, 1824. Two months earlier, rumors circulated in Vienna that Beethoven also had been in correspondence with Count Brühl in Berlin regarding a premiere of the Ninth Symphony in that city.

Why would Beethoven have considered allowing the Ninth Symphony to have its premiere away from his adopted home? And what circumstances influenced him to change his mind? The answer to these questions lies in the nature of public concerts in Vienna in the years following the Congress of Vienna, the peace convention which took place during the winter of 1814–15. Conditions for the performance of symphonies were not nearly as propitious as they had been between 1800 and 1814, the period that witnessed the premieres of Beethoven's first eight symphonies. The business and sociology of concert-giving—and along with it the status of the symphony—had changed, due in no small measure to the accomplishments of Beethoven himself. Furthermore, the problems that Beethoven faced in arranging the first performance of the Ninth Symphony were far more numerous and complex than one might imagine.

Beethoven's personal and professional life started to take a decided turn for the worse in the wake of Napoleon's defeat. Biographers have offered many reasons to explain the quantitative decline in Beethoven's compositional output during these years. His legal struggle against his hated sister-in-law over the custodianship of his nephew Karl and his deteriorating health were a drain on his time and energy. The devaluation of the Austrian currency in 1811 caused a depletion of his income, reducing his annuity of 4000 to only 1600 florins.[1] Between 1812 and 1816, death had claimed three of Beethoven's most loyal patrons—Karl Lichnowsky, Ferdinand Kinsky, and Franz Joseph von Lobkowitz. Count Razumovsky was financially ruined in 1814 by a tragic New Year's Eve fire that destroyed his Viennese palace; two years later economic woes forced him to disband his string quartet, thereby causing the temporary removal from Vienna of Beethoven's trusted friend and interpreter, Ignaz Schuppanzigh (who fortunately returned from St. Petersburg in sufficient time to play an important role in the premiere of the Ninth Symphony). While successful litigation with the estate of the Kinsky heirs and the continuing support of Archduke Rudoph had saved Beethoven from complete financial ruin, the aggregate effect of the weak Austrian economy on Beethoven's patrons cannot be overestimated.

VIENNESE CONCERT LIFE IN THE 1820S

It has long been known that in Vienna an indescribable amount of music is made, publicly and privately. For awhile it seemed that the Music-mania had reached its peak here, and yet the number of music instructors and performers continues to climb. Whether art itself benefits from this is a difficult question to answer. . . . It is certain that those who seek to gain profit from music have suffered, whether in the

theater or in the concert institutions, whether native artists or visit-
ing. One can presently hear so much music—and often good music—
for free in Vienna that few are willing to pay money for it. . . . Foreign musical artists must bring great calling and commensurate talent
with them if they wish to make pecuniary gains from their concerts
here. Only the lucky chosen few are able to make a profit from their
talents. . . .

In the realm of opera, the public became too accustomed, early on,
to the style of Rossini's operas by ever-increasing numbers of performances. As a result, it is no longer receptive to other styles of composition. In music more than in any other art it is more striking how
quickly and surely the ear becomes seduced by dint of repetition to the
same master, while at the same time losing interest in others.[2]

So described the journal *Caecilia* the state of concert life in Vienna in
1824. While there was an abundance of music making, programs featuring
symphonies were few and far between in the early 1820s.[3] The 1824–25
concert season was filled, as was usual for this period in history, with
theatrical farces, ballets, and Italian operas. The last category was dominated, of course, by works from the pen of the ever popular Rossini. Concert
programs featured various musical fairy tales, satires, and pantomimes
composed by Beethoven's contemporaries such as Seyfried, Romberg, Mayseder, and Gläser. Pianists and violinists dazzled Viennese audiences with
virtuoso potpourris and fantasias derived from the most fashionable opera
or ballet. An occasional symphony could be heard at these concerts, but
such a work served as an addition to the program, and not as its centerpiece.

Performances with symphonies as the principal fare were the province
of the Concerts Spirituels (founded in 1819), and a glance at this institution's programs shows that its directors did not neglect Beethoven's music.[4]
Upon closer examination, however, one can understand how Beethoven
could hardly have taken solace at the support of the Concerts Spirituels,
since its ranks were filled with amateur musicians. The players were of
limited proficiency, and their performances offered audiences only a vague
idea of Beethoven's true greatness. According to Adam Carse, an orchestra
numbering fifty players was engaged for each concert, but only the ten or
twelve wind players were paid professionals.[5] There was little rehearsal for
the Concerts Spirituels programs, and the peformances amounted to little
more than sight-reading sessions. So poor was the result that Schubert
once dejectedly left the auditorium during the playing of one of his own

works. An attempt was made in 1824 to salvage the Concerts Spirituels by removing their programs from the public eye and offering only private concerts. The frequency and popularity of these events dwindled, however, and by 1848 they disappeared from the scene altogether.[6]

The merits of the concerts sponsored by the Gesellschaft der Musik-freunde (Society for the Friends of Music), or Musik-Verein, placed this organization only slightly higher than the Concerts Spirituels in the arena of orchestral music. Founded in 1814 for the purpose of fostering musical performance, composition, and education in Vienna, the Society held Bee-thoven in great esteem, even if the feeling was not always reciprocated by the composer.[7] Vincenz von Hauschka and Leopold Sonnleithner, two ama-teur leaders of the organization, were largely responsible for the choice of music played by its orchestra. Sonnleithner, nephew of Joseph von Sonn-leithner, one of the Society's founders, was a personal friend of Beethoven, Schubert, and Franz Grillparzer. Beethoven's music figured prominently in the Society's concerts, and the composer had become financially indebted to the Society by accepting a cash advance for an oratorio based on a text by Grillparzer—a project that remained incomplete. According to Pohl, when Sonnleithner sought to procure the honor of giving the first performance of the Ninth Symphony, Beethoven at first accepted the proposal with a proviso that a portion of the receipts be directed toward the settlement of the oratorio debt. But when the Society learned how difficult the music was, and the considerable expenses involved, they refused to assume the sole responsibility for producing the event.[8] As it will be seen, the Society nev-ertheless played a significant, if supportive, role in the premiere of the Ninth Symphony by augmenting the ranks of the orchestra and chorus.

According to the *Caecilia* account of 1824, the orchestra at the Imperial Royal Theater beside the Kärntnerthor, which would form the nucleus of the ensemble for the premiere of the Ninth Symphony, was the best or-chestra in Vienna. The writer noted, however, that even this orchestra's quality had suffered of late because too many new and inexperienced play-ers had been admitted into its ranks.

Politics and Censorship

It is sometimes difficult to measure the impact of politics on artistic activity. In the Austrian Empire of Franz I, however, many writers and musicians, including Beethoven, suffered demonstrably. Although Franz reigned with the outward appearance of generosity toward his subjects, his secret police enforced a strict and cumbersome policy of censorship and obscurantism.[9] Beethoven's friend Grillparzer, whose *König Ottokars Glück und Ende* had been banned by the Viennese censors, remarked in one of the Beethoven Conversation Books that composers were lucky because their work was immune to censorship. This statement seems rather naïve in light of the fact that the libretti of vocal music were no less prone to the heavy hand of the censor than purely literary works. In 1823–24 Beethoven was engaged in setting a poem by Schiller, a poet whose *Wilhelm Tell* had been heavily cut and whose *Piccolomini* had for a time been banned. One cannot dismiss the possibility that political considerations governed the composer's choice of which sections of "An die Freude" to use.[10] Given the anti-Enlightenment bias of the censorship system, many of the sentiments expressed in "An die Freude"—especially in its more overtly political version of 1785—would have been anathema to Viennese officials. Beethoven, whose personal political philosophy remained committed to Enlightenment ideals, had occasion more than once to lament the deleterious effect of Austrian censorship.

Berlin, London, or Vienna? The February Petition

As noted earlier, Beethoven considered premiering the Ninth Symphony in Berlin rather than in Vienna. When word of this plan became known in the early months of 1824, Viennese admirers quickly sprang into action, approaching the composer with a petition that was later published in the Vienna *Allgemeine musikalische Zeitung* and the Vienna *Theater-Zeitung*.[11] The author of the petition is unknown, but according to Thayer, Count Lichnowsky was "the most active agent in securing signatures."[12] This interesting document attests to the difficult political situation in Vienna and to the desire of Beethoven's followers to keep the Ninth on Austrian soil:

To Herr Ludwig van Beethoven:
Out of the wide circle of those who in reverent admiration surround your genius in this your second native city, there approach you today a

small number of disciples and lovers of art to express long-felt wishes, humbly to present long-suppressed requests.

But since the number of the spokesmen bears but a small proportion to the multitude who joyfully acknowledge your worth and what you have come to be for the present and for the future, in like manner the wishes and requests are in no wise limited to the number of those who speak for others who feel as they do. They assert in the name of all to whom art and the realization of their ideal is more than a means and object of pastime that what they request is echoed aloud or silently by all those in whose breasts there lives a sense of the divine in music.

It is the wishes of those of our countrymen who reverence art that we present here, for although the name and the creations of Beethoven belong to all the world and to those lands where art finds a welcoming spirit, yet it is Austria that may claim him as its own. There still lives in its people the appreciation of the great and immortal works that Mozart and Haydn created within its bosom for all time, and with happy pride they know that the sacred triad, in which their names and yours shine as symbols of the highest in the spiritual realm of tones, sprang from the earth of the Fatherland.

It must cause you all the more sorrow that a foreign power has invaded this royal citadel of what is finest, that over the graves of those who have passed and around the dwelling of the one of that band that still remains with us, spectres are leading a course that can have no kinship with the princely spirits of this royal house; that shallowness is sullying the name and the insignia of art; that in unworthy dalliance with sacred things the feeling for the pure and ever-beautiful is being beclouded and dissipated.

For this reason they feel more strongly and actively than ever before that the great need of the present moment is a new impulse led by a powerful hand, a new appearance of the ruler in his domain. It is this need that leads them to you now, and these are the pleas that they present to you on behalf of all who hold these wishes dear and in the name of the art of the Fatherland.

Do not withhold longer from popular enjoyment, do not withhold longer from the oppressed appreciation of what is great and perfect a performance of the most recent masterworks of your hand. We know that a great sacred composition has been added to that first one in which you made immortal the emotions of a soul permeated and

transfigured by the power of faith and by divine light. We know that a
new flower glows in the garland of your noble and still unequalled
symphonies. For years, ever since the thunder of the 'Victory of Vic-
toria' died away, we have waited and hoped to see you once again
distribute new gifts within the circle of your friends from the fulness of
your riches. Disappoint no longer the hopes of all! Enhance the ef-
fectiveness of your newest creations by the joy of first making them
known by you yourself. Do not allow these your youngest children to
be introduced as foreigners in the city of their birth, perhaps by those
to whom you and your spirit are strange. Appear soon among your
friends, among those who admire and honour you! This is our nearest
and first plea.

But still other claims upon your genius have been made public. The
wishes and offers extended to you more than a year ago by the direc-
torate of our Court Opera and then by the Society of Austrian Friends of
Music have too long been the unspoken wish of all admirers of art and
of your name. They had stimulated hope and expectation too much not
to have attained the swiftest public knowledge near and far, not to have
awakened the most widespread interest. Poetry has done her utmost to
support such fair hopes and desires. Worthy material from the hand of
the estimable poet awaits your imagination to charm it into life. Do not
allow these intimate summonses to so noble an objective to be in vain.
Delay no longer in leading us back to those departed days in which the
song of Polyhymnia powerfully seized and delighted the initiates of art
and the hearts of the multitude alike!

Need we tell you with what deep regret your withdrawal from public life has long filled us? Need we tell you that as all glances turned
hopefully to you, all perceived with sorrow that the one man whom we
are compelled to name as the foremost of all living men in his field
looked on in silence as foreign art invaded German soil, the place of
honour of the German muse, while German works gave pleasure only
as they echoed the favourite tunes of foreigners, and where the might-
iest had lived and worked a second childhood of taste threatened to
follow the golden age of art?

You alone are able to assure a decisive victory for the best among
us. From you the native Art Society and the German opera await new
blossoms, renewed life, and a new supremacy of the true and the
beautiful over the dominion to which the spirit of the day would sub-

ject even the eternal laws of art. Give us hope that the wishes of all to whom the sound of your harmonies has come will soon see this fulfilled. This is our most urgent second plea.

May the year that has now begun not come to an end without rejoicing us with the fruits of our pleas, and may the coming spring, if it brings the unfolding of one of the gifts that we seek, become for us and the world of art a time of twofold flowering.

Vienna, February 1824.

Signers

Fürst C. Lichnowsky	Ferdinand Graf v. Palffy	Moritz Graf v. Dietrichstein
Artaria und Company	Eduard Frh. v. Schweiger	Ig. Edler von Mosel k. k. Hofrath
von Hauschka	Graf Czernin	Carl Czerny
M. J. Leidesdorf	Moritz Graf v. Fries	Moritz Graf Lichnowsky
J. E. von Wayna	I. F. Castelli	Zmeskall
Andreas Streicher	Deinhardstein	Hofrath Kiesewetter
Anton Halm	C. Kuffner	Leopold Sonnleithner Dr.
Abbé Stadler	Fr. Nehammer Ständ Secretär	S. A. Steiner & Comp.
von Felsburg Hofsecretär	Stainer von Felsburg Bank-liquidator	Anton Diabelli
Ferdinand Graf Stockhammer		Lederer [?] J. N. Bihler[13]

The signatories represented some of Vienna's most distinguished musicians and patrons.[14] The petition probably would have included the names of other prominent citizens had Lichnowsky not been anxious to get it into Beethoven's hand before the composer could reach an agreement with Brühl. Beethoven reportedly derived great satisfaction from the expression of support from so many well-wishers, although the subsequent publication of the document in two Viennese journals caused him dismay, since he feared that some would accuse him of having encouraged its publication. The petition nevertheless achieved its main purpose: after receiving it Beethoven resolved to perform his new symphony in Vienna after all.

The First Performance of the Ninth

By the third week in April, Beethoven decided to present the Ninth in an *Academie* which would also include the "Consecration of the House" Overture, op. 124, and the Kyrie, Credo, and Agnus Dei from the *Missa solemnis,* op. 123. The publication of the petition in April served to heighten expectations among the Viennese musical public, and for the first time since 1812, Beethoven was returning personally to the concert stage:

> This *Academie* will offer friends of German music one of the most beautiful festivities and will bring recognition to the national master. France and England certainly will envy the pleasure of having the opportunity to offer homage to Beethoven himself, who is acknowledged throughout the world to be the most ingenious composer. Anyone whose heart beats warmly for greatness and beauty will surely not be absent on this evening.[15]

The Vienna *Allgemeine musikalische Zeitung,* in a notice written by its editor, Friedrich August Kanne, showed similar enthusiasm for the upcoming event:

> Beethoven's great creative spirit has earned the eternal admiration of the world in the last ten years by dint of the ever-growing dissemination of his works, and all educated lands count the original creations of his fantasy among the prime works of German art. However, it seems that in Vienna, where we have always heard his work performed first, he has found no favorable moment to appear before the public, which most certainly comprises the largest number of his genuine admirers, with a grand performance of a new work. . . .
>
> He who could create a grand world within himself merits no reproach when the activity of the outside world was ever foreign to him! All the more, those who proved themselves active in the planning and arrangement of a well-prepared public performance of Beethoven's newest works have earned our rightful thanks. If the worthy master's joy over the recognition of his friends and compatriots is raised a degree by this, then we therefore not only bring a fitting offering to art, but this hour surely will arouse the genius himself to a newly-inspired creativity, and will fire his energies to renewed productivity.

It can only be concluded that the ever-communicative national character of the Viennese has placed itself, on this occasion, in the brightest light.[16]

But many problems remained to be solved, including the choice of an auditorium, the selection of vocal soloists and personnel for the orchestra and chorus, the setting of ticket prices, the scheduling of rehearsals, and the copying of the orchestral and choral parts. The Conversation Books contain numerous entries that demonstrate how Beethoven often became distrustful of the small army of friends and advisors who assisted him with preparations for the event. They also reveal that the choral forces used at the first performance included boys (who apparently had great difficulty learning their parts) and that the members of the Kärntnerthor orchestra, the wind players in particular, were inadequately prepared to negotiate the difficulties of their parts. A passage from the Conversation Book of March 20 to April 1, 1824, also sheds interesting light on the cello and contrabass recitative:

SCHINDLER: How many *Contrabasses* should play the *Recitative?*
———
Could that be possible? All of them!
———
To play it in strict time would not be difficult, but to play it in a singing fashion will cost great pains in rehearsal.
———
If only the old *Krams* were still alive, one could leave such things without worry, because he used to lead 12 *Basses,* who had to do as he wished.
———
So entirely thus, as if words were written below?
———
If need be, I will set down words underneath, so that they learn to sing.[17]

Despite all obstacles, the long-awaited *Academie* took place on May 7 at seven o'clock in the evening at the Imperial Royal Court Theater next to the Kärntnerthor. The orchestra and chorus were augmented by members of the Gesellschaft der Musikfreunde and boy sopranos. The string section included fifty-eight players: twenty-four violins, ten violas, twelve cellos

132   THE PERFORMANCES OF 1824

and twelve basses. It is unclear whether or not the "Doubled Harmonie" mentioned in one of the Conversation Books means that the wind section was twice as large as the score indicates. Given the exceptionally large size of the string section (when all of them would be playing in louder moments), it seems likely that the kind of "tutti" and "solo" alternation specified in sources for the Fourth Symphony also obtained on this occasion. The choir comprised approximately ninety voices.[18] Beethoven followed the normal Viennese practice of inviting amateurs to participate in the concert, and a few prominent professional musicians from the city—Mayseder, Böhm, Jansa, Linke, and Thalberg—are also known to have joined in.

It is impossible to determine the number of sectional rehearsals that preceded the concert. We know that Ignaz Dirzka, the chorus-master of the Kärntnerthortheater, directed the choral rehearsals, Schuppanzigh was responsible for working with the strings, Beethoven and Michael Umlauf both rehearsed the vocal soloists, and Ludwig Schwarzböck directed the boy sopranos. Ferdinand Piringer and Leopold Sonnleithner also worked with some of the performers. Because of the busy schedule of the Kärntnerthortheater and the performers, Louis Antoine Duport, the manager of the theater, allowed only two full rehearsals. Excessive delays and the postponement of the concert proved costly in terms of attendance.[19] The regular Vienna concert season was over, and many aristocrats and members of the court, most notably Archduke Rudolph, had left the city.

The May 7th concert was reviewed in numerous journals, ranging from local Viennese periodicals to the widely read Leipzig *Allgemeine musikalische Zeitung.* Here is the report from Bäuerle's *Allgemeine Theater-Zeitung:*

> A musical high feast took place on May 7 in the I. R. [Imperial Royal] Court Opera Theater. Beethoven gave a grand musical academy and performed from his compositions a grand Overture, three Hymns (sections from his new Mass), and a grand Symphony on Schiller's Lied An die Freude with solo and choral voices entering in the finale.
>
> The solo voice parts were performed by Demoisellen Sonntag and Unger, and Herren Haitzinger and Seipelt. Herr Schuppanzigh directed the orchestra, Herr Kapellmeister Umlauf had the general direction, and the Musik-Verein bolstered the chorus and orchestra. The composer himself took part in the overall direction.
>
> The ticket prices were the usual ones and the house was very full.

The public received the tone-hero with the most respectful sympathy and listened to his wonderful, gigantic creations with the most intense attentiveness, and they broke out in jubilant applause—often during movements—but repeatedly after each of them.

After one hearing of these immense compositions, one can say scarcely more than that he has heard them. It is impossible for anyone who only attended the performance to present an informed discussion. Because of this, the reader must be satisfied with the promise that these pages will return to these works of art by Beethoven in greater detail.

Imagine the highly inspired composer, the musical Shakespeare, to whom all means of his arts readily are available at the slightest wave of his hand, how, in the innermost belief in the holy work of redemption, he sings God's praise and the hope of humanity. Only then, perhaps, can one gain a slight notion of the impact of this Kyrie, Credo, and Agnus Dei!

The Overture that opened the concert was indeed a real treat, but this masterpiece seems rather ordinary when one recalls the Hymns and the immense Symphony.

Through his symphonies Beethoven has shown for so long such a high level of artistic creation in this branch of composition that it has become difficult for any composer to succeed in the wake of this Helicon, and this newest symphony is certainly the greatest work of art that Beethoven, with full Titan's power, has brought into existence. Each individual part of it, especially the scherzo, made the most decided impact, and this symphony would have distinguished itself even more in the striking fantasy which introduces the final chorus, and by the chorus itself, had it been possible for the performers to render this movement as perfectly as it demanded.

Regarding the orchestra, one can only say that it is inconceivable how they were able to perform these uncommonly difficult compositions so masterfully with only three rehearsals, and they rendered them most worthily indeed. And this orchestra was composed, for the most part, of dilettantes. Only in Vienna can one find that!

The singers did what they could. Opera singers are accustomed to learning their task by dint of many rehearsals, especially when the style is unfamiliar to them. Herr Seipelt [bass] acquitted himself most gallantly. Herr Haizinger [sic; tenor] had the more difficult assignment. This composition is uncommonly difficult to sing from the standpoint of intonation alone, and to this is added the problem of frequent meter changes.

Herr Schuppanzigh and Herr Umlauf have long been celebrated, but by the efforts made today, Umlauf has made himself unforgettable to all Viennese friends of music.

The most earnest wish of a large public is that these works of art that so beautifully reveal the divine in human nature, be heard again soon. May this wish be fulfilled![20]

A review by Friedrich August Kanne described the event in similarly enthusiastic language, although he was unhappy with the choice of auditorium:

The performance . . . finally took place on May 7 before an unusually large audience in the theater by the Kärntnerthor.

Beethoven's genius evidenced itself to us as entirely in its youth and original strength again in these grand, gigantic compositions. His rich, powerful fantasy holds sway with lofty freedom in the realm of tones familiar to it, and it raises the listeners on its wings into a new world that excites amazement.

The great realm of instrumental music, in which the celebrated master of so many beautiful creations has chosen to reign throughout his entire life, can still await many treasures from him, because his lofty fantasy, which transcends time and taste, proves itself to be an inexhaustible fount of beauty with each new product.

Even though it would have been preferable to have heard the three pieces from his grand new Mass that were presented on this occasion in another locale, because the variability in the seating in the auditorium also denotes a discrepancy in the sophistication of the audience, and also because neither the chorus nor the solo singers were sufficiently prepared for such difficult and deeply intricate music, still the grandiose style with which Beethoven has drawn this work revealed itself in evident clarity.

The effect that so heavy an orchestration ought to have had was weakened because the sound faded away and dissipated in the bare spaces between the wings to such an extent, that we could barely hear half of the noteworthy effect in the lively moving mass of sound.

The Overture and the grand Symphony with the chorus entering in the finale, however, were heard to better effect.

We therefore earnestly hope that the efforts of several distinguished men of art may be crowned with happy success in preparing a second—and in all particulars improved—performance in another locale that is better suited for music, thereby fulfilling all demands of the art in the accompaniment of the orchestra and in the precision of the execution.

It is impossible for contemporaries of the great composer to look with an indifferent eye, and it should be taken very much to heart, if the exertion in bringing forth these grand works should not yield him at least some profit, which in no way could be equal to that which he offers the world, but which nevertheless is of great importance for the "artist's pilgrimage on earth."

The second performance will elevate to the highest degree the enthusiastic applause that honored the great master, who personally took part in the overall direction [of the concert], and the composer will find therein renewed reward for his efforts.

The excellent Kapellmeister Umlauf, who directed this performance, has earned the grateful recognition to the highest degree of all friends of art for his zeal and skill.[21]

The Vienna correspondent for the Leipzig *Allgemeine musikalische Zeitung* had a great deal to say about the concert. His long review has been reprinted in several sources, and only those portions relevant to the Ninth Symphony are given here:

Grand musical *Academie* of Herr Ludwig van Beethoven, honorary member of the Royal Academies of Arts and Sciences in Stockholm and Amsterdam, also honorary citizen of Vienna, where his newest works were produced, namely: 1. Grand Overture; 2. Three Grand Hymns with solo and choral voices; 3. Grand Symphony with solo and choral voices on Schiller's "Lied an die Freude" entering in the finale. The soloists were the Demoiselles Sonntag and Unger, Herren Haitzinger and Seipelt; the Musikverein augmented the orchestra and chorus. Herr Schuppanzigh directed at the violin, Herr Kapellmeister Umlauf directed with the baton, and the composer himself participated in the general direction of everything. He stood, namely, by the side of the presiding marshall and indicated the beginning of each new tempo, following his original score, because due to his hearing deficiency, the higher enjoyment was sadly denied him. But where can I find the words about these giant works to relate to my readers, especially after a performance that in no way could suffice in light of the extraordinary difficulties, especially in the vocal sections, and after only three rehearsals; therefore neither any imposing power, nor necessary differentiation of light and shade, secure intonation, or fine shading or nuanced execution, could exist. And still the effect was indescribably great and magnificent, jubilant applause from full hearts was enthusiastically given the master, whose inexhaustible genius revealed a new world to us and unveiled never-before-heard, never-imagined magical secrets of the holy art! . . .

The symphony may measure itself fearlessly with its eight sisters; it certainly will not be obscured by any. Only its originality reveals its father, otherwise everything is new and unprecedented. The first movement is a defiantly bold *Allegro* in *D Minor*, most ingeniously invented and worked out with real athletic power. From the first chord (A Major) [!] until its gradual development into the colossal theme, expectation is kept in uninterrupted suspense, but is resolved most happily. It is impossible to give a sketch of it and it would provide only an insufficient portrayal. The wildest mischief plays its wicked game in the Scherzo (also D Minor). All instruments compete in the banter, and a brilliant march in the major mode is, indeed, an unusually refreshing alternate section. Whoever sets out with the idea that there could be no *Andante* more enjoyable and delectable than that of the Seventh Symphony [*Allegretto*] should hear this one (in B-flat Major) and he will at least start to question his assumption. What heavenly song; how overwhelming the variations and combining of motives; what artful and tasteful development, how natural everything in most sumptuous fullness; what grandeur of expression and grand simplicity! The master demands much, very much, nearly overstepping the human ability of his instrumentalists, but he also thereby brings forth such magical effects after which others fruitlessly strive, even using similar means, but without [his] Promethean fire! The finale (D Minor) announces itself like a crushing thunderclap with a shrill cutting minor ninth over the dominant [sic] chord. Potpourri-like, in short phrases, all previously-heard principal themes are paraded before us once again in colorful succession, as if reflected in a mirror. The contrabasses then growl a recitative that seems to question: "What is to happen next?," answering themselves with a soft, swaying motive in the major mode that, through the gradual entrance of all the instruments in wonderfully beautiful connections, without Rossinian eyeglass basses and third-passages develops into an all-powerful crescendo in measured steps.[22] Finally, after an invitation by the solo basso, the full chorus also intones the song in praise of joy with majestic splendor. Then the glad heart opens itself widely to the feeling of delight in this spiritual enjoyment, and a thousand voices rejoice: "Hail! Hail! to the divine music! Honor! Praise! and thanks to its worthiest high priest!"

The critic now sits with regained composure at his desk, but this moment will remain for him unforgettable. Art and truth celebrate here their most glowing triumph, and with right one could say: non plus ultra! Who, in fact, could succeed in excelling these unnameable moments? It therefore is impossible for the remaining strophes of the poem—now set for solo voices, now for choral, with changing tempos, keys, and meters, no matter how excellently handled as individual moments—to produce a similar effect. Even the work's most glowing worshippers and most inspired admirers are convinced that this truly unique finale would become even more incomparably imposing in a more concentrated shape, and the composer himself would agree if cruel fate had not robbed him of the ability to hear his creation. Only one wish, only one request, is for the early repetition of these masterpieces.

Parenthetically: the revenue, because the ticket prices for the loges and orchestra seats were not raised, amounted to 2200 Fl. W. W. The administration received 1000 Fl. from that as overhead for the evening, and for orchestra and vocal personnel; the copyists cost 700 Fl.; incidental costs: 200 Fl.; profit: netto 300 Fl. W. W. or 120 Fl. in silver. . . . [23]

Finally, a correspondent from *Caecilia* also presented a brief, but telling, report of the event:

This musical winter season could not have closed more worthily and brilliantly than it did with a grand musical *Academie,* in which the greatest genius of our time proved that the true artist knows no

standstill. Forward, upward, is his watchword, his battle cry. Beethoven gave a grand Overture, three Hymns from his new Mass, and
his new Symphony, whose last movement ended with a chorus on
Schiller's song, An die Freude. One can say no more than that the
connoisseurs judged and spoke with unanimity: Beethoven has once
again forged ahead!!

These new artworks appear as the immense products of a son of the
gods, who snatched the holy animating flame directly from heaven
itself. But they are too important for us not to make an independent
report about them to follow soon.[24]

These initial reviews of the Ninth Symphony augured well for the success of the piece, although they contain clear warnings of problems that
would plague future performances. All four critics clearly supported Beethoven and his art, even to the point of referring to the composer's fiscal
circumstances. Despite the obvious shortcomings of the first performance,
the spirit of the composition nevertheless came through with sufficient
force to make a deep impression. Beethoven succeeded in demonstrating
that he was still capable of producing great things. Entries in the Conversation Book of May 8 record the enthusiasm of Beethoven's friends as well as
giving evidence about the cheering audience—cheers that Beethoven himself, sadly, was unable to hear.[25]

The Second Performance: May 23, 1824

Now that it had been performed publicly, the Ninth Symphony would have
to make its way in the world. But before this would happen, the composer
had one last opportunity to supervise a performance of it. From the start,
Beethoven and his supporters considered a second *Academie* in which the
Ninth Symphony would be featured. The problems that forced the delay of
the first concert also caused difficulties for the second. Duport was unable
to offer the Kärntnerthortheater, and it was decided that the large Redoutensaal would be used, with the concert commencing at half past noon.
Duport recommended that the program be changed so that the event might
attract a larger audience. The overture, the Kyrie from the Mass, and the
symphony were retained, but to these were added Beethoven's terzetto,

"Tremate, empi, tremate" (which was misleadingly listed as a new composition), and "Di tanti palpiti" from Rossini's *Tancredi* (transposed a fourth higher for the popular Viennese tenor David).[26] As well-intentioned as Duport's idea—not to mention his generosity in paying all expenses and offering a guarantee of 500 florins (1200 fl. W. W.)—may have been, the concert turned out to be a commercial failure. Thayer blamed it on the unfavorable hour, the beautiful Sunday weather, and Beethoven's refusal to appear personally on stage during the performance.[27] But confusion in the press also contributed to the poor attendance. The Vienna *Theater-Zeitung* of May 15 announced that the concert would take place on May 18 in the Kärntnerthortheater, only later to print on May 20 that the concert would take place the next day, again in the Kärntnerthortheater. The Vienna *Allgemeine musikalische Zeitung* finally announced the correct date, time, and place on May 22, only one day before the event took place and, apparently, too late for many to make arrangements to be there. Given these circumstances, the Viennese could hardly be blamed for the poor attendance.

But the second *Academie* offered the critics an additional opportunity to consider the Ninth Symphony in greater depth. Kanne, hearing the work for a second time, compared Beethoven's art to that of many of his contemporaries and complained that the sensibilities of musicians and audiences alike had become tainted by the Viennese cult of virtuosity. Beethoven, on the other hand, was a composer who never succumbed to such trivialities, concerning himself instead with using his resources in the service of the music's spiritual content and poetic depth:

> The first *Allegro* in D minor [of this new Symphony], which ought to be designated a colossal fantasy for orchestra if one wishes to describe it precisely, likewise offers again the power of instruments decided opportunity for shining moments of effect. Like a volcano, Beethoven's power of imagination makes the earth, which tries to impede the rage of his fire, burst, and with an often wonderful persistence, develops figures whose peculiar formation, at first glance, not seldom expresses an almost bizarre character, but which become transformed under the artful master's skilled hand into a stream of graceful elaborations that refuse to end, swinging upward, step by step, into an ever more brilliant loftiness.
>
> The master, with never-exhausted creative power, places ever new

obstacles in the path of his upward-rushing stream of fire, impeding it by tied figures that continually encounter each other in imitation, thus in parallel running forms in diagonal directions. He inverts his phrases, forcing them down into a terrifying abyss, from which his inflamed genius now leads them all, united in a ray, against the clouds, in order to make them disappear, high up, in a sharply [and] entirely unexpected unison, which itself rises still, stepwise, above its own high level. But he grants the eye no rest! New powers develop from the middle, sometimes streaming to all sides, at other times rolling forth in gentle planes like the waves of a river.

Beethoven's masterly hand with great art thrusts the musical bolts in the midst of this wonderful tumult of all the elements of art, and, like a scene painter, transforms the entire mass of his figures into a trans-figured blue fire.

Kanne's imagery and enthusiasm are striking. So powerful was the ef-fect of the first movement on him, he expressed the wish that Beethoven would have followed it with the "gentle, songful, and melancholy *Adagio*," rather than with the tumultuous scherzo. But this was not to say that he was any less enthusiastic about the second movement:

Whoever has never known Beethoven's humor from one of his works will find its quintessence in all gradations in this *Scherzo*. Who would question whether the tempo is furious? The metric feel can hardly follow the rapid flight of the figures, the colorful changes of the droll, often strange, changes of harmony!

The uncommon tuning of the kettledrums, which right at the start announces the humorous style, already gives the listener information as to what he may expect. The running, ever-tripping theme that gains more in character by the its sharp staccato articulation, shows the wonderful naïve spirit in which Beethoven's soul found itself when he wrote it.

The grotesque leaps that Beethoven's genius makes in the *Scherzo* at hand are often of such a bold nature, and are executed with such rapid power, that one readily understands how he could interpolate an *Al-labreve* into this tempo, by which the ear at once regains new strength.

One sees in the staccato runs of the oboe, flute, bassoon, etc., the little Colombine tripping with her Harlequin, who springs in bold leaps from one modulation point to another, and changes at every moment. Indeed, whoever brings such an inspired imagination to his listening, as Beethoven did in his composing, will not be amazed when we perceive again in the humorous beating of the two kettledrums tuned in [octave] F[s], sometimes leaping from the higher to the lower, Harlequin enlivening all his company with his wooden sword. Even more, the basses, with their wide steps and diverse gestures, represent the long-armed Pierot. . . .

Kanne's review also sheds light on how the performers fared at this concert, as well as on the acoustics of the Redoutensaal:

> The performance of this movement was far more successful in the Kärntnerthortheater than it was in the large Redoutensaal because the reverberation of sound was suppressed (understandably, since the orchestra was placed on the stage), and the pointed staccato tones were more well-defined as individual sounds, without any reverberating echoes that could muffle them. The very large orchestra there [Kärntnerthortheater], augmented by the participation of many dilettantes, was also of greatest benefit to the sound. One hardly needs to add that a movement such as this one, created with the highest freedom of spirit and unchecked enthusiasm, scarcely gives an experienced violinist enough time to work out a good fingering, by which token then, relatively weak violinists—that is those who play variations or concertos readily enough, but who are unaccustomed to the fast passages in orchestral performance—would be horrified at first by such difficult passages. They would therefore set down their bows and sit out so many measures, thereby disregarding the difficult passages until such time as they once again can join in the easier passages, taking their place with the orchestra in progress. The reliable ones with true artistic expression had to compensate during such passages by playing louder to compensate for the performers who stopped playing.
>
> The truth of what is being said may indeed seem monstrously difficult to prove to many laymen, but the connoisseur, who is our true reader, will understand us entirely and find no iota unimportant!

The review next turns to the Ninth's third movement, whose execution by Schuppanzigh and Umlauf merited particular praise:

The *Adagio* in B♭ is a most highly personal song—full of warmth
and flowing in heavenly melancholy—in which Beethoven's grandeur
manifests itself in great clarity. A short concluding phrase which the
composer attaches to each of the phrases, melting in graceful ecstasy
like an echo, adds an attractiveness to the entire piece. He breathes his
yearning into the most flowing melodies, which die away softly over a
very interesting harmony that is not interrupted by too many changes,
and which—especially right before the final cadence—soars from the
peace-seeking sixth, still hesitantly, to a higher tonal level, until the
spirit is once again calmed by the attainment of the long-delayed
resolution....

Kanne was deeply impressed with the enormity of Beethoven's plan in
the finale, as well as by the way in which the composer unified seemingly
"contradictory" elements. The sheer size of the movement, in Kanne's
opinion, forced Beethoven to create "entirely new structures." The addition
of Turkish instruments (triangle, cymbal, and bass drum) was motivated
by the need for a "still greater measure of . . . force," and not by the desire for
exoticism for its own sake. But as enthusiastic as Kanne himself may have
been about the work, he readily acknowledged that other opinions had
been expressed:

> The passionate nature of the finale, battling and struggling with all the
> elements and powers of music, indeed is not to be grasped upon a first
> hearing, and it may, therefore, also very well have been the case that
> there were those who, among the ranks of inspired listeners, did not
> want to agree with the enthusiastic applause of Beethoven's admirers.
>   The more such a work exceeds all customary norms, the more
> freedom it develops in its course, the less one finds therein that which
> is familiar and popular for us, the more, lastly, it stretches the expecta-
> tion by its dimension; then the easier it becomes for differing opinions
> to grow in which the public, either because of its duty, its numbers, or
> also its custom, has given its voice. Many a view, therefore, previously
> expressed in other publications have been in disagreement with it.
>   But all those in sympathy with the highly educated musical world
> expressed themselves all the more decidedly and clearly in perceiving
> Beethoven's originality and free individuality as a great phenomenon
> of the century.[28]

Kanne was not the only critic to file a review for the May 23 concert. An unnamed reviewer in the Vienna *Theater-Zeitung* also waxed enthusiastic, though not without the caveat that many in the audience had failed to understand Beethoven's latest works, including "many professionals," but quickly adding that there were also "many, very many, present who had understood."[29] A brief notice in the Leipzig *Allgemeine musikalische Zeitung* commented on the poor attendance at this concert, blaming it on the unfavorable hour and high ticket prices. The correspondent further reported that the performance of the Symphony "here and there left something to be desired, for which the unfavorable locale was also in part to blame."[30] A report in *Caecilia* placed the economic problems of the May performances in a larger perspective:

> In general ... the interest in compositions of this genre [the symphony] is declining substantially, and the artistic disciple who travels this road, unrewarded for his effort, without profit, often without applause, must fight with unspeakable difficulties even to bring his work to performance.
>
> Evidence of this, and unpleasant evidence at that, is offered by the results of the Academies by Beethoven held last year, in which his magnificent new symphony, an overture, and part of his second Mass were given. At the first performance in the Kärntnerthor Theater, the income was: 2220 fl., 57 kr. W. W. (250 gulden equal 100 silver gulden); the expenses were nearly 1900 fl, leaving, therefore, not quite 400 fl. W. W. People showered the genial master with applause and testimonials of praise, but *molto onore, poco contante* [much honor, little contentment].[31]

In producing these two concerts, Beethoven had taken a large financial and artistic risk. Gottfried Weber, the editor of *Caecilia,* deemed the first performance of the Ninth Symphony worthy of inclusion in a list of the most significant dates in musical history since the sixteenth century.[32] The critics of 1824 were favorably disposed toward Beethoven and his new symphony. But even in these positive reviews, the seeds of future dissension—particularly regarding the integrity of the finale—were sown. Of the critics, it was Kanne who evoked the most poetic descriptive language for describing the Ninth. Both he and the correspondent from the Leipzig *Allgemeine musikalische Zeitung* exhibited an acute sensitivity to the differences between the musical style of the Ninth Symphony and that of Rossini's operas and the composers of virtuoso keyboard music. One senses that many German musicians and critics lived in a kind of Messianic age, an age that looked hopefully to Beethoven and his Ninth Symphony as agents of redemption for a musical culture that was losing its way. But, as the next chapter will show, not everybody was a true believer. One thing was certain, however: the composition and performance of symphonies, a genre that once was the sole province of the courts of nobility, had now moved permanently onto the stages of public concerts. The symphony and its performance would never be the same again.

Chapter 6

IN THE SHADOW OF THE NINTH

The following inscription was seen over the entrance to an instrument dealer:
  "Genuine Viennese and English Pianos [Flügel]."
Underneath this was written the motto:
  Alle Menschen werden Brüder,
  Wo dein sanfter Flügel weilt.[1]

The first two performances of the Ninth Symphony in May 1824 were the only ones over which Beethoven had direct control. Any success that the piece would enjoy afterward would depend on musicians who were brave enough to perform the work and critics and audiences who would accept or reject the piece based upon their experience of it. The story of the Ninth's reception, and of the immense shadow that the work cast, is as complex as the masterpiece itself. The respect that Beethoven's name commanded assured that the Ninth would be performed. But the efficacy of the composer's "late" style became a lively issue in terms of how the work was perceived. The fact that the Ninth continues to generate controversy in our own day is but a confirmation of the important issues that the piece raises.

In chapter 7 we will deal more specifically with performance issues, but these issues cannot be isolated entirely from the story of how the Ninth

Symphony made its way into the concert life. The circumstances under which the Ninth Symphony was performed form a vital part of its reception history, because written opinions were often based on inadequate performances. As important as performances were in spreading the reputation of the work, discussion of the piece was by no means limited to concert reviews. *Rezensionen,* or analyses based on the published score, usually written by a theorist and/or composer, stood aloof from the vicissitudes of performance and greatly influenced the public's perceptions of the work. The Ninth also was transmitted through transcriptions for piano, the earliest being an arrangement of the finale and issued by Schott in 1826. Carl Czerny's transcription for piano four-hands appeared in 1829, published by Probst and Schott. Liszt arranged the work for piano, two hands, in 1851 (published 1853), and then, in 1865, printed his version for piano solo, perhaps the best-known arrangement today. The transcriptions were critical because they spread the piece to localities where people were unlikely to encounter the work in its original form.

As the Beethoven myth grew after the composer's death, the Ninth Symphony also became the subject of essays, short stories, and novellas. These literary forums succeeded in bringing the work and its issues before a general public that had no interest in reading the more specialized musical journals that flourished in nineteenth-century Europe. The story of the Ninth's dissemination, then, is a complex and varied tale.

The Rise of the "Concert" Orchestra

Hector Berlioz, one of the Ninth Symphony's most enthusiastic supporters, observed that by dint of repeated performances, operas stood a greater chance of becoming known to audiences than symphonies. His argument went as follows:

> This cannot happen with symphonies that are given only at wide intervals. Instead of obliterating the bad impressions they produced on their first appearance, the interval gives these impressions time to take root and to produce theories, indeed written doctrines, to which the talent of the writer who utters them lends more or less authority according to the degree of impartiality he seems to show in his critique

and the apparent wisdom of the advice he gives the composer. Frequency of performance is therefore a prerequisite to the redress of errors of opinion about works such as Beethoven's, which were conceived outside the musical habits of those that hear them. . . .

What is needed then, let me repeat, is that Beethoven's works should receive frequent performances of irresistible power and beauty. But I do not honestly believe there are six places in the whole world where one can hear, say, six times a year all his symphonies properly performed. In one place the orchestra is unselected, in another it is too small in numbers, in yet another it is badly led, or the concert hall is no good, and the players have no time to rehearse—in short, almost everywhere one runs into obstacles which, in the last analysis, bring disaster upon these masterpieces.[2]

Berlioz, as composer, critic, and conductor, was uniquely placed to make such an observation. The very idea of a "symphony concert" performed by a professional orchestra as we know it today was a fledgling concept in the musical world into which the Ninth Symphony was born. The same may be said for the art of conducting. As seen in chapter 5, even Vienna—the city that gave birth to all of Beethoven's symphonies—had no standing professional orchestra dedicated solely to the performance of symphonic music until 1842, when Otto Nicolai established the Philharmonic Concerts. Expert orchestras, such as the one hired by Beethoven for his *Academie* concerts in 1824, had to be performed from the ranks of musicians who performed in Vienna's principal theaters.

Institutions featuring "concert" orchestras already existed in London (Philharmonic Society), Paris (Société des Concerts), Leipzig (Gewandhaus Concerts), and Berlin (Symphony Soirées), and it is not surprising that these metropolitan centers were among the first outside of Vienna to host performances of the Ninth Symphony. The sizes of these orchestras varied greatly. The orchestra for the Gewandhaus concerts in Leipzig in 1830, for example, numbered thirty-eight players with a string section of twelve violins, two violas, two cellos, and two basses. The Société des Concerts orchestra of 1828, by comparison, numbered over eighty-two musicians with thirty violins, eight violas, twelve cellos, and eight basses. As time went on, however, the size of the orchestras generally expanded to the one-hundred-or-so piece ensemble encountered today.[3]

The methods used to direct rehearsals and concerts in the early part of the century were quite different from those used today. François-Antoine Habeneck, the "conductor" of the Société des Concerts in Paris, for example, stood before his orchestra as its leader with violin bow (and often violin) in hand, but he led performances with a violin part on his desk instead of a score. In London, on the other hand, a new "leader" (concertmaster) and "director" or "conductor" (a keyboardist, whose role had become particularly ill defined after the era of the basso continuo) were appointed by the Directors of the Philharmonic Society to prepare and execute each concert, often with only one rehearsal. This antiquated practice continued until the appointment of Michael Costa in 1846 as a baton conductor (Louis Spohr's claim that he supplanted the old system as early as 1820 is exaggerated). Baton conductors were more commonly found when choral forces were involved, as in the performance of oratorios. The choral part of the finale of the Ninth Symphony was probably led in this fashion. Rehearsal time for the preparation of a given concert was, as a rule, short, although Habeneck, at least, is known to have been especially generous where the preparation of Beethoven's symphonies was concerned.

By the middle of the nineteenth century the modern art of conducting became firmly established. The inadequacies of the older methods yielded to the new phenomenon known as the conductor, whose personal vision and awareness of the intricacies of complex scores would galvanize each performance into a coherent whole. While the use of a conductor had distinct advantages, it also led to a new problem—the emergence of the "star" conductor whose ego at times came into conflict with the instructions of the composer. It would be safe to say that the Ninth Symphony, a work that calls for several changes of tempo and meter within single movements, helped to bring about a change in the way orchestral concerts were directed.

Between 1825 and 1846 more than eighty performances of the Ninth Symphony can be documented.[4] The most important local premieres can be summarized as follows:

Location	*Date*	
London	March 21, 1825	Philharmonic Society, directed by George Smart and led by Ferdinand Cramer, finale sung in Italian
Frankfurt	April 1, 1825	
Aachen	May 23, 1825	2nd day of Niederrheinische Musikfest, directed by Ferdinand Ries, scherzo omitted, *Adagio* curtailed

Leipzig	March 2, 1826	Gewandhaus, directed by Heinrich August Matthäi and Johann Philipp Christian Schultz (finale). Second and third performances on March 30 and October 19
Berlin	November 27, 1826	directed by Karl Möser. On November 13, Mendelssohn played a piano transcription before a select audience
Prague	March 9, 1827	
Bremen	1827 season	
Magdeburg	1827 season	
Paris	March 27, 1831	directed by François-Antoine Habeneck on 5th program of Société; 1st two movements played at beginning of program, last two at end
Dessau	1834 season	
Munich	February 1835	
Halle	1834/35 season	
St. Petersburg	March 7, 1836	Philharmonic Society
Hanover	April 9, 1836	
Freiburg	1835/36 season	
Dresden	November 7, 1838	
Oldenburg	1840 season	finale omitted
Breslau	1839/40 season	
Cologne	Pfingstfest 1841	23rd Rheinische Musikfest, directed by Konradin Kreutzer with 700 performers participating
Düsseldorf	Spring 1845	Musikfest
Bonn	August 10, 1845	Beethoven Monument Dedication Ceremony directed by Louis Spohr
Hamburg	August 11, 1845	Beethoven-Feier und Festkonzert
New York	May 20, 1846	Philharmonic Concert, American premiere

Each of the performances played an important role spreading the reputation of the Ninth. Because of the coverage they received in the major musical journals, however, the first performances in London, Aachen, Leipzig, Berlin, Paris, and Bonn (which was as much a political event as it was a musical one) were particularly influential.

It would require an entire volume to account for all of the performances of the Ninth Symphony in the first half of the nineteenth century. However, an examination of the fate of the piece in one city, London, is instructive, for it illustrates well the issues that were germane to the reception of the Ninth Symphony elsewhere. London was the site of the first performance of the Ninth Symphony after its Viennese premiere, and it was the commission of London's Philharmonic Society that had been a principal motivational force for the work's completion. Also, as seen in chapter 2, one of the most significant primary sources for the work is the copy of the score that Beethoven's copyists made for the Philharmonic Society. As far as the Londoners were concerned, the Ninth Symphony had been composed "expressly" for them.

TRIALS, TRIBULATIONS, AND TRIUMPHS: THE NINTH IN LONDON

In preparing for a performance of the Ninth Symphony on March 21, 1825, the Directors of the Philharmonic Society followed their customary practice of choosing both a "director" and "leader." They also scheduled a "trial," the Society's normal mechanism for determining whether a new piece was feasible or worthy of public performance. The Directors of the Society had hoped that Beethoven himself would travel to London to supervise the first performance of his new symphony, but the composer declined to come. George Smart and Ferdinand Cramer, the "director" and "leader," respectively, selected by the Directors, would have to make do without the personal guidance of the great master.

The Philharmonic Society did not maintain its own chorus. Whenever one was needed, it turned to the combined forces of smaller professional choirs (including those of St. Paul's Cathedral, Westminster Abbey, and the Chapel Royal) as well as singers who worked at London's opera houses. Carse suggests that these vocal forces were also used by other orchestras in London (such as the Concerts of Ancient Music) "for the simple reason that no other choir was available at the time in London."[5] Curiously, Beethoven's vocal recitative and Schiller's poem were translated into Italian, presumably because it was the *lingua franca* of singers in London. The minutes of the Society's Directors' Meeting, however, sheds further light on the issue:

> Resolved that Mr. Neate be requested to consult Mr. Pagliardino respecting the translating the words of Beethoven's New Symphony into Italian. Resolved that Mr. Charles Clementi be informed that the difficulty of singing the English words [of Schiller's poem] has induced the Directors to have it performed in Italian.[6]

The English critics in the *Harmonicon* and the *Quarterly Musical Magazine and Review* in 1825 wasted no time in exhibiting hostility toward the Ninth. Witness the *Harmonicon* report of the trial reading:

> Previously to the re-commencement of these concerts, the Philharmonic Society had three private meetings in the months of January and February, for the purpose of trying, with the full orchestra, new compositions, and deciding on their fitness for public performance. Amongst these were, a symphony by Mr. Cipriano Potter, an overture by Mr. Goss, Weber's overtures to *Preciosa* and *Euryanthe,* and a Grand Symphony recently composed for the society, by Beethoven. All of these we shall have to notice when they are regularly before the public. But much curiosity having anticipated in part our regular criticism on it, by observing, that it manifests many brilliant traits of Beethoven's vast genius; that it imbodies [sic] enough of original matter, of beautiful effects and skilful [sic] contrivances, to form an admirable symphony of ordinary duration: but that unfortunately, the author has spun it out to so unusual a length, that he has "drawn out the thread of his verbosity finer than the staple of his argument," and what would have been delightful had it been contained within moderate limits, he has rendered wearying by expansion, and diluted his subjects till they became weak and vapid. When we add that the time which it is calculated this composition will take in performing, cannot be much less than an hour and twenty minutes, our readers, though they have not heard it, may almost judge for themselves of its inadequacy to fix the attention of any audience, or to produce such an effect as the admirers of Beethoven must earnestly wish.[7]

The initial bone of contention in London, then, was the unprecedented length of the symphony. The critics in Vienna who reported on the first performances of the work in 1824 also shared this concern. It is not clear, however, by what method the *Harmonicon* reporter was able to estimate a performance time of eighty minutes from a preliminary reading that undoubtedly was interrupted by frequent stops and starts. Smart, who was fastidious about keeping track of the duration of pieces he performed, surely must have found this prediction preposterous.[8] No objection was offered (yet) to the inclusion of a vocal component in a symphony, nor was there any reference to the Italian translation of the text. The English press had damned the work even before it had been heard by the Philharmonic's audience.

The London premiere of the Ninth Symphony formed the second "act" of the third concert of the Philharmonic Society on March 21, 1825. The first "act" was characteristically long, including a symphony by Haydn, a string quartet by Mozart (chamber music often was included on these programs), a woodwind quintet by Reicha, an overture by Cherubini, and vocal selections by Mozart and Handel. The Ninth Symphony was listed as "Symphony (MS.) with Vocal Finale, 'Choral Symphony'/Mme Caradori, Miss Goodall; Messrs, Vaughan, Phillips and Chorus./(First performance; composed expressly for this Society.)/Leader, Mr. F. Cramer. Conductor, Sir G. Smart."[9]

The contrabass and cello recitative in the early London performances is an interesting issue in its own right. The Directors of the Society, in their belief that Beethoven had composed the work for London, assumed that the unusual instrumental recitative was composed as a solo for the celebrated bassist Domenico Dragonetti and his desk partner, the cellist Lindley.[10] When Smart visited Beethoven in Vienna later that year, he told the composer, with the assistance of Schuppanzigh: "H.[err] Smart wanted to know exactly how he [Beethoven] wishes to have the recitative in the symphony performed. He said it had caused them a great deal of trouble."[11]

The March 21 performance of the Ninth caused the *Harmonicon* reviewer to soften his criticism of the work's length, although he still found it too long for his taste. He remained unrepentant for his earlier chastisements, and now raised additional objections:

> The new symphony of Beethoven, composed for, and purchased at a
> liberal price by, this society, was now first publicly produced. In our
> last number we mentioned it, and we see no reason for altering the

opinion we there offered. We must, however, correct our statement as
to its duration. At a rehearsal, where so many interruptions occur, it is
next to impossible to ascertain exactly the length of a piece: we now
find this to be precisely one hour and five minutes; a fearful period
indeed, which puts the muscles and lungs of the band, and the patience of the audience, to a severe trial. In the present symphony we
discover no diminution of Beethoven's creative talent; it exhibits many
perfectly new traits, and in its technical formation shews amazing
ingenuity and unabated vigour of mind. But with all the merits that it
unquestionably possesses, it is at least twice as long as it should be; it
repeats itself, and the subjects in consequence became weak by reiteration. The last movement, a chorus, is heterogeneous, and though
there is much vocal beauty in parts of it, yet it does not, and no habit
will ever make it, mix up with the three first movements. This chorus
is a hymn to joy, commencing with a recitative, and relieved by many
soli passages. What relation it bears to the symphony we could not
make out; and here, as well as in other parts, the want of intelligible
design is too apparent. In our next [issue] we shall give the words of the
chorus, with a translation; in the present number our printer has not
been able to find room for them. The most original feature in this
symphony is the minuet, and the most singular part, the succeeding
trio,—striking, because in duple time, for which we are not acquainted
with anything in the shape of a precedent. We were also much pleased
by a very noble march, which is introduced. In quitting the present
subject, we must express our hope that this new work of the great
Beethoven may be put into a produceable form; that the repetitions
may be omitted, and the chorus removed altogether; the symphony
will then be heard with unmixed pleasure, and the reputation of its
author will, if possible, be further augmented.[12]

These are the words of a critic who preferred a Beethoven of Haydn-
esque proportions. The scherzo ("minuet" according to our conservative
critic) is the only movement to call for any literal repetition, leaving us to
wonder as to how—besides omitting the finale—he would propose to get the
piece into a "produceable form." The *Harmonicon* critic at least believed
that the Ninth Symphony could be salvaged. Not so for the writer for the
Quarterly Musical Magazine and Review, whose displeasure on hearing the
trial performance outstripped that of his colleague:

Before I enter into a brief detail of the beauties and defects of this symphony, it may be right at once to say, that its length alone will be a never-failing cause of complaint to those who reject monopoly in sounds, as it takes up exactly one hour and twenty minutes in performance, which is not compensated by any beauty or unity of design, taking the composition as a whole. . . .

The fourth and last movement, upon which the violent admirers of Beethoven seem to place all their ill-judged vehemence of approbation, is one of the most extraordinary instances I have ever witnessed, of great powers of mind and wonderful science, wasted upon subjects infinitely beneath its strength. But I must at the same time declare, that parts of this movement, one especially where the basses lead off a sort of fugal subject of about twenty bars, in a bold and commanding style, afterwards answered by the other parts, are really beautiful, and would be sufficient to have raised fame for any composer less known—but even here, while we are enjoying the delight of so much science and melody, and eagerly anticipating its continuance, on a sudden, like the fleeting pleasures of life, or the spirited young adventurer, who would fly from ease and comfort at home, to the inhospitable shores of New Zealand or Lake Ontario, we are snatched away from such eloquent music, to crude, wild, and extraneous harmonies, that may to some ears express a great deal, but whether it is my misfortune or my fault I know not, I must confess, the impression made upon my ear resembled the agitations and contradictions of "restless couples," or reminded me of the poet's lofty figure, "chaos is come again." . . . The chorus that immediately follows is also in many places exceedingly imposing and effective, but then there is so much of it, so many sudden pauses and odd and almost ludicrous passages for the horn and bassoon, so much rambling and vociferous execution given to the violins and stringed instruments, without any decisive effect or definite meaning—and to crown all, the deafening boisterous jollity of the concluding part, wherein, besides the usual allotment of triangles, drums, trumpets, &c &c. all the known acoustical missile instruments I should conceive were employed, with the assistance of their able allies, the corps of Sforzandos, Crescendos, Accelerandos, and many other *os,* that they made even the very ground shake under us, and would, with their fearful uproar, have been sufficiently penetrating to call up from their peaceful graves (if such things were permitted) the revered shades of

Tallis, Purcell, and Gibbons, and even of Handel and Mozart, to witness and deplore the obstreperous roarings of modern frenzy in their art. . . .

One great excuse remains for all this want of perfection. It is to be remembered, that the great composer is afflicted with an incurable disorder (deafness), which to powers like his must be a deprivation more acute and distressing than any one can possibly imagine. May not this disturb a mind gifted with such extraordinary genius? Age is stealing upon him, and every one must see from daily experience, that age, unaccompanied by domestic happiness, seldom improves the temper, and now the homage of the world is divided as it were between himself and Von Weber. . . . He writes to suit the present mania, and if this be so, he has succeeded in his purpose, for everywhere I hear the praises of this his last work.[13]

The review is revealing on several counts. The critic's reference to "flattering accounts from Germany" and the "violent admirers of Beethoven" indicates that he, like his colleague from the *Harmonicon,* had read the Viennese reviews of 1824, but concluded from his own experience that the German critics' enthusiasm had been "ill-judged." A distinctly British bias also is evident in the reference to the "shades of Tallis, Purcell, and Gibbons, and even of Handel and Mozart" as silent deplorers of "obstreperous roarings of modern frenzy." The British enthusiasm for Weber, whose music was considered the paragon of the modern style, led the critic to suppose that Beethoven was self-consciously competing with the composer of *Der Freischütz.*

A retrospective view of the 1825 season of the Philharmonic concerts in the *Quarterly Musical Magazine and Review* served to seal the fate of Beethoven's Ninth Symphony in London for many years to come:

The compositions newly introduced were Beethoven's symphony (purchased up by the society at an expence of 250 guineas), Spontini's overture to *Olimpia,* and an overture by Mr. Onslow. Of the first a correspondent has already given so detailed an account, and his criticism has been so completely borne out by the performance, that we should only repeat what he has said were we to enter again upon an analysis of its parts. The impression on the auditors was certainly a mixed feeling of pleasure and dissatisfaction—of pleasure arising from the casual and bright gleams of talent that every now and then broke

forth—of dissatisfaction at the exaggeration of several of the parts, at
the disjointed nature of the whole composition, and at its immoderate
length; it lasted an hour and five minutes. The expence it entails in the
engagement of a chorus, the necessity of repeated rehearsals, &c &c
may perhaps forbid its ever being done again, and will certainly im-
pede both its frequent repetition or its general reception. Yet it is the
work of a great mind.[14]

The dual blows of performance difficulties and adverse criticism im-
peded the progress of the Ninth Symphony in London, and the Philharmonic Society gave no further performances of the work until 1837.

This is not to say, however, that the Ninth went unheard in London.
Charles Neate, a founder and Director of the Philharmonic Society and a
personal acquaintance of Beethoven, presented it in a concert at the King's
Theatre on April 26, 1830. The performance was reviewed by the *Harmonicon,* whose correspondent reluctantly admitted that there were those in
the audience who were happy to hear Beethoven's masterpiece. Another
London performance of the Ninth took place on June 20, 1835, in the Hano-
ver Square Rooms, the site of the Philharmonic Concerts. The performers
on this occasion were students and professors from the Royal Academy of
Music (some of the latter, no doubt, were Philharmonic members). The
conductor of the concert was Charles Lucas, a cellist, organist, and professor of composition at the Academy. Instead of performing the entire
work, Lucas and his ensemble decided to tackle the most controversial
part, the choral finale. A critic from the *Times* had this to say:

> The pupils gave their last concert for the season on Saturday morn-
> ing at the Hanover-square Rooms, which was extremely well attended.
> Its chief distinction over those which have preceded it was the perfor-
> mance of the latter portion of Beethoven's Ninth Symphony, for which
> Schiller wrote his "Ode to Joy," and into which the composer had
> thrown all the grandeur of the effect to be derived from the combina-
> tion of orchestra and chorus, with a degree of power which has ob-
> tained for it with musicians the highest rank among the modern pro-
> ductions of the art. To those aware of the difficulty of the performance,
> its announcement by the Academy pupils was treated as a rash at-
> tempt, certain to end in failure, but they have nevertheless passed
> through the ordeal in a manner which has surprised the profession,

who attended in great numbers to witness the experiment. The whole reflects, it must be allowed, the highest credit on the establishment. They accomplished all that their limited numbers permitted; and increase of power was all that was wanted to the original design, but its outline and character were brought out with admirable precision. This has been thought heretofore too elaborate a work for the public, but it is evident now, that it only requires to be well executed to be perfectly understood even by an ear not trained to scientific combinations. Its structure is essentially simple, and it was easy, as it was played on this occasion, to trace the plain chant and beautiful subject, with which the basses lead off, amidst the apparent complexity of the succeeding movements. The orchestra, which was led by Mr. Patey, one of the pupils still in the Academy, must have rehearsed its share of the performance with great industry; and in the chorusses [sic], which are under the management of Mr. Elliott, the same careful preparation is manifest. The solo voices were sustained by Mr[s] H. R. Bishop, Miss Birch, Mr. Burnett, and Mr. Stretton, and the management of the whole devolved upon Mr. Lucas, as conductor, to whose judgment and industry the success of the whole performance is mainly owing. Beyond the Academy, that success will do infinite good to the art itself, by stimulating other societies of musicians to similar attempts, for much treasure of the same sort lies buried, or is suffered to fall into utter neglect. Above all, it is hoped that the sleeping virtue of the directors of the Philharmonic Society will be awakened by it, and induce them to rescue the state of art in England from the reproach justly cast on it by foreigners, of consigning to utter oblivion one of its noblest productions. They alone have the means at their disposal to do it complete justice, and their shame and disgrace in continuing to neglect it will be doubled, as it was the Philharmonic Society that Beethoven composed this symphony. We forgot to mention, as proof of the care with which it has been brought out by the Academy, that a new and very good translation of Schiller's ode has been made expressly for the occasion. A clumsy Italian version of it was, we believe, the only one that previously existed.[15]

The performance and favorable review presented an important turning point for the Ninth Symphony in London. The Società Armonica quickly responded to the reviewer's challenge by placing the Ninth Symphony on a program at the King's Theatre on March 24, 1836. The performance was led by Henry Forbes, with the vocal solos performed by Bishop, Shaw, Hobbs, and Balfe.

Encouraged by their success in performing the finale, and perhaps spurred by the Società Armonica performance, the students of the Royal Academy presented the Ninth in its entirety on April 15, 1836. Again, a critic from the *Times* was present:

> The Royal Academy pupils gave their second concert for the season yesterday morning. After a miscellaneous act in which little was done to acquire distinction, with the exception of a fantasia on the flute by Mr. Richardson, a pupil of Nicholson, the 9th Symphony of Beethoven was given, and occupied the remainder of the concert. The very attempt at this noble composition is a species of distinction for the Academy, but the manner in which they gave some of its finest passages yesterday entitles the pupils to high rank as musicians. The minuet and trio [!] with the latter part of the slow movement were, perhaps, the most distinctly brought out. The vocal part of the symphony, which occupies nearly one half of it, is one grand sustained effort of genius. More beautiful, yet more simple melodies, are not to be found in this composer, who is always clear and intelligible, if justice is done him by the performers. The solo parts devolved on Mrs. Bishop, Miss Birch, Mr. Bennett, and Mr. Stretton. The number of the chorus was too small for the purpose, but they had studied the composition with great care, and did credit to the skill of Mr. Lucas, the conductor, who was himself one of the pupils, and has gone into the profession with a reputation which reflects honour on the institution. The room was well filled, and a large proportion of the leading professors attended the performance.[16]

The reviews of performances of the Ninth Symphony that appeared in the *Times* reflected a remarkable change from the tone of those found in the *Harmonicon* and the *Quarterly Musical Magazine and Review.* Seemingly overnight, the highly conservative critics had fallen mute. The older journals had yielded their authority to the critics who wrote for the *Times* and the *Musical World* (founded in 1835). Charles Neate and Charles Lucas also deserve much of the credit for having the courage to perform the Ninth Symphony in the face of the dubious reputation that its earliest London critics had given it. The Ninth Symphony seemed to have been given a new lease on life in London.

The Directors of the Philharmonic Society could no longer ignore the chastisements of the new generation of London critics, and the Ninth Symphony was placed on the Philharmonic program of April 17, 1837, with Moscheles as conductor and Loder as leader. A review of the concert that appeared in the *Musical World* placed this event in an historical perspective.

On the 21st of March 1825, twelve years ago, the Philharmonic Society produced the Sinfonia Caractéristique, of the Passion of Joy, which was composed for that body by Beethoven. From that day until last Monday, the Society has laid it aside as useless lumber. Written in the prime of life, in the full flower of his genius, following the wonderful trio 'Tremate, empi, tremate,' and succeeded by the still more wonderful Missa for eight voices—it was pronounced "the aberration of a great mind!" The old gentlemen who wrote indifferent glees, and kept up a society for mutual applause, set to work on the 'Harmonicon' and 'Musical Magazine;' in the one it was averred, with a hardihood surpassing belief, that the symphony presented "the most extraordinary instance of great powers of mind and wonderful science wasted upon subjects infinitely beneath its strength;" in the other, that it was "full of repetition," "without intelligible design," and what relation the ode had to the music "they could not make out." This was enough; down went the MS. into an obscure a corner of the library, the law and the gospel were both against it. Beethoven dies; the symphony is published by subscription—but the English musicians referred to the critiques and withheld their patronage. On the 17th day of April 1837, the symphony is reproduced, meets with enthusiastic applause, and absolutely overwhelms the auditors with ecstasy and astonishment at its marvellous beauty. We never saw a more unanimous feeling of approbation, or one demonstrated with greater cordiality at any meeting of this society. The truth is, that in the first instance the symphony was mercilessly butchered—we state this on the best authority. On Monday it was, barring a few exceptions, understood, and executed with a seriousness and earnestness which reflected the highest credit on the association. Mr. Moscheles conducted, and every attitude testified how completely he was absorbed in the beauty of the scene: how his spirit bowed down and worshipped the mighty genius of his master. For the way in which he led the band to draw out some few points, we thank him with feelings of gratitude and admiration; and we really think

now our enthusiasm has in some measure subsided, that had we met
him coming out of the concert room, we should have knelt to him, and,
through him, done homage to the memory of the magician, whose
mighty conception he had been so instrumental in developing. We
have received a communication from a contributor respecting this
symphony, which shall appear in our next number; and thus render
any further detail on our part unnecessary. Mrs. Bishop, Miss Hawes,
and Mssrs. Horncastle and Phillips, were the solo singers.[17]

The return of the Ninth Symphony to the Philharmonic Society concerts
represented a true watershed for the piece in London. Its honored place in
the repertory of the Society assured, the work would never again fall into
disrepute.

OTHER REACTIONS TO THE NINTH

The fate of the Ninth Symphony in London was echoed in other locations
throughout Europe. A vigorous debate regarding its worthiness was waged
in 1826 in the pages of the Berlin *Allgemeine musikalische Zeitung,* a debate
that prefigured one between François-Joseph Fétis in Paris and an anonymous London critic, "Dilettante," in 1828.[18] The Berlin combatants were
the journal's Leipzig correspondent and its editor, Adolph Bernhard Marx
(1795–1866). Marx, a staunch Beethoven enthusiast who was to write one
of the earliest biographies of the composer, declared the work to be "the
profoundest and most mature instrumental composition by the greatest
genius and the most conscientious of living composers"—an opinion based
solely on his study of the score. On the other hand, the Leipzig correspondent, placing great stock in the ability of the Gewandhaus orchestra to
render Beethoven's symphonies in an intelligible manner, found little that
was praiseworthy in the Ninth Symphony, indicating moreover that the
majority of the Leipzig audience agreed with his judgment. A critic writing
for the Leipzig *Allgemeine musikalische Zeitung* was even more severe than
his colleague from Berlin, accusing Beethoven of being "an exorcist, whom
it has pleased this time to demand from us something superhuman. To this
I do not consent."[19] The nature of the reviews from Leipzig began to change
after Felix Mendelssohn ascended the podium of the Gewandhaus orches-

tra and conducted his first performance of the Ninth on March 13, 1836. Reviews of Mendelssohn's later Leipzig performances (in 1838, 1841, 1843, and 1846) reveal, among other things, that he was the first conductor in the city to use women's voices in the chorus instead of a boys' choir. But above all, it was Mendelssohn's skill as a conductor and musician that won the day for the Ninth Symphony in Leipzig.

Rezensionen of the work are as idiosyncratic as the work itself. Interpretive analyses sometimes were enfolded into reviews of performances, such as Kanne's essay given in chapter 5. Chrétien Urhan, writing in *Le Temps,* and Henry John Gauntlett writing in the *Musical World,* also attempted to interpret the Ninth Symphony for their readers in the context of a concert review.[20] Urhan's essay, fueled by an intense religiosity, characterizes the work as Beethoven's "moral autobiography." Taking quotations from Dante's *Inferno* to illustrate his interpretation of the first movement, Urhan calls it the representation of a "night of disasters," a piece that bears witness to "one of the tempests of Beethoven's soul." The second movement portrays the composer performing a lusty German dance against the backdrop of nature, while the *Adagio* is a "pure" representation of love, tinged "with melancholy and all sort of poetic sadness." The finale finds the long-suffering composer rejecting the materialism of this world and seeking spiritual consolation in the presence of his creator. The cherub standing before the throne of God, says Urhan, is Beethoven himself. The essay ends with a quote from a fellow Parisian who claims that Schiller's "Brothers!" refers to the fraternal spirit of Freemasonry. To this Urhan can only add, "Perhaps we are as mad as that fellow! But if our explanation is only a dream, it is a dream of good faith, and a pure dream. . . . Forgive us for it!"

After the publication of the Ninth, analytical essays appeared in various places. Three separate critiques were published in the 1828 volume of *Caecilia.* The first was written by Franz Joseph Fröhlich, a professor of aesthetics at the University of Würzburg. The other two writers were a Dr. Grossheim of Kassel and Ignaz von Seyfried, a personal acquaintance of Beethoven. Robin Wallace has pointed out that the vocal component in the finale was not in itself a problem for these writers, who discussed the finale as if it were merely an extension of Beethoven's instrumental music.[21] Marx stood alone in his view that the vocal element of the finale represented the victory of song—the most innately human type of musical expression— over purely instrumental music. The work's fundamental "idea," in Marx's words, is that sonata yields to cantata. Fröhlich's "idea," by way of contrast, was that the Ninth represented the struggle that begins in sorrow and long-ing and leads to the eventual attainment of joy. Grossheim also viewed the work as a spiritual pilgrimage, with the relationship of the first part of the symphony to its finale representing "a marriage of opposites" (the absence of joy, and its attainment). Seyfried, on the other hand, rejected a program-matic interpretation in favor of a more technical discussion of the work's content.

The Ninth Symphony—more than any of Beethoven's other composi-tions—inspired, and even demanded, new and different ways of writing about music. Criticism itself was forced to find a balance between analysis and interpretation. In this sense, the Ninth Symphony became a catalyst for change in music criticism in much the same way that it fostered new ap-proaches to orchestral performance practices. The seeds planted by the critics of the 1820s bore rich fruit later in the century, especially in the im-portant analytical essays on the Ninth Symphony written by Hector Berlioz and Richard Wagner.

Berlioz's extensive article on the Ninth Symphony was the concluding essay in his series, "Symphonies de Beethoven," published over several issues of the *Revue et Gazette musicale* in 1838, and it formed—with minor modifications—the basis for the "Études Critiques" of *A Travers Chants*, published in 1862.[22] The essay on the Ninth Symphony was prompted by the January 14, 1838 performance by Habeneck—the very same concert that inspired Urhan's article in *Le Temps*. Berlioz's essay is distinguished by the depth of its technical insight, the eloquence of its descriptions, and its candor. While Berlioz's enthusiasm for the Ninth Symphony is manifest, he uses little of the powerful symbolic imagery found in his essay on the "Eroica" Symphony with its allusions to a soaring eagle "athirst for the infinite." Although each essay could be read separately, Berlioz doubtlessly hoped that the patrons of the *Revue et Gazette musicale* would read the entire series of essays on the Beethoven symphonies. He constructed the essays to read in a logical progression, while at the same time finding language appropriate to each work. Berlioz admits at the beginning of his article on the Ninth Symphony that a discussion of the work is "a difficult and dangerous task that we have long hesitated to undertake," especially in light of the diverse opinions that the piece had elicited. He does not hesitate to inform his readers that he deems the piece to be "the most magnificent expression of Beethoven's genius." Berlioz pays tribute to Urhan's essay in

Le Temps, but avers that he wishes to determine "if the novelty of the form would not be justified by an intention independent of all philosophical or religious thoughts, equally reasonable and beautiful for the fervent Christian, as for the pantheist and for the atheist, by an intention, finally, purely musical and poetical." Berlioz believed the instrumental recitative in the finale to be a "bridge" over which the instruments must pass to form an "alliance" with the human voice. The text of the vocal recitative in turn becomes the oath of "treaty" between the opposing forces. Having established this premise, Berlioz then begins his detailed survey of the entire piece, a survey in which he frankly admits that there are problematic moments in the work that he can not explain.

Berlioz's almost prosaic approach to Beethoven's last symphony seems to have been intentional. His feigned reluctance to commit his ideas about the piece to writing becomes, in this light, a literary ruse. By acknowledging certain "anomalies" in the work, and by describing them in graphic detail, Berlioz assumes the role of devil's advocate. Berlioz thereby informs those enemies of the Ninth Symphony that the piece's occasional peculiarities are insufficient grounds on which to dismiss a work of its magnitude.

Richard Wagner had a great deal to say about the Ninth Symphony, a work that took on a mystical significance to him:

> On first looking through the score, which I obtained only with great difficulty, I was struck at once, as if by force of destiny, with the long-sustained perfect fifths with which the first movements begins: these sounds, which played such a spectral role in my earliest impressions of music, came to me as the ghostly fundamental of my own life. This symphony surely held the secret to all secrets; and so I got busy over it by painstakingly copying out the score. Once, after having spent a night at this task, I remember being startled by the dawn, which affected me so strongly in my excited condition that I buried myself under the bedclothes with a loud shriek as if terrified by an apparition.[23]

Wagner's enthusiasm, inspired by his study of the score (which he, too, transcribed for piano in 1828, but failed to get published), was followed by initial disappointment two years later upon hearing the work badly performed at a Gewandhaus concert. More polished rehearsals and performances by Habeneck in Paris (1839–42) restored his faith in the Ninth, but it would not be until 1846, when serving as Vice-Kapellmeister in Dresden, that Wagner would at last find himself positioned to make a significant public statement about the work, both as conductor and as a writer.

Wagner believed that his audience needed preparation for his performance of the Ninth Symphony, especially since an earlier performance of the work in Dresden had failed miserably. His Paris years afforded him the opportunity to see how other writers, Berlioz and Urhan in particular, had found effective ways of writing about the piece that meant so much to him. Indeed, it was during the Paris years (1840) that Wagner penned his *A Pilgrimage to Beethoven,* a piece of quasi-autobiographical fiction that contains his earliest publicly expressed thoughts about the Ninth Symphony. Following in the footsteps of Marx in Berlin, one who also had recognized the value of good advance publicity, Wagner anonymously published three notices (on March 24 and 31, and April 2) in the *Dresdener Anzeiger* for the purpose of generating enthusiasm for his forthcoming Palm Sunday performance of the Ninth. Members of the audience at the concert itself were handed Wagner's exegesis of the work, illustrated with quotations from Goethe's *Faust.* An excerpt from Wagner's description of the first movement gives an idea of the entire "program":

> The first movement appears to be founded on a titanic struggle of the soul, athirst for Joy, against the veto of that hostile power which rears itself 'twixt us and earthly happiness. The great chief-theme, which steps before us at one stride as if disrobing from a spectral shroud, might perhaps be translated, without violence to the spirit of the whole tone-poem, by Goethe's words:

> *Entbehren sollst du! Sollst entbehren!*   Go wanting, shalt thou!
> Shalt go wanting.[24]

What is wanting, of course, is joy, whose attainment in the finale is the goal toward which the entire symphony is oriented. No less important is the "crisis" that Beethoven perpetrates by means of the instrumental recitative, a crisis that makes the arrival of the human voice "a positive necessity," so that the addition of words may make the achievement of joy possible. Following the sequence of events in Beethoven's finale, Wagner declares that "*every human soul is made for Joy*" (italics in the original). The particular becomes the universal.

The path that led Wagner from the enthusiast of 1846 to the revolutionary of 1849 was a short one. On Palm Sunday of that year Wagner directed
his third Dresden performance of the Ninth Symphony. The rebellion began shortly thereafter, and as the opera house—now a symbol of the tyran-
nical old order—burned down, a guard remarked to the composer, "Well,
Mr. Conductor, joy's beautiful divine spark has made a blaze." Schiller's
poem and Beethoven's symphony now had become, in some quarters, an
unofficial anthem of revolutionary politics.

Wagner's own revolutionary bent was more artistic than political. The
Ninth Symphony for him became a justification of his own creative agenda.
But there were others operating in the Ninth Symphony's shadow who had
become inflamed by the political implications of the great work's finale. One
of the earliest of these individuals was the Braunschweig critic, playwright,
and occasional contributor to Schumann's *New Zeitschrift für Musik*, Wolfgang Robert Griepenkerl (1810–68). Griepenkerl's contribution to the discussion of the Ninth Symphony was a novella published in 1838, *Das Musikfest oder die Beethovener* (*The Music Festival, or the Beethovenists*). The plot of
Das Musikfest revolves around the plans for a music festival that is to be
managed by Count Adalbert von Rohr, a young Beethoven enthusiast who
had been summoned especially for the purpose of convincing the skeptical
local backers of the festival that Beethoven's Third and Ninth Symphonies
should be the featured works. He is joined by two local "Beethovenists," the
organist Pfeiffer and the clergyman Vikarius, who assist Adalbert in his
difficult task. They later are joined by the contrabassist Hitzig (see Plate 6–
1), "the Atlas, who balances the heaven of an entire symphony on his
shoulders," and who waxes rhapsodic at the mere mention of the Ninth
Symphony. Griepenkerl also presents the opposing camp—three local busi-
nessman, one of whom, tellingly, is the editor of the local newspaper. Beethoven, his music, and his admirers are beyond the ken of this latter trio of
stolid citizens.

Each "Beethovenist" is given the opportunity to offer a personal point of
view regarding the Ninth Symphony. The common link between them all is
Griepenkerl's idiosyncratic idea of humor. He sees humor as resulting from
the placement of opposite moods in close proximity with one another.
Griepenkerl finds this characteristic to be present not only in Beethoven's music, but also in the writings of proto-romantic author Jean Paul
and, even more pointedly, in Shakespeare. "Beethoven is Shakespeare's
brother," shouts Adalbert in a moment of enthusiastic transport. Adalbert

Plate 6–1. Frontispiece to *Das Musikfest oder die Beethovener* (1838)

also is the political firebrand who characterizes the Ninth Symphony as a creation that represents the revolutionary *Zeitgeist*. Beethoven is the new Messiah, the "secular evangelist" of a new age:

> Beethoven is the first . . . to raise true music, that is, instrumental music, to the height of self-understanding, so that one has no doubt about the true colors of his intentions. All these symphonies carry the character of our time, whose directions he recognized in his prophetic soul. Anticipating the great drama of the July revolution, played behind a curtain that was held down only with great difficulty, of the stirred stage of the people, he condemned light play with forms. In art, his symphonies were the first battle cry of that occasion. One need only travel to Paris to see how this audience sits there and listens to

these works. One would have to say that in Beethoven's symphonies, chords are struck that are as powerful as the blustering wings of the period itself. Then the result there is enormous, almost unbelievable. I saw an entire auditorium spring to its feet as if smitten by a magical stroke, and with a cry that one could call a cry of horror as much a cry of enchantment. Where has one ever seen music, oft-neglected music, arrive at that? With Beethoven, the first epoch of this art in world-historical meanings begins.[25]

As the finale of the Ninth is being rehearsed, the Vikarius exclaims triumphantly, "Whoever knows what whore this disguised 'Joy' of Schiller's was at her birth, let him grasp her!" In a footnote attached to this phrase, the author adds in explanation, "Es war die Freiheit"—"It was freedom."[26]

Eighteenth-century audiences understood Schiller's "Freude" in a context that embraces the concepts of aesthetic, moral, and political freedom. *Das Musikfest*, while largely occupied with political questions, also addresses the topic of art as religion. The characters in the novella see Beethoven as both prophet and Messiah, with the Ninth Symphony representing his "testament." But Griepenkerl recognized—and he wished to impart this to his reader—the danger of confusing art and revelation. The festival ends disastrously. Under the duress of excess ideological baggage, the Ninth Symphony leads to neither joy nor freedom.

The Ninth continued to garner both admirers and detractors. Even Wagner, who continued to wave the Ninth Symphony's banner in public, admitted privately to Liszt that he found the finale to be the least satisfactory part of the work. Other musicians voiced their serious misgivings about it publicly. Louis Spohr, for example, who conducted the work on several occasions, penned this famous invective in a discussion of Beethoven's late composition:

I confess freely that I could never get any enjoyment out of Beethoven's last works. Yes, I must include among them the much-admired Ninth Symphony, the fourth movement of which seems to me so ugly, in such bad taste, and in the conception of Schiller's Ode so cheap that I cannot even now understand how such a genius as Beethoven could write it down. I find in it another corroboration of what I had noticed already in Vienna, that Beethoven was deficient in esthetic imagery and lacked the sense of beauty.[27]

The final sentence is telling. To Spohr, Beethoven, in his desire to express the "sublime," had forsaken the "beautiful." And Spohr was by no
means the only one to raise such a complaint. Robert Schumann, in an
essay of 1835, took note of the various ways in which some people expressed their admiration of the Ninth Symphony:

> "What do you suppose Beethoven meant by those basses?" "Sir," I
> replied gravely enough, "a genius often jests; it seems to be a sort of
> night-watchman's song." Gone was the exquisite moment, once again
> a Satan was set loose. Then I remarked the Beethoven devotees—the
> way they stood there goggle-eyed, saying: "That's by our Beethoven.
> That's a German work. In the last movement there's a double fugue.
> Some reproach him for not excelling in this department, but how he
> has done it—yes, this is *our* Beethoven." Another choir chimed in with:
> "It seems as though all forms of poetry are combined in the work: in
> the first movement the epic, in the second the humorous, in the third
> the lyric, in the fourth—the blend of them all—the drama." Still another
> choir really applied itself to praising: "It's a gigantic work, colossal,
> comparable to the pyramids of Egypt." Still another went in for de-
> scription: "The symphony tells the story of man's creation: first chaos,
> then the divine command 'Let there be light,' then the sun rising on
> the first man, who is delighted with such splendor—in short, it is the
> whole first chapter of the Pentateuch."[28]

Schumann, in observing the aesthetic climate of his own day, was as
prophetic as he was astute. Other writers were prepared to use the Ninth
Symphony as a metaphor for whichever myth suited them. Even Friedrich
Nietzsche saw the Ninth Symphony as fitting into his Dionysian world
view:

> How strong metaphysical need is and how difficult nature renders our
> departure from it may be seen from the fact that even in the free spirit,
> when he has cast off everything metaphysical, the loftiest effects of art
> can easily produce a resounding of the long silent, even broken, meta-
> physical string,—it may be, for instance, that at a passage in Beetho-
> ven's Ninth Symphony he feels himself floating above the earth in a
> starry dome with the dream of *immortality* in his heart; all the stars
> seem to shine round him, and the earth to sink farther and farther

away.—If he become conscious of this state, he feels a deep pain at his heart, and sighs for the man who will lead back to him his lost beloved, be it called religion or metaphysics.[29]

Nietzsche's paean to Wagner, *The Birth of Tragedy*, similarly invokes the finale of the Ninth Symphony:

> The chariot of Dionysus is covered with flowers and garland; panthers and tigers walk under its yoke. Transform Beethoven's "Hymn to Joy" into a painting; let your imagination conceive the multitudes bowing to the dust, awe-struck—then you will approach the Dionysian. Now the slave is a free man; now all the rigid hostile barriers that necessity, caprice, or "impudent convention" have fixed between man and man are broken. . . . In song and in dance man expresses himself as a member of a higher community; he has forgotten how to walk and speak and is on the way toward flying into the air, dancing. . . . He is no longer an artist, he has become a work of art.[30]

But how does one sustain the Dionysian? The Schopenhauerian gulf between what is and what ought to be remains as wide as ever. One can understand how Thomas Mann's Adrian Leverkühn, seeing the chasm between the idealism of the Ninth Symphony and the reality of the world, would express a desire to rescind the work. But would the world truly be a better place without the utopian vision? Does mankind truly aspire to become a member of a higher community, to become part of a work of art? These questions, in the final analysis, may be unanswerable. But the Ninth has yet to be rescinded, and with each new performance lies the infinity of possibility.

THE MUSICAL LEGACY OF THE NINTH

The first compositions to be influenced by the Ninth Symphony were by Beethoven himself. The fourth of his six Bagatelles for piano, op. 126, features a tune (Ex. 6–1) that somehow gives the impression that the composer is trying to exorcise the "Freude" melody. But not even Beethoven could so easily escape from under the shadow that his own symphony had

Example 6–1. Beethoven: Bagatelle, op. 126, no. 4, mm. 52–59

Example 6–2. Beethoven: String Quartet in B♭ Major, op. 130, *Cavatina*, mm. 7–10

cast. The lyricism of the Ninth's *Adagio,* for example, with the characteristic echo at the end of each of its phrases, found its way into the famous Cavatina of his String Quartet in B♭ major, op. 130 (Ex. 6–2). As is the case in the finale of the Ninth Symphony, Beethoven again applied a four-movement structural scheme in the *Grosse Fuge,* op. 133, the movement that originally served as the finale of this same quartet.

Example 6–3. Beethoven: String Quartet in A Minor, op. 132, transition to finale

Other immediate by-products of the Ninth are the recitative-like passage, marked *Beklemmt*, in the middle of the Cavatina, as well as another recitative passage in the String quartet in A minor, op. 132 (Ex. 6–3). Turning to a work by Beethoven's fellow Viennese, Franz Schubert, is not the opening of the development from the finale of his "Great" C major Symphony an homage to the "Freude" theme (Ex. 6–4)?

In one sense the Ninth Symphony was inimitable, a work that threatened to stifle composers who wished to write new symphonies in its wake. As Carl Dahlhaus has written:

Example 6–4. Schubert: finale to Symphony No. 9 in C Major, D. 944, mm. 386–393

> The history of the symphony . . . looks almost like a history of the
> conclusions that composers were able to draw from Beethoven's vari-
> ous models of the symphonic principle: from the Third and Seventh
> Symphonies in the case of Berlioz, the Sixth in the case of Mendels-
> sohn, and the Ninth in the case of Bruckner. Yet the line of develop-
> ment breaks off in mid-century. Mendelssohn and Berlioz strangely
> rub shoulders in the history of the symphony immediately after Bee-
> thoven, and from the 1870s to the early years of our century the sym-
> phony experienced a "second life."[31]

As is the case with most generalizations, Dahlhaus's observation contains a modicum of truth. But to suggest that Bruckner was the sole heir to
the Ninth Symphony is misleading. If this were the case, how does one
account for Berlioz's contrapuntal combination of two distinct themes in
the finale of the *Symphonie fantastique?* What work other than the Ninth
Symphony could have inspired the thematic recall of the earlier movements in the finale of *Harold en Italie?* How does one explain the use of
vocal forces in Berlioz's *Roméo et Juliette,* Mendelssohn's Symphony No. 2
("Lobgesang"), not to mention the later manifestation of the "choral" symphony in works such as Liszt's *A Faust Symphony* (in its 1857 revision) and
Mahler's Second and Eighth Symphonies? And what of the most obvious of
all symphonies modelled after the Ninth—Brahms's imposing First Symphony? Bruckner most certainly was not the only composer after Beethoven to draw conclusions from the Ninth.

The shadow of the Ninth extended into other genres as well. The bare
fifth that opens the Ninth's first movement is the unmistakable progenitor
of Wagner's *The Flying Dutchman* and can be heard in the opening of *Das
Rheingold.* Brahms's Piano Concerto No. 1 in D minor, op. 15, a work that
originally was intended to be a symphony, carries the imprint of the Ninth
Symphony on a thematic level as well as on a structural level; the juxtaposi-

tion of D minor and B♭ major in this work could only have resulted from a careful study of the Ninth Symphony.[32] *Ein Deutsches Requiem,* too, is filled with borrowings, the most obvious of which being the passage that precedes the double fugue of the third movement.

The examples cited thus far may be said to be, at one level or another, self-conscious borrowings. Dahlhaus refers to a break in the development of symphonic writing in the middle of the nineteenth century, a "dry period" that was filled with offshoots such as concert overtures and symphonic poems. If he is correct in this judgment, then the Ninth Symphony truly was a terminal point rather than the progenitor of any new tradition. Such a view, furthermore, would lend support to Wagner's propaganda which held that "absolute" music after the Ninth was an impossibility. But not everybody accepted Wagner's thesis. The various ways in which Brahms patterned his First Symphony after the model of Beethoven's Ninth certainly points in a different direction.[33]

Tovey asserted that if "a great work of art could be made responsible for all subsequent failures to imitate it, then Beethoven might have had cause for doubting whether the opening of his Ninth Symphony was worth the risk."[34] No doubt Tovey was thinking primarily of the mysterious beginning of Bruckner's Third and Ninth Symphonies and Mahler's First Symphony (all in D minor) when he wrote these words. One suspects, however, that Tovey also had something more in mind. Perhaps the greatest overriding legacy of the Ninth Symphony is its sheer monumentality, a scale of writing that indeed opened wide the door for Wagner, Bruckner, and Mahler. These three composers, more than any others, stood toe to toe with the Ninth Symphony. Others sought to circumvent it. None could escape its immense shadow.

Chapter 7

PERFORMANCE TRADITIONS

The conductor has always stood in the vanguard of the battle to gain an audience for the Ninth Symphony. We have seen, in chapter 6, how the demands of the Ninth, especially the difficult changes of tempo and meter within its movements, required a fundamental change in the way orchestral rehearsals and performances were directed. The problems that plagued the earliest performances of the Ninth were gradually solved by the enlistment of a conductor, the provision of adequate rehearsal time, and the general rise in performance standards. But above all, it was the conductor who began to place an indelible imprint on the work. Many conductors achieved fame through their performances of the Ninth Symphony. Among the earliest important interpreters were Felix Mendelssohn, François-Antoine Habeneck, Hector Berlioz, Ignaz Moscheles, Michael Costa, Otto Nicolai, and Richard Wagner. Later conductors whose readings have proven to be of particular significance were Gustav Mahler, Felix Weingartner, Wilhelm Furtwängler, Arturo Toscanini, and Roger Norrington. The list is by no means exhaustive, for virtually every conductor who has led a performance of the Ninth has placed a stamp of individuality on the work. But the conductors mentioned here have, in one way or another, made a demonstrable contribution to the performance tradition of this pivotal composition.

Many of the issues concerning the performance of the Ninth Symphony

commenced before the advent of sound recording. For the earliest performances, one must rely on the authority of written accounts. But even the
most detailed description cannot give sufficient information to recreate a
particular concert. Still, we can identify certain landmark performances of
the Ninth, beginning with the Vienna premiere under Beethoven's supervision (1824). Felix Mendelssohn's first performance of the work in Leipzig
(1836), thanks to adequate rehearsal time and Mendelssohn's leadership
skills, went far in winning over the hitherto resistant Gewandhaus audience. Otto Nicolai's Vienna Philharmonic performances (1843 and 1846)
permitted the Viennese to hear at last an adequately prepared rendition of
the work. Richard Wagner's Palm Sunday concert in Dresden (1846) also
should be included, if for no other reason than for the extraordinary efforts
he made to sell the piece to his audience, even to the point of distributing an
elaborate program to explain it (in the spirit of Berlioz's program for the
Symphonie fantastique). Wagner's concert to mark the laying of the foundation for the Festspielhaus in Bayreuth (1872) may be said to have be-
queathed upon the Ninth its exalted status as a ceremonial work.

These concerts all expanded the public's understanding of the Ninth in
significant ways. Unfortunately, however, contemporary reviews of them
shed very little light on the performance practice issues—tempo, articulation, and the size of the performing forces—that interest modern players
and scholars most. Of these issues, tempo is perhaps the most controversial, and much of the controversy can be traced to the composer himself.

TEMPOS

The metronome markings will be sent to you very soon. Do wait for
them. In our century such indications are certainly necessary. Moreover I have received letters from Berlin informing me that the first
performance of the symphony was received with enthusiastic applause, which I ascribe largely to the metronome markings. We can
scarcely have *tempi ordinari* any longer, since one must fall into line
with the ideas of unfettered genius.

Thus wrote Beethoven to Schott, the publisher of the Ninth Symphony, in
the fall of 1826. The metronome markings for the Symphony soon followed

in a letter dated October 13, 1826. The missive is in the hand of Beethoven's nephew, Karl, but was signed by the composer himself.[1] The markings are as follows:

Movement 1:
  All°. ma non troppo   88 = ♩

Movement 2:
  Molto vivace   116 = ♩. (dotted half)
  Presto   116 = 𝅗𝅥 (half)

Movement 3:
  Adagio, tempo 1ᵐᵒ   60 = ♩
  Andante moderato   63 = ♩

Movement 4:

Finale presto	66 = 𝅗𝅥. (dotted half)		Adagio divoto	60 = 𝅗𝅥 (half)
All°. ma non troppo	88 = ♩		All°. energico	84 = 𝅗𝅥. (dotted half)
Allegro assai	80 = 𝅗𝅥 (half)		All°. ma non tanto	120 = 𝅗𝅥 (half)
Alla Marcia	84 = 𝅗𝅥. (dotted half)		Prestissimo	132 = 𝅗𝅥 (half)
Andante maestoso	72 = 𝅗𝅥 (half)		Maestoso	60 = ♩

These markings were published in *Caecilia* in 1827 and were included in the second edition of the score issued by Schott later that year.

   Despite Beethoven's public endorsement of Mälzel's metronome, many have questioned the reliability of the composer's markings, not only for the Ninth Symphony, but for other works as well. Some have chosen to dismiss all of Beethoven's markings, citing as reasons: a) Beethoven's metronome was unreliable, b) many of the movements (and not only the faster ones) are unplayable at the indicated speeds, c) the markings stand at variance with the traditional verbal indications (*Allegro, Adagio,* etc.), d) the speeds that Beethoven imagined in his mind were faster than he actually meant, e) the transmission of some of these markings has been faulty, either with respect to the speed or to the note value indicated, and f) discrepancies abound when certain speeds are compared with analogous passages from other works.

   Only arguments e) and f) can be weighed empirically. In a letter written to Ignaz Moscheles on Beethoven's behalf by Anton Schindler, dated March 18, 1827, the metronomic indication for the opening of the finale appears as $\dot{\jmath}$. = 96 instead of 66, for example. Curiously, the compositor for Beethoven's publisher Schott also inverted the first digit in the 1827 edition of the score. There can be no doubt that 96 is a mistake, as the music is absolutely unplayable at this speed. (The edition of the full score published by Dover, itself taken from Litolff's edition, transmits this faulty marking.) The 1826 letter to Schott contains another mistake—an omission of the dot after the half note in the tempo for the scherzo. In *Caecilia* the stem on the half note for the *Presto* trio of the scherzo is omitted: thus, o = 116.

But was the omission of the stem a misprint? The most controversial tempos for the Ninth are those of the trio and the Turkish March in the finale, which is marked ♩. = 84. Some conductors and scholars believe the markings given in the Schott letter to be *half* as fast as they ought to be.[2] In their view, the *Caecilia* "misprint" is not a mistake, but rather a clue to the correct tempo. Other conductors have attempted to perform the trio and Turkish March at the Schott speeds. The effects produced by the two approaches could not be more extreme: the tempos suggested by those who double the markings sound frenetic; the tempos taken by the literalists sound lethargic. In the end, most conductors compromise and take a middle ground.

It is impossible to tell from verbal evidence (reviews, etc.) whether or not these two metronome markings represent the speeds that were observed in early performances of the work. The review in the Leipzig *Allgemeine musikalische Zeitung* of the 1824 premiere identified the trio as "a brilliant march in the major mode"—certainly too ambiguous a description to be conclusive about speed. The original German, *brillanter Marsch*, may not refer to tempo at all. Friedrich August Kanne, writing in the Vienna *Allgemeine musikalische Zeitung*, spoke in general terms of Beethoven's "powerful tempos" that "pull the listener along, as if in a torrent," but he also mentioned the trio as offering a chance for the ear to gain "new strength." Unfortunately, he gave no clearer indication of the tempo at which this and other passages were played at the premiere. The reviews of the first performance in Berlin, the concert to which Beethoven alluded in his letter to Schott, fail to indicate anything regarding speeds.

The meter of the trio is 2/2—that is *alla breve*—but the autograph manuscript suggests that Beethoven considered notating it in 2/4 time, as shown by the placement of the barlines (Plate 7–1). The scherzo and trio are joined by a *stringendo* (quickening of speed) that links the *Molto vivace* in 3/4 time ($\dot{\jmath}$. = 116 in the Schott letter) to the *Presto* in 2/2 time ($\jmath$ = 116 in the Schott

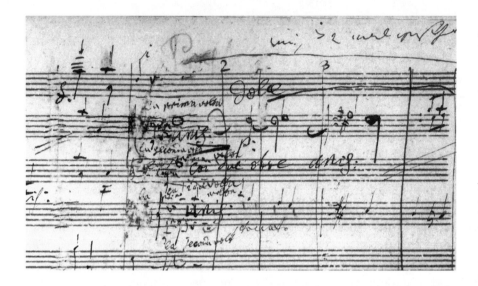

Plate 7–1. Autograph manuscript of Ninth Symphony/II, beginning of trio. Courtesy Staatsbibliothek zu Berlin–Preußischer Kulturbesitz, Musikabteilung mit Mendelssohn-Archiv.

letter)—a relationship that suggests a speeding up to a *slower* speed.[3] This process, taken at face value, is perplexing, and until such time as scholars can satisfactorily resolve the issue, conductors and listeners will have to decide for themselves which tempo for the trio—slower or faster—produces the most satisfying musical results. To judge from the past, conductors will continue to chose whatever tempo they wish, even should conclusive evidence emerge.

A slow performance of the Turkish March from the finale ($\downarrow$. = 84, according to the Schott letter) is even more startling than the trio. Marches exist in a wide variety of speeds, and Beethoven's verbal identification of this passage—*Allegro assai vivace*—does not automatically preclude a slower tempo, especially if *assai vivace* (very lively) is viewed as an indication of character rather than speed. As discussed in chapter 4, this particular march, with its reference to "Happily flying like his suns / Through Heaven's splendid firmament" (is "flying" a fast activity by cosmic standards?) may be read as a metaphor for a wedding, an interpretation for which a slower performance tempo would be suitable. The tempo for the 6/8 march ought to take into consideration the speed of the *Allegro ener-*

gico, a parallel passage in 6/4 meter (and also a double fugue) whose marking, ♩. = 84, is often observed by conductors without producing controversy. As with the indication *assai vivace,* the *energico* could be interpreted not as an indication of speed, but of articulation. Ultimately, we must acknowledge that these terms and numbers present confusing contradictions.

Another much-pondered passage from the finale is the cello and contrabass recitative.[4] By the time the work was published, Beethoven had added the well-known performance note, "*Selon le charactère d'un Récitatif, mais in Tempo*"—"In the manner of a recitative, but in tempo." It is commonly believed that Richard Wagner was responsible for establishing a tradition that renders this passage more slowly and freely than the Schott metronome marking indicates: ♩. = 66. But already in 1841, five years before Wagner was to conduct the work for the first time, Schindler objected to a performance by Habeneck in Paris that took the recitative too slowly, and pointed to several conductors in Germany who had made the same error. Corroborating evidence that Beethoven wished the passage to be performed quickly was offered in a letter published in 1864 by Leopold Sonnleithner, who stated that the recitative was performed at "a rapid pace, not in the sense of presto, but neither as an andante."[5]

An additional point of contention is the tempo of the third movement. Beethoven indicated ♩ = 60 for the *Adagio* and ♩ = 63 for the *Andante moderato,* tempos considerably faster than one usually encounters today. If these markings are correct, then the speed of this movement has grown slower over the years, and it is not hard to guess why. The decorative counterpoint in the violins that embroiders the *Adagio* theme is difficult to execute at a fast speed, especially by a large group of players. Practical considerations may have resulted in a slower pace. A decided advantage of a faster tempo is that the violin lines sound like background decorations, which they are, rather than foreground melody, which they are not. The woodwinds play the *Adagio* theme more or less at its orginal speed in each of its varied reprises, and an extremely slow tempo makes it difficult not only to sustain the line of the slower moving melody, but to hear it with any clarity. The sonority and activity of the violins always threaten to obscure the woodwind line, regardless of the tempo at which the music is played. A performance at a quicker speed at least helps to render the melodic line more distinct.

When Sir George Smart visited Beethoven in 1826 to learn more about the composer's intentions concerning the performance of the Ninth, he was astounded to hear that the Viennese premiere lasted only forty-five minutes. Even if the faster speeds for the most controversial passages were observed, and no repeats were taken in the scherzo, this reckoning seems to be impossible—a conclusion already reached by Smart. Impossible or not, it points to a brisk performance, and it is unlikely that Beethoven would have been in sympathy with some of the extremely slow tempos for the Ninth Symphony that conductors adopted after his death. Over time, tempos have been dictated more by the circumstances of individual performances and the judgment of conductors rather than by Beethoven's sometimes confusing indications. Beethoven's reference to *tempi ordinari*—most probably an allusion to eighteenth-century practice in which meter alone dictated the *tempo giusto,* or judicious tempo, of a piece—was more prophetic than even he could have imagined. A slavish adherence to the metronome markings, on the one hand, would be unmusical, and perhaps even patently "inauthentic," given Beethoven's own antityrannical leanings. Excessive deviation from given speeds, on the other hand, takes the listener farther from the essence of the composition.

Repeats in the Scherzo

Debate also surrounds the repeats in the scherzo. To what extent were repeat marks in minuets and scherzos observed in the reprise after the trio? Current research suggests that in Beethoven's time the repeats were taken, unless otherwise specified. Conductors today, however, generally omit them. In the case of the scherzo of the Ninth Symphony we have one pertinent document: a letter from Beethoven to Charles Neate in London in which he instructs Neate to perform the reprise of the scherzo without repeats ("*sans répétition*").[6] This same instruction was sent to Schott along with the correction of a printing error that omitted the *da capo dal segno* at the end of the trio. Beethoven's autograph manuscript also notes at the end of the trio, "from here without further repetition." Unfortunately, no edition of the Ninth includes Beethoven's remark, and consequently conductors have decided for themselves whether or not to observe any or all of the repeats in the scherzo.

ORCHESTRATION

The Ninth Symphony calls for the largest orchestra that Beethoven ever used, one including four horns, three trombones, piccolo, and contrabassoon in addition to the normal pairs of winds, trumpets and timpani, and strings. These instruments are augmented in the finale by the bass drum, triangle, cymbals, and vocal forces. The autograph manuscript and other documents discussed in chapter 2 show that Beethoven continued to add details to the orchestration of the Ninth Symphony right up to its first performance, and even afterward. Although early partisans and critics often discussed Beethoven's deafness with regard to the Ninth Symphony, they never assailed the composer's orchestration. The use of "Turkish" instruments attracted attention, as did the overall difficulty of the wind and string writing and the high tessitura of the vocal parts. But otherwise, no one suggested that Beethoven was deficient as an orchestrator. Still, we know that Beethoven, following the traditions of the time, occasionally encouraged doubling of woodwind parts when large numbers of strings were used.[7] Such doubling may have been used at the premiere of the Ninth Symphony in the large orchestra gathered for the occasion. Several subsequent performances of the piece involved large ensembles, and there, too, the winds may have been doubled to maintain the delicate balance between wind and string tone.

But later, Wagner and other conductors who followed him—most notably Mahler and Weingartner—went farther, reorchestrating parts of the Ninth altogether. Why? The earliest performances Wagner heard were poorly led by conductors who, in his opinion, did not understand the work. The players and singers, furthermore, were underrehearsed. Changes in orchestration, Wagner reasoned, would help to ameliorate part of the problem. Wagner also was eager to exploit the capabilities of valved trumpets and horns—instruments that were a novelty in Beethoven's day—but which by the 1840s had improved to the point where they could play the entire chromatic range of pitches denied to their valveless predecessors. In "On Performing the Ninth Symphony," Wagner used the two fanfares from the opening of the finale to demonstrate how modern, fully chromatic brass instruments could be used to fill in the gaps left by Beethoven's limited horns and trumpets (Ex. 7-1). Wagner also felt it necessary to reinforce the melodic line in mm. 93–108 of the second movement by adding French

Example 7–1. Wagner's reorchestration of the trumpet parts for the "horror fanfares"

Example 7–2. Wagner's reorchestration of the second theme in the scherzo (mm. 93–97)

horns to the wind choir (Ex. 7–2). Quite often the ear often misses the line because of the volume of sound produced by the *tutti* strings.

Beethoven, in his orchestral music at least, never wrote higher than a³ for the violin or flute, even though each instrument could play higher pitches. Wagner concluded that "modern" orchestras should therefore extend these instruments to encompass b♭³, a note that would be appropriate at points, especially in the first and second movements, in order to maintain continuity of the melodic line.

Wagner's notion of melodic line, in fact, is central to his justification for reorchestrating passages from the Ninth Symphony. Referring to his experience with the Ninth Symphony in Paris, Wagner described with admiration how the French musicians under Habeneck had discovered the true "melos" of music, enabling these musicians to truly "sing" Beethoven's melodies. Also citing Liszt's transcription of the Ninth's first movement as a model, Wagner offered suggestions for rewriting the flute and oboe parts in mm. 138–145, including several changes in register in the flute part, in order to achieve the ideal line that he believed Beethoven to have had in mind in composing this passage (Ex. 7–3). It should be added that Wagner, ever mindful of the "melos," also made several suggestions for adding dynamic and articulation expressions. He even went so far as to simplify the tenor part in the last passage for the vocal quartet in the finale.

Wagner's changes to Beethoven's scoring were relatively modest compared to those offered by Mahler and Weingartner. Mahler, whose reorchestration of the Ninth dates from 1895, was keenly aware of Wagner's pronouncements on the subject, and his aim, like that of his predecessor, was to realize what he understood to be Beethoven's intentions. He also was able to draw on his own experiences as a conductor of the work in 1885 in Kassel and Prague. While Mahler did not choose to adopt all of Wagner's modifications (the rewriting of the tenor part in the finale, for instance), he did follow Wagner's advice regarding the smoothing out of octave displacements in the winds and first violins and the use of the valved brass instruments' capability to fill in notes that were not available to Beethoven's natural horns and trumpets. But Mahler elected to make revisions more far-reaching than even Wagner envisioned. Most striking among these are the addition of four horns and an extra pair of timpani and the expansion of dynamic indications to range from *pp-ff* to *pppp-ffff*. Occasionally Mahler added entirely new contrapuntal lines in certain passages. Many of Mahler's reorchestrations are relatively subtle and escape detection by most

Example 7–3a. Wagner and Liszt's simplification of the melodic line of the first movement, mm. 138–145.

listeners. But the general sound produced by Mahler's expanded instrumentation stands out, especially in some of the louder passages, and reflects a post-Wagnerian aesthetic, rather than Beethoven's.

Weingartner, an experienced and highly regarded conductor, also proposed changes and additions to Beethoven's scoring and expression marks. A student of Franz Liszt and a successor to Mahler at the Vienna Opera, Weingartner's contributions to the debate on a "proper" performance of the Ninth Symphony include an essay, "On the Performance of Beethoven's

Example 7–3b. Ninth Symphony/I, mm. 137–145, woodwinds

Example 7–3b. (Continued)

Symphonies," his own live performances, and two recordings of the work (1926 and 1935).[8] The purpose of Weingartner's essay was not merely to expand upon Wagner's recommendations (and occasionally to correct them), especially those concerning orchestration, tempo, and expression, but also to provide a rational and practical response to the excesses of certain unnamed conductors who were unable to discern the difference between Wagner the composer and Wagner as the interpreter of Beethoven. Although Weingartner's own additions to Beethoven's original scorings are considerable, it is important to bear in mind that he advocated changes only "if they spring from a pressing need, and not if they are based on a difference of opinion." The Ninth Symphony may have been a prime *inspiration* for Wagnerian opera, but it was not itself Wagnerian opera. Weingartner understood this better than most of his peers.

The Ninth and the "Historical Practices" Movement

According to Adrian Boult, Weingartner, toward the end of his career, allegedly recanted his ideas about altering the orchestration and adding expressive nuances to the scores of Beethoven's symphonies.[9] Although Weingartner himself may have undergone a change of heart, his *Ratschläge* continued to influence many conductors, who felt enfranchised to make a contribution to the collective "tradition" of performing the Ninth Symphony that began with Wagner's essays. Even so-called purist conductors such as Arturo Toscanini felt free to make changes where it was deemed appropriate. In the absence of an authoritative text, and with the widespread disagreement regarding Beethoven's tempos and metronomic markings, the aesthetic of the late nineteenth-century orchestra became the accepted model for performing Beethoven's symphonies.

More recently, however, as the historical practices movement has branched out from the early repertory to the music of the late eighteenth and early nineteenth centuries, musicians, scholars, and critics have started to reevaluate the Wagner tradition in light of insights revealed by the use of historical instruments (valveless horns and trumpets, smaller timpani with skin heads and wooden mallets, string instruments with gut strings and pre-Tourte bows, and pre-Boehm winds) and from the study of early nineteenth-century treatises. The conductors associated with the historical approach, Christopher Hogwood, Roy Goodman, Roger Norrington, and others, have argued that traditional conductors and performers have lost touch with the conventions of Beethoven's day regarding sonority, articulation, phrasing, and—most importantly—tempo. Even orchestral seating plans have been held up to question.

Norrington and the London Classical Players have been in the vanguard of the historical movement, not only performing Beethoven's symphonies on period instruments but adhering relatively strictly to the published metronome markings. Conductors before and after Norrington have experimented with the Schott markings, but no one has been able to take all the indications literally. Benjamin Zander, for one, had been an advocate for the slow tempos of the trio of the scherzo and Turkish March in the finale. More recently, however, he has concluded that both these tempos were incorrectly transmitted, and has consequently abandoned them.

But aside from the trio and the Turkish March, Norrington has demonstrated that Beethoven's markings for the Ninth Symphony are not only doable but can produce musically convincing—even revelatory—results. In the process, he has challenged the notion of ignoring the single most precise performance indication that Beethoven has left to posterity.

Richard Taruskin, writing in *Opus*, has called Norrington's approach to the Beethoven symphonies "inspired literalism," praising his readings (particularly of the Second Symphony) for the way in which they bring to mind and the ear the sense of novelty that these works had inspired when they were first performed.[10] But at the same time, Taruskin has taken Norrington severely to task for ignoring the spirit of the Ninth Symphony. Norrington's literalism, Taruskin argues, reduces the grand work to no more than the sum of its parts. By stripping the Ninth of the layers of interpretation that had accrued to it over the years, Taruskin's argument continues, Norrington produces a trivial, albeit skillful, representation of the piece, one that is unfaithful, not only to the received tradition as history, but to the work itself.

The bogeyman that lies behind the debate is the question of "authenticity." Some of the more zealous proponents of historical performance practices believe that a truly "authentic" rendition of music from the past is possible: "Beethoven as Beethoven's contemporaries heard him" is their motto. More circumspect advocates, on the other hand, set more limited goals for the use of period instruments and the application of early performance practices. Norrington, Hogwood, and Goodman's efforts have demonstrated that the heterogenous sonority of the winds and brass of Beethoven's day *can* stand up to, and, when necessary, penetrate the less brilliant sound of gut strings. The angularity of Beethoven's lines that troubled Wagner may have been dictated by the limitations of his instruments. But such problems, if they be such, were a fact of Beethoven's professional life. The late quartets and piano sonatas of Beethoven also contain "awkward" voice leading. Has anyone seriously suggested that it needs to be corrected?

An exact recreation of the first performance of the Ninth Symphony, in light of the evidence presented in chapter 5, would be neither possible nor desirable. If, by the same token, one assumes that the nineteenth-century repertory will continue to hold center stage in orchestral programming (and there is little evidence to the contrary), can one find a way to keep this music fresh and vital? Without question, the historical practices movement has forced audiences to listen to the Beethoven symphonies—including the Ninth—in "new" ways, by stripping away the patina applied by Wagner, Mahler, Weingartner, Furtwängler, and others.

History is an ongoing process. Interest in performing Beethoven's music in the style known to the composer is but the most recent chapter in a continuum that will last as long as the Ninth Symphony occupies the imagination of humanity. The debate on performance can yield fruitful results, but only if the overarching goal remains a transmission of Beethoven's last symphonic testament that is faithful to the spirit of the composer's time and meaningful to our own.

Some Thoughts Concerning the Bärenreiter "Urtext" Edition

The Breitkopf & Härtel 1864 edition of the Ninth Symphony that formed part of the so-called Gesamtausgabe of Beethoven's works represented, for its time at least, the gold standard redaction of the work. Various subsequent editions, issued by Litolff, Schott, Breitkopf & Härtel (again), C. F. Peters, Eulenburg, and Philharmonia have appeared, each one claiming to represent corrections, emendations, and improvements. Our understanding of the work has been based largely upon performances derived from one or more of these editions, informed by whatever idiosyncracies or insights that have been imposed by conductors, performers, critics, and analysts.

The most important event in the ongoing life of the Ninth Symphony since the appearance of the original edition of this book has been the publication and subsequent adoption by conductors of the Jonathan Del Mar's *Urtext* score and parts. I have expressed my views about the relative pros and cons of this edition at greater length elsewhere but feel that a few words here are appropriate, as this edition is generating new—and in some cases false—performance traditions in its own right.[11]

The *New Harvard Dictionary of Music* defines *Urtext* as a "text in its presumed original state, without subsequent alterations or additions by an editor; an edition purporting to present a work in such a state."[12] If Del Mar had given such authority entirely over to Beethoven's autograph manuscript, then part of the dilemma presented by his edition would have been eliminated. But Del Mar acknowledges that the *Stichvorlage*—the score prepared by Beethoven's copyists and proofread by the composer to be sent to Schott—must share that authority, even to the point (correctly) of giving its content greater weight at times than the autograph. Del Mar is aware, of course, that there are significant discrepancies between the autograph and *Stichvorlage,* and he decided, in his own words, to "combine circumstantial evidence with musical judgement in order to decide which text to follow."[13] If things were only so simple. Among the other important primary sources for the text of the Ninth Symphony we must also count surviving performance materials, a copy of the score that was sent to London, the dedication copy (*Widmungsexemplar*) sent to King Friedrich Wilhelm III in Berlin, the first edition of the full score published by Schott, and several other documents over which Beethoven had a modicum of control.[14] Many of these sources disagree with each other in many important details.

The principal problem with Del Mar's edition is that Bärenreiter has aggressively marketed it as if it were a critical edition that transmits Beethoven's last word (*Fassung letzter Hand*). An *Urtext* and a critical edition are *not* the same thing. Furthermore, while an *Urtext,* insofar as establishing one is possible, may be useful, it should be used in consultation with, but not in lieu of, a carefully prepared critical edition.[15] Regretfully, Bärenreiter has opted to market Del Mar's edition as the new paragon of textual accuracy. "Can you afford to give your audiences anything but the *real* Beethoven?" the publisher's brochure asks rhetorically.

Example 7–4. Ninth Symphony/IV, mm. 532–542, horns 1 and 2 as found in First Edition

Example 7–5. Ninth Symphony/IV, mm. 532–542, horns 1 and 2 as found in Autograph, Stichvorlage, and Urtext Editions

Example 7–6. Ninth Symphony/IV, mm. 532–542, horns 1 and 2 as found in Widmungsexemplar

Let us examine the most problematic passage of all—the articulation markings in the first and second horn parts between m. 532 and m. 540. The horns play F# in octaves from m. 517 until m. 540, with the following rhythmic pattern: quarter note, eighth note, dotted quarter note tied to quarter. All editions up to now, including the first edition based on the *Stichvorlage,* show mm. 532 to 540 with the articulations shown in Ex. 7–4. The autograph and *Stichvorlage,* the sources upon which Del Mar bases his *Urtext,* show the ties in mm. 532–533, 538, and 540 shifted, as shown in Ex. 7–5. To make matters even more confusing, the *Widmungsexemplar* shows a tie between the eighth note and the dotted quarter note in m. 532, but has all remaining ties as they appear in the first edition (Ex. 7–6). Which source, then, represents Beethoven's true intentions and final thoughts on this passage? Del Mar and Bärenreiter certainly have convinced a number of conductors—John Eliot Gardiner, Roy Goodman, Simon Rattle, and Philippe Herreweghe among them—to perform it as it appears in the autograph, even though these ties may be a mistake.[16] While a reading of the primary sources yields pitches (such as D instead of B♭ in the flute and oboe in m. 81 of the first movement) and articulations (the passage just examined) that are strikingly different from the ones transmitted in later sources, this does not necessarily mean that they represent Beethoven's last word or that later redactors got things terribly wrong. Beethoven was not always the most reliable of proofreaders.

Given the multiplicity of discrepancies in the primary sources, then, no text for the Ninth Symphony can claim the ultimate authority of authenticity. It is unfortunate that this most recent redaction of the Ninth Symphony has been marketed—misleadingly in my opinion—as a performing edition under the pretense of an *Urtext.*[17] Until such time as the critical edition authorized by the Beethoven-Haus Archiv appears, however, it is likely we shall continue to experience more and more performances and recordings that follow the contents of Del Mar's edition literally. *Caveat emptor!*

NINE NINTHS: A SELECT DISCOGRAPHY

---- ✍ ----

$\mathscr{M}$ost listeners have a highly personal concept of what constitutes an ideal performance of the Ninth Symphony. Such an ideal might have its roots in the cherished memory of a live performance. Another source might be a recording that brings together a favorite conductor, orchestra, chorus, and vocal soloists. For others, the ideal performance exists only in their imaginations.

Theoretically, the best possible performance would bring into perfect balance fidelity to Beethoven's score and inspired musical intuition. As we have seen in chapter 7, however, a fully authoritative score of the Ninth Symphony does not yet exist, and as chapters 5 and 6 have demonstrated, interpretive insight is very much a matter of time and circumstance, as well as individual taste. How, then, could *any* performance (recorded or live) be defined as faithful?

To begin, one ought not stray far from the published metronome markings, as problematic as some of these may seem. Only two of the fifteen Schott metronome markings for the Ninth Symphony are truly controversial: the trio of the scherzo (*Presto, ♩ = 116*), and the Turkish March from the finale (*Allegro assai vivace, Alla Marcia, ♩. = 84*). With the exception of the trio and the Turkish March—and scholarship has thus far failed to prove them wrong—the other tempos are playable, effective, and reasonable. The metronome markings of ♩ = 60 for the *Adagio molto e cantabile,* and $\downarrow = 63$ for the *Andante moderato* in the third movement strike most listeners as being too fast. This perception, however, has arisen because some conductors perform them at *much* slower speeds (Furtwängler's 1942 performance, for example, takes them at $\downarrow = 26$ and $\downarrow = 32$).

Beethoven's expression marks also ought to be carefully observed. It is hard to understand why in the first movement, for example, many conductors delay the *a tempo* in mm. 196, 214, 507, and 511, especially when Beethoven took care to indicate it each time. Many of the *sforzatos* in the voice parts in the finale also rarely come through in performance. These expressive gestures, far from being incidental, are essential features of Beethoven's style. In the finale they also reflect Beethoven's interpretation of "An die Freude" (such his accent on "nie" in mm. 281 and 289, on the words "feuertrunken" and "Heiligtum" in mm. 553 and 557, and on "Brüder" in mm. 570 and 586).

Changes in orchestration are less problematical, especially if the rewriting is limited to an occasional addition of bb^3 for the flute and violins, or some filling in of notes that were unavailable to the valveless brass instruments of Beethoven's day. In chapter 7, however, we observed how some conductors—Wagner, Weingartner, and Mahler, in particular—went considerably further in making wholesale changes to Beethoven's orchestration. These conductors believed that they were faithful servants of Beethoven's spirit—if one can, indeed, identify such a thing—and while the primary motivation for their changes was to clarify Beethoven's melos (to use Wagner's favorite term), it sometimes seems as if they had their *own* melos in mind.

Here then, in chronological order, are "nine Ninths" from the more than seventy recordings currently available on compact disc. These recordings, whether made in the studio, or taken from live performances, represent a wide range of interpretations. Each recording was selected based on its intrinsic interest, either as a document of a significant cultural event, or as the representation of a particular performance tradition.

Oskar Fried Conducting the Berlin State Opera Orchestra and the Bruno Kittel Choir (Lotte Leonard, Jenny Sonnenberg, Eugen Transky, and Wilhelm Guttmann, Soloists); Pearl Gemm CD 9372

Oskar Fried (1871–1941) was one of the first conductors whose reading of the Ninth Symphony—recorded for Polydor in 1928—was preserved by means of electrical recording.[1] This digital remastering is remarkably free of the surface noise and distortion from old recordings that can be a distraction from the music itself. Purity of intonation and precision are not the strong points of this recording, yet the standards of playing and singing are high.

Fried, a composition student of Humperdinck and a disciple of Mahler, was one of the great conductors of the post-Wagner generation. His reading of the Ninth is relatively free from overinterpretation, with crisp, yet flexible, tempos that are pushed when the music becomes impassioned. Save for some touches of reorchestration, Fried's vision of the Ninth is remarkably faithful to the letter of the score.

Fried omits repeats in the scherzo proper in this recording, but observes them in the trio section. His interpretation of the *stringendo* that leads up to the trio is particularly interesting. Taking ♩. = 108 (his tempo for the scherzo) as a starting point, he pushes the speed beyond that of the trio, and begins the *alla breve* at a very fast pace ♩ = 192. He then shifts suddenly to a rather leisurely pace (♩ = 122, quite near the published markings!) for the remainder of the trio. His tempo for the Turkish March in the finale is ♩. = 116, faster than the Schott 84, and he moves it along at a faster pace (♩. = 132) by the beginning of the orchestral double fugue.

Timings: I = 14'01"; II = 10'05"; III = 13'59"; IV = 23'30"

Felix Weingartner Conducting the Vienna Philharmonic Orchestra and the Vienna State Opera Chorus (Louise Helletsgrüber, Rosette Anday, Georg Maikl, and Richard Mayr, Soloists); Music Memoria MM CD 30270[2]

Here is the 1935 recording by the conductor whose book on the performance of Beethoven's symphonies influenced a whole generation of conductors. Weingartner's reading of the work offers much to recommend it, and this remastering on CD has a very clear sound that allows its many nuances to be heard quite distinctly.

Weingartner's recording of the Ninth Symphony does not observe all of the performance suggestions found in his own *Ratschläge*. In his book, for example, he advocates a "moderate" slowing of the tempo for mm. 138–149 (and mm. 407–418) of the first movement. In his recording, however, his moderation of the tempo is rather severe, reducing the speed from ♩ = 74 to 60. In the same movement, he also extends the ritard in m. 510 through mm. 511–512, despite his advice to the contrary in his book.

As with Oskar Fried's recording, Weingartner omits the repeats for the scherzo, but observes them in the trio. Weingartner's tempo for the trio is rather fast ($\flat$ = 159), but his speeds for the third movement are, by way of contrast, slow and quite elastic. Flexible tempos also are the rule in the finale, with a Turkish March that starts at $\flat$. = 108, but speeding up to a brisk 122 by the beginning of the double fugue.

Timings: I = 15′29″; II = 10′04″; III = 14′39″; IV = 22′33″

Wilhelm Furtwängler Conducting the Berlin Philharmonic Orchestra, the Bruno Kittel'scher Chorus (Tilla Briem, Elisabeth Höngen, Peter Anders, Rudolf Watzke, Soloists); Hunt Productions CDWFE 357

Four of the nine complete recordings of the Ninth Symphony under the direction of Furtwängler are currently available on CD, all of which are taken from live performances.[3] Each of them gives an idea of the eccentric nature of this great German conductor, and no two recordings are alike. The variances from performance to performance may be attributed in part to the idiosyncracies of the particular orchestra, chorus, and soloists that Furtwängler led for each recording. The variability of human nature also accounts for many of the differences. Time and circumstance were, in my judgment, the most crucial factors that shaped the character of a given performance.

The recording under consideration here was made in Berlin on March 24, 1942. If ever an artist was faced with the dilemma of how to conjure beauty in the face of evil, it was Furtwängler leading a performance of the Ninth Symphony in the Berlin of Nazi Germany. On April 19 of the same year, he was compelled against his will to do something he hitherto had carefully avoided; to lead a performance of the Ninth in the presence of Adolf Hitler on the Führer's birthday.

To hear Furtwängler's rendition of the Ninth from 1942 is to bear witness to one of the greatest ironies of modern history. The specifics of this performance—its extremely slow and fast tempos, its greatly exaggerated ritards and accelerandos, its spectacularly wide range of dynamics—do not tell the entire story. No work meant more to this conductor than the Ninth. Furtwängler knew that it had become a stranger in its own land, a prophecy falling on deaf ears. With all the urgency he could muster, Furtwängler sought through the Ninth to restore humanity where humanity itself was nowhere to be found. Indeed, the fraility of that humanity is captured eloquently in one moment of all-too-human error. The fourth hornist in the *Adagio* is called upon to repeat the same three-note figure eight times in mm. 118–120. The Berlin hornist on this occasion lost count (was it a case of nerves or Furtwängler's slow tempo?). In moving to the last beat of m. 120 too soon—spoiling not only the harmony, but the grandeur of the climactic fanfare that follows—we are reminded of just how fragile even the greatest of edifices can be.

In these days, when studio recordings are concerned more with super-human accuracy and acoustical ambience than with musical honesty, the 1942 Furtwängler recording should be in the collection of anyone who truly cares about the Ninth Symphony and what it has come to represent.

Timings: I = 17′20″; II = 11′30″; III = 20′23″; IV = 24′26″

Arturo Toscanini Conducting the N.B.C. Symphony Orchestra and Westminster Choir (Jarmila Novotna, Kerstin Thorborg, Jan Peerce, and Nicola Moscona, Soloists); Legato LCD-136-1

This recording was made from a live performance at Carnegie Hall in 1944 (the specific date is not indicated).[4] As such, it forms an interesting and poignant comparison to that other wartime document—Furtwängler's 1942 performance in Berlin. Toscanini and Furtwängler did more than work on opposite sides of the Atlantic during World War II: they have been touted as representatives of opposing schools of thought regarding the art of con-ducting. Toscanini has been identified as an objective purist, for whom the composer's score represented the supreme authority, while Furtwängler was considered to be the deeply subjective interpreter who looked for the essence of the music beyond the signs and symbols of the printed page.

This kind of polarization, of course, can lead to overgeneralizations. It is true, on the one hand, that Toscanini kept a steadier beat than his German colleague, but it was not completely inflexible. Its shadings were simply less extreme. Furthermore, Toscanini—like nearly all conductors of his generation—freely tampered with Beethoven's score. The 1944 perfor-mance of the Ninth, for example, abounds in octave changes, added dy-namic nuances, and even wholesale re-orchestrations (especially notice-able in the second theme of the scherzo).

Two characteristics distinguish all Toscanini-led performances: pin-point precision and rhythmic drive. This performance of the Ninth does not disappoint on either count. The first movement moves along briskly (for the

most part at ♩ = 88, exactly as the Schott markings have it) and offers tre-
mendous dramatic intensity. The scherzo, with its fixation on a single rhythmic motive, seems tailor-made for Toscanini. The maestro also observes
Beethoven's repetition scheme exactly. Toscanini's tempo for the trio is on
the fast side (♩ = 152), but shows allegiance to neither ♩ = 116 nor 𝅝 = 116.

The *Adagio,* at ♩ = 46 (the *Andante* at ♩ = 50), is somewhat slower than
the Schott markings, but Toscanini does not treat it, as does Furtwängler, as
if it were from a Bruckner symphony. As for the finale, one can point to
many details where Toscanini takes liberties with the printed score. Among
these are an *extremely* fast horror fanfare (with added notes in the trumpets
and horns), the omission of the second bassoon part in mm. 116ff. (he evi-
dently had not seen the evidence discussed in chapter 4), the addition of
a rearticulated "freuden" for the vocal recitative at the word "freuden-
vollere" in m. 234, a staccato articulation for the vocal statement of the
"Freude" theme (presumably to match the pizzicato strings), and the
stretching of time for "alle Menschen" in mm. 806f.

Timings: I = 12′28″; II = 12′20″; III = 12′43″; IV = 22′50″

George Szell Conducting the Cleveland Orchestra and Cleveland Orchestra Choir (Adele Addison, Jane Hobson, Richard Lewis, and Donald Bell, Soloists); Sony Essential Classics SBK 46533

This studio recording of the Ninth, made in 1961 by one of the great orchestras and conductors of its time, remains one of the best available today,
and sounds superb on compact disc. It also was one of the first stereo
recordings of the Ninth.

This excellent performance's shortcomings are small in comparison to
its many virtues. Szell's tampering with the score is limited mainly to the
customary octave rewritings for the violins and flutes in the first and second movements. His tempo for the first movement, at ♩ = 82, is only slightly
slower than the 88 in the Schott letter, and maintains throughout a wonderful dramatic tension. One of the only places where Szell deviates noticably
from the score is at mm. 507 and 511, where he ignores the *a tempo* indications in favor of a general ritardando into the funeral march.

The main drawback in Szell's reading of the scherzo is the omission of
the repeat of the second, longer, section of the movement. Szell's tempo for
the trio is ♩ = 128, a compromise speed that leans closer to ♩ = 116 than 𝅝 =
116. As with so many other recordings, Szell adds horns to the woodwinds

for the second theme at mm. 93 and 330 of the scherzo. He also has the
timpanist add a D (not in the score) at the very end of the movement, a note
that Beethoven's timpanist would not have had available with his drums
both tuned to F, but is possible for modern drums equipped with tuning
pedals.

Szell's tempos for the third movement—♩ = 46 and ♩ = 51—are slower
than the Schott speeds, but they never seem to drag. Furthermore, the balance between the winds and violins in the 12/8 section (mm. 99ff.) is nearly
ideal, with the principal melodic line in the winds holding the foreground.
Unfortunately, however, Szell elected to make a conspicuous, and rather
unmusical, reduction in speed in mm. 107–110 that interrupts the flow of
the music.

The performance of the finale crackles with excitement, aided by excellent vocal soloists and choristers (prepared by Robert Shaw). In the established Wagner/Weingartner tradition, Szell fills in the gaps in the brass
parts in the horror fanfare. Another notable feature is the emphasis placed
on the horns in mm. 313–320 ("Küße gab sie"). Beethoven's orchestration
at this point calls for two horns to reinforce the soprano line in the chorus,
but rarely is the doubling as prominent as it is in this recording.

Szell's tempo for the Turkish March is a compromise, beginning at ♩. =
116, but increasing to 134 for the double fugue. The *Allegro energico*, 6/4 at
♩. = 92, comes closer to the Schott marking of 84.

Timings: I = 15′34″; II = 11′23″; III = 15′20″; IV = 24′06″

Roger Norrington Conducting the London Classical Players and the Schütz Choir of London (Yvonne Kenny, Sarah Walker, Patrick Power, and Petteri Salomaa, Soloists); EMI CDC 7 49221 2

This 1987 recording has provoked great controversy, mainly because of
Norrington's strict adherence to the Schott metronome markings—a characteristic that distinguishes his recordings of the other Beethoven symphonies. Norrington's recording of the Ninth was also the first one to feature period instruments.

The Ninth, as Norrington states in the "performance note" that accompanies this recording, is a work that belongs to the Classical period, and
the use of period instruments and historical performance techniques provide insight into that style. Indeed, the sounds produced by the gut strings,
the skin-headed kettledrums played with wooden sticks, and the valveless

trumpets and horns—note the colors produced by the handstopping in the C♭ scale in the third movement—are particularly revelatory. Beethoven's metronome markings, Norrington's notes continue, provide the most significant clue about the character of the music, and to disregard these indicators is to ignore the "only information we have [about tempos] from one of the world's great musical minds." Norrington pretty much toes the line, and it is much to his credit—and that of his skillful players and singers—that the tempos generally work. The sole exception is the Turkish March, which, starting at ♩. = 94, is slow enough to command the listener's attention, since nearly every other conductor takes the passage much faster.

If the Turkish March seems unduly slow, the Schott metronome markings for the third movement will shock the listener by how fast they sound. Yet, thanks to the excellence of Norrington's players, the movement dances along with grace and charm. From time to time one wishes that Norrington—eager to prove his point about the tempos—would relent a little, and give the music a chance to breathe.

Norrington is no purist with respect to other details of the score. In the double fugue that follows the Turkish March, for example, Norrington adds several diminuendos and other changes in dynamics (for the sake of contrast, no doubt) that are not in the score. His flutist sometimes plays b♭³— a pitch that Beethoven never notated, but which Norrington's recording shows was possible on the instrument of the period. Norrington also adds accents to the timpani part that are not present in the score (the recapitulation of the first movement is a conspicuous example).

For all the controversy that it has evinced, Norrington's recording is an exciting rendition of the Ninth that gives a perspective offered by none of its competitors, forcing conductors and listeners alike to think twice about received tradition. Traditionalists and historical performance adherents all have benefitted enormously from Norrington's bold experiment.

Timings: I = 14′13″; II = 14′20″; III = 11′08″; IV = 22′39″

Christopher Hogwood Conducting the Academy of Ancient Music and the London Symphony Chorus (Arleen Augér, Catherine Robbin, Anthony Rolfe Johnson, Gregory Reinhart, Soloists); L'oiseau-Lyre 425 517-2

Recorded in 1989, Hogwood's recording on period instruments forms an interesting comparison to Norrington's. Many of the personnel of the

Academy of Ancient Music are the same as the London Classical Players, drawn as they are from the pool of specialists on period instruments based in London. Hogwood had a head start on Norrington in recording the Beethoven symphonies, even though Norrington's Ninth was released earlier. Hogwood also had the experience of recording all the Mozart symphonies (as well as many of Haydn's) under his belt before undertaking the Beethoven project.

The principal difference between Hogwood and Norrington's recordings of the Ninth is that Hogwood's orchestra uses "double" winds (including brass and percussion), as opposed to Norrington's single winds. The extra instruments are used only in the louder passages to counterbalance a string section of forty-nine players. The one hundred-voice chorus is divided into twenty-five singers per part. While Norrington's recording of the Ninth has attracted the most attention, Hogwood's contains many of the same virtues, and fewer of its vices. Hogwood, who undoubtedly was looking over his shoulder at his rival, stays fairly close to the Schott metronome markings in the first three movements. He falls noticeably under speed at the instrumental statement of the "Freude" theme ($\downarrow$ = 66 as opposed to the Schott 80) in the finale, but the vocal statement at 74 is only a shade off. The Turkish March at $\downarrow$. = 90 begins quite close to the 84 of the Schott marking, speeding comfortably up to 97 by the end of the double fugue. Hogwood's most conspicuous abandonment of a Schott tempo comes in the *Andante maestoso*, which at $\downarrow$ = 60 is considerably slower than the original 72.

Hogwood pays closer attention to more of Beethoven's dynamic and articulation nuances than do other conductors. One example that may serve for many is the observation of the *diminuendo* in the kettledrum in m. 330 (the last "Gott" before the Turkish March). It is this kind of attention to detail that distinguishes this recording, making it one of the best available to date.

The gravity of Hogwood's enlarged orchestra makes this recording likely to please listeners who prefer a weightier Ninth in the Wagnerian tradition, while, at the same time, satisfying those for whom faithfulness to historical performance practices is important.

Timings: I = 13'56"; II = 13'34"; III = 10'44"; IV = 25'00"

Leonard Bernstein Conducting the Bavarian Radio Symphony Orchestra with Members of the Dresden Staatskapelle, the Orchestra of the Kirov Theatre, Leningrad, the London Symphony Orchestra, the New York Philharmonic, the Orchestre de Paris and the Bavarian Radio Chorus with Members of the Berlin Radio Chorus and Dresden Philharmonic Children's Chorus (June Anderson, Sarah Walker, Klaus König, Jan-Hendrik Rootering, Soloists);
DGG 429 861-2

This international cast was put together for a performance given on December 25, 1989 as an "Ode to Freedom" at the Schauspielhaus in (formerly East) Berlin. The extraordinary event was occasioned by the razing of the Wall in November, marking the unofficial end of the Cold War. The concert was broadcast throughout the world, and may also be obtained on videotape or laserdisc in addition to compact disc. Aside from the large and diverse assemblage of performers, this concert was unusual because Bernstein and his singers substituted the word "Freiheit" (freedom) for the "Freude" (joy) of Schiller's poem. As seen in chapter 1 and 6, Bernstein was not the first to think of this idea.[5]

This recording is the only one to use boy's voices in the finale. As we saw in chapter 5, a boy's choir participated in the 1824 premiere of the Ninth. Bernstein may not have been aware of this fact; of this we can be certain: his decisions regarding this performance of the Ninth were governed more by sensitivity to nineteenth- and twentieth-century political history than to interest in historical performance practices. As the cultural response to an important event in international politics, this performance, at times, is deeply moving. As a rendition of the Ninth, however, it is more faithful to Bernstein's self-indulgence than it is to Beethoven's score.

This performance, with its extremely slow tempos (especially in the third movement), is bound to invite comparison with Furtwängler. A comparison of the timings of the individual movements bears this out. But where Furtwängler at his slowest offers depth, Bernstein only offers weight. One can measure how far Bernstein strays from the Schott tempos by the length of time that elapses between the opening of the finale and the end of the instrumental recitative. The opening is marked $\downarrow. = 66$. Assuming that the recitative is performed *a tempo,* as the score indicates, the passage should last about two minutes (Norrington takes 1'52"). Bernstein's rendition lasts 4'28". Even with the omission of both repeats in the scherzo, this performance, at over seventy-seven minutes, is the longest one currently available.

Bernstein was one of the most influential conductors of the second half of the twentieth century, as well as a man admired for his humanity and deeply felt convictions. "Ode to Freedom" is a prime example of an artist self-consciously trying too hard to make history. As a symbolic media event, it is a triumph. As a performance of the Ninth Symphony, it is sadly wanting.

Timings: I = 17'54"; II = 10'41"; III = 20'10"; IV = 28'45"

Peter Tiboris Conducting the Brno Philharmonic Orchestra and Janáček Opera Choir (Leah Anne Myers, Ilene Sameth, James Clark, and Richard Conant, Soloists); Bridge BCD 9033

This recording, released in 1992, is included because it is based on Gustav Mahler's reorchestration of 1895. As discussed in chapter 7, many of Mahler's changes are too subtle to be detected by most listeners. Peter Tiboris's detailed notes that accompany this recording, however, make rather extravagant claims to the contrary. Regarding mm. 14–35 of the first movement, for example, Tiboris writes that a doubling of the number of violinists in the upper register and the addition of cellos in octaves gives a "more soaring" quality and adds "more fiber to the inner structure of the movement." This claim seems somewhat exaggerated in light of the recording itself. Tiboris further claims that Mahler's doubling creates "less harmonic space" (whatever that may mean) and "more weight." The latter quality is true enough, but it is as much a product of Tiboris's ponderous tempo ($\quarternote$ = 68—a full twenty ticks slower than the Schott marking) as it is of Mahler's scoring. This slow speed, as well as Tiboris's other idiosyncratic tempos, is surprising, especially since the conductor's own performance notes draw attention to the fact that Mahler called for no changes in Beethoven's original tempo indications.

There are moments, however, where Mahler's changes do make a difference. The addition of a new line for the horns in mm. 316 ff. of the first movement, for example, is striking, as is the horn doubling of the viola and cello line at mm. 512 ff. of the trio of the scherzo (Mahler doubles the second theme of the scherzo with horns and trumpets, but reorchestration of this passage is the rule, rather than the exception).

One would expect that Mahler's reorchestrations would make a larger impact on the finale than it actually does. The opening fanfares sound even less imposing on this recording than they do on Norrington's or Hogwood's, which do not fill in the "missing notes" in the horns and trumpets. Mahler's decision to add violas to the contrabass and cello recitative does add volume and depth to this passage, but it hardly makes it "more dramatic," as Tiboris claims. The addition of a tuba to the lower brass and choral basses at the *Andante maestoso* (mm. 595ff.)—not even mentioned by Tiboris in his notes—is striking, however, as are the isolated moments when Mahler allows the trumpets to soar with the choral sopranos.

Timings: I = 15′55″; II = 11′40″; III = 15′31″; IV = 24′45″

Notes

INTRODUCTION

1. See Ralph Vaughan Williams, *Some Thoughts on Beethoven's Choral Symphony* (Oxford: Oxford University Press, 1953), 40, to find a similar expression that describes the opening of the last movement.

2. Ludwig van Beethoven, *Symphonie Nr. 9 in d-moll = Symphony No. 9 in D minor, op. 125*, ed. Jonathan Del Mar (Kassel: Bärenreiter, 1996). Ludwig van Beethoven, *Sinfonie Nr. 9 d-Moll, op. 125, Taschen-Partitur. Einführung und Analyse von Dieter Rexroth* (Mainz: Goldmann-Schott Verlag, 1979).

3. The scores of Symphonies nos. 6–9 are to be found in vol. 3.

CHAPTER 1
From "Rescue from the Chains of Tyrants"
to "All Men Become Brothers": The World of the Ninth

1. Associated Press, June 3, 1989.

2. See Lewis Lockwood, *Beethoven: The Music and Life* (New York: Norton, 2003), 411–412, who reminds us that the Ninth has figured into every Olympic Games since 1956.

3. Schiller never identified "An die Freude" as an ode, and the popular title "Ode to Joy" cannot be found in either the original published version of the poem or its 1803 revision. Beethoven, however, called it an ode on the title page of the dedication copy of the score that was sent to Berlin, as well as in the copy forwarded to B. Schott Söhne, the publisher of the Ninth.

4. Klaus L. Berghahn, ed., *Briefwechsel zwischen Schiller und Körner* (Munich: Winkler-Verlag, 1878), 2:358–359.

5. Frank E. Kirby, "Beethoven and the 'geselliges Lied,'" *Music and Letters* 47 (1966): 116–125.

6. See Maynard Solomon, "Beethoven and Schiller," *Beethoven Essays* (Cambridge, Mass.: Harvard University Press, 1988), 205–215 for an interesting examination of Beethoven's reception of Schiller's works and philosophy.

7. Friedrich Schiller, *On the Aesthetic Education of Man,* trans. Reginald Snell (London: Routledge and Kegan Paul, 1954), 12.

8. Karl-Heinz Köhler and Grita Heere, eds., *Ludwig van Beethoven's Konversationshefte,* vol. 1, (Leipzig: VEB Deutscher Verlag für Musik, 1972), 235.

9.   Maynard Solomon, "Beethoven's Ninth Symphony: The Sense of an End-ing," *Critical Inquiry* 17 (1991): 303–304.

10.   I will return to these issues in chapter 4.

11.   Susan McClary, *Feminine Endings: Music, Gender, and Sexuality* (Min-neapolis: University of Minnesota Press, 1991).

12.   McClary, *Feminine Endings,* 127–130. In an earlier version of this essay, McClary's phrase "murderous rage" read even more graphically, as "throttling murderous rage of a rapist incapable of attaining release." See Pieter C. van den Toorn, "Politics, Feminism, and Contemporary Music Theory." *Journal of Musicol-ogy* 9 (1991): 275–299.

13.   Ruth A. Solie "What Do Feminists Want? A Reply to Pieter van den Toorn," *Journal of Musicology* 9 (1991): 399–410, refers to *A Clockwork Orange.*

14.   Anthony Burgess, *A Clockwork Orange* (New York: Norton, 1963), 48–49.

15.   Burgess, *A Clockwork Orange,* 114.

16.   Furtwängler continuously sought to distance himself from official Nazi ac-tivities and there is reason to believe that he participated in the 1942 Birthday Con-cert against his will. See Sam H. Shirakawa, *The Devil's Music Master* (Oxford: Ox-ford University Press, 1992), 271–279.

17.   Burgess, *A Clockwork Orange,* 116.

CHAPTER 2
The Genesis of the Ninth

1.   Hitherto unknown "revisions, alterations and corrections" for the Ninth Symphony in the hand of Beethoven and his copyist Ferdinand Wolanek were sold to an unidentified buyer at a Sotheby's auction in London on May 5–6, 1988. Accord-ing to the auction catalogue, the four pages that comprise this pencil-drawn manu-script contain several changes not found in the autograph manuscript of the Sym-phony housed at the Staatsbibliothek zu Berlin but which were incorporated in the published first edition of 1826.

2.   Maynard Solomon, *Beethoven* (New York: Schirmer Books, 1977), 311.

3.   Among the most significant of Nottebohm's studies are *Ein Skizzenbuch von Beethoven* (Leipzig: Breitkopf und Härtel, 1865), *Beethoveniana* (Leipzig and Win-terthur: C. F. Peters 1872), *Ein Skizzenbuch von Beethoven aus dem Jahre 1803* (Leip-zig: 1880), and *Zweite Beethoveniana* (Leipzig: C. F. Peters 1887). Some sources that were described by Nottebohm have since been lost.

4.   Beethoven used desk sketchbooks when working at home and pocket sketchbooks when away from his residence. The most important inventory is Doug-las Johnson, Alan Tyson, and Robert Winter, *The Beethoven Sketchbooks* (Berkeley, Calif.: University of California Press, 1985).

5.   See Douglas Johnson, "Beethoven Scholars and Beethoven's Sketches,"

19th Century Music 2 (1978): 3–17 and Joseph Kerman, "Viewpoint: Sketch Studies," *19th Century Music* 6 (1982): 174–180.

6.   Sieghard Brandenburg, "Die Skizzen zur Neunten Symphonie," in *Zu Beethoven,* (Berlin: Neue Musik, 1984), 2:88–129; Robert Winter, "The Sketches for the 'Ode to Joy'," in *Beethoven, Performers, and Critics* (Detroit: Wayne State University Press, 1977), 176–214, and Jenny L. Kallick, *A Study of the Advanced Sketches and Full Score Autograph for the First Movement of Beethoven's Ninth Symphony, Opus 125* (Ann Arbor: UMI Press, 1987). The seminal study of sketches for the Ninth Symphony was Gustav Nottebohm, "Skizzen zur neunten Symphonie," *Zweite Beethoveniana* (Leipzig, Neue Musik, 1887), 157–192.

7.   This table is patterned after Kallick, *A Study of the Advanced Sketches,* 25–26. Sigla for the sources are taken from Johnson, Tyson, and Winter, *The Beethoven Sketchbooks.*

8.   See Frank E. Kirby, "Beethoven and the 'Geselliges Lied'," *Music and Letters* 47 (1966): 116–125, James Parsons, *Ode to the Ninth: The Poetic and Musical Tradition Behind the Finale of Beethoven's "Choral Symphony"* (Ph.D. diss., University of North Texas, 1992), 324–433, Maynard Solomon, *Beethoven Essays,* 205, and Rey M. Longyear, *Schiller and Music* (Chapel Hill, N.C.: University of North Carolina Press, n.d.), 117, 133, and 141.

9.   The attributions to Winter in respect to the musical examples in this chapter refer to "The Sketches for the 'Ode to Joy'." Examples attributed to Nottebohm are taken from *Zweite Beethoveniana,* and those attributed to Brandenburg are from "Die Skizzen zur Neunten Symphonie."

10.   *"Sinfonie / erster Anfang / in bloß 4 Stim[m]en / 2 Vi[oli]n Viol Basso / dazwischen forte mit andern Stim[m]en u. wenn möglich jedes / andere Instrument nach u. nach eintreten lassen—"*

11.   Nottebohm, *Zweite Beethoveniana,* 163.

12.   The original German of this letter is given in Dieter Rexroth's annotations to the score of the Ninth Symphony (Mainz: Goldmann-Schott Verlag, 1979), 329. The allusion to North America stems from an unfulfilled request from the Handel and Haydn Society in Boston for an oratorio. Alexander Wheelock Thayer, *Thayer's Life of Beethoven,* rev. ed. Elliot Forbes (Princeton, N.J.: Princeton University Press, 1967), 834.

13.   Rochlitz published this account in Volume 4 of *Für Freunde der Tonkunst* and an earlier printing of it may be found in the Leipzig *Allgemeine musikalische Zeitung* 30 (1828): 5–16. See Maynard Solomon, "On Beethoven's Creative Process: A Two-part Invention," *Music and Letters* 61 (1980): 272–283.

14.   See Barry Cooper, *World Premiere: Beethoven Symphony No. 10.* London Symphony Orchestra, Wyn Morris, conductor. MCA Classics, MCAD-6269 (1988), "Newly Identified Sketches for Beethoven's Tenth Symphony," *Music and Letters* 66 (1985): 9–18, and "The First Movement of Beethoven's Tenth Symphony: A

Realization," *Beethoven Newsletter* 3 (1988): 27. For a challenge to Cooper's conclusions, see Robert Winter, "Of Realizations, Completions, Restorations and Reconstructions: From Bach's *The Art of the Fugue* to Beethoven's Tenth Symphony," *Journal of the Royal Musical Association* 116 (1991): 96–126. See also Winter, "Noch einmal: Wo sind Beethovens Skizzen zur zehnten Symphonie?" *Beethoven Jahrbuch* 9 (1973/77): 536–537 and Brandenburg, "Die Skizzen," 110–115.

15. Jenny L. Kallick, *A Study of the Advanced Sketches,* and Winter, "The Sketches for the 'Ode to Joy'." Winter does not discuss the instrumental and vocal recitative.

16. Beethoven's metronomic indication for the Andante theme is $\flat$ = 63. It is interesting to note that the English critic Henry John Gauntlett, writing in 1837, identified this theme as a polacca. Chapter 7 will examine issues of tempo for this and other passages. Some scholars believe that the *Andante* theme may not originally have been part of this movement.

17. The information that follows is based in part on Ludwig van Beethoven, *Sinfonie Nr. 9, Einführung und Analyse von Dieter Rexroth* (Mainz: Goldmann-Schott, 1979), 303–314, supplemented by information provided by Kallick, *A Study of the Advanced Sketches,* 151–153, and the 1988 Sotheby catalogue.

18. Since unification, the two Berlin State Libraries have become the Staatsbibliothek zu Berlin–Preußischer Kulturbesitz.

19. See Otto Baensch, "Die Aachener Abschrift der neunten Symphonie," *Neues Beethoven Jahrbuch* 5 (1933): 7–20.

20. See Pamela J. Willetts, *Beethoven and England* (Edinburgh: T. and A. Constable, 1970), 49–50.

21. The most extensive investigation of these sources may be found in the Critical Commentary that accompanies Jonathan Del Mar's *Urtext* edition.

22. See Parsons, *Ode to the Ninth,* 51ff.

23. The translation is by William Mann. EMI CDC 7499652, Hayes Middlesex, 1990.

CHAPTER 3
The Ninth: Movements I–III

1. Here I find myself in disagreement with Richard Taruskin, "Resisting the Ninth," *19th Century Music* 12 (1989): 251. Taruskin argues that the sextuplets, being at odds with the meter, enhance the "blur" that he believes the opening is intended to produce.

2. There are exceptions to the rule regarding introductions to sonata-form movements. The first movement of Haydn's "Drum Roll" Symphony (no. 103) comes to mind. The introduction to the first movement of Mozart's Serenade, K.320 ("Posthorn") is brought back in the recapitulation, cleverly integrated into the meter and tempo of the *Allegro*. Another case is Beethoven's Piano Sonata, op. 13 ("Pathé-

tique"), itself possibly influenced by Clementi's Sonata, op. 34, no. 2, where the *Grave* introduction is brought back at key structural points within the *Allegro* movement, but always in its original tempo. Throughout his career, Beethoven reassessed the role of the introduction, and this continued well into his late style, by which time he found ways to blur the line between introduction and main body of a sonata-form movement (e.g., the first movements of the String Quartets, opp. 127 and 130). The Ninth Symphony differs from all the examples mentioned here in that there is only one tempo indication for the entire movement, and the so-called introduction is not set off by a different tempo or meter.

3.   Donald Francis Tovey, *Essays in Musical Analysis* (Oxford: Oxford University Press, 1935), 2:6.

4.   Tovey, *Essays in Musical Analysis* (Oxford: Oxford University Press, 1935), 1:68. for another view of the significance of this opening, see Leo Treitler, "History, Criticism, and Beethoven's Ninth Symphony," *Music and the Historical Imagination* (Cambridge, Mass.: Harvard University Press, 1989), 19–45.

5.   This is not the only minor key sonata form movement by Beethoven where he substitutes VI for III, as witnessed by the first movements of opp. 95, 111, and, from a later work, op. 132.

6.   Beethoven similarly disguises the beginning of the development section in the first movement of op. 59, no. 1. Here, too, there is no repeat of the exposition.

7.   Martin Cooper, *Beethoven: The Last Decade* (Oxford: Oxford University Press, 1985), 291, identifies this cadential formula as a "refrain," correctly pointing out that it marks the "end of each episode in the development section." But each time it returns, its harmonization is slightly different. We will return to this passage later.

8.   The manuscript copy of the Ninth Symphony in the British Library (BL MS 21) includes a "correction" made by Ignaz Moscheles in which the E♭ and G in the oboes is altered to F and A♭ in order to agree with the violas.

9.   See pp. 57–59 of the Peters facsimile of the autograph. See also Igor Markevitch, *Die Sinfonien von Ludwig van Beethoven: historische, analytische und praktische Studien* (Leipzig: Peters, 1981 and 1983).

10.   With the sole exception of Markevitch's edition.

11.   Given the density of sound at this moment, it could be argued, of course, that the discrepancy between the manuscript and the published score is too small to be noticed. Beethoven or his copyist changed the placement to its familiar place in the *Stichvorlage* sent to Schott.

12.   Many conductors try to make too much of this effect by extending the *ritardando* in m. 510 and ignoring the *a tempo* in m. 511. The same complaint holds true for the appearances of the cadential formula in the development section.

13.   Maynard Soloman, "The Ninth Symphony: A Search for Order," *Beethoven Essays* (Cambridge, Mass.: Harvard University Press, 1988), 28.

14.   The Fs in the timpani in the Eighth Symphony, however, represent the tonic, and not the mediant.

15. Beethoven used the same tonal scheme in the second movement of his Piano Trio, op. 70, no. 1 ("Ghost").

16. For an analysis of this movement based on metrical groupings, see Richard L. Cohn, "The Dramatization of Hypermetric Conflicts in the Scherzo of Beethoven's Ninth Symphony," *19th Century Music* 15 (1992): 188–206.

17. This repeat frequently is omitted in performance. Regarding the observance of repeats in the reprise of the scherzo after the trio, see below and chapter 7.

18. Beethoven's metronome marking for the scherzo is ♩. = 116, while the tempo for the trio is set at the rather leisurely pace of ♩ = 116. This has, understandably, raised serious questions about the role of the *stringendo*. But since this question cannot be separated from the larger issue concerning all of Beethoven's metronome markings for the Ninth Symphony, a discussion of this issue will be taken up in chapter 7.

19. Joseph Kerman, *The Beethoven Quartets* (New York: Knopf, 1966), 200–203. Kerman cites the "vocal" quality of the Ninth Symphony as the progenitor of the intense lyricism found in Beethoven's last quartets.

20. For more on this, see Solomon, "The Ninth Symphony," 14–17.

21. François-Joseph Fétis, *Revue Musicale* (April 2, 1831), 68–70 reported that the shift to F major elicited a "cry of admiration from the entire audience" in Paris.

22. *The Letters of Beethoven*, ed. and trans. Emily Anderson, vol. 3 (London: 1961), 1166–1167. ("Il me semble avoir été oublié dans la 2ᵈᵉ partie de la Symphonie, qu'à la répétition du minore après le Presto il faut commencer de nouveau du signe et continuer *sans répétition* jusqu'à la ferma; alors on prend aussitôt la Code.").

23. An excellent case in point is the *Adagio* from Haydn's Symphony no. 102, a movement that was taken from his Piano Trio in F-sharp Minor, Hob. XV:26. In the symphony, Haydn greatly modified and simplified the movement.

24. Tovey, *Essays in Musical Analysis*, 2:29–31, 29–31, argues that the reorchestrated second appearance of the *Andante* theme in a different key (G major) constitutes, in itself, a variation. He cites the *Allegretto* from the Seventh Symphony, the slow movement of the Piano Trio in E♭ Major, op. 70, no. 2, and the second movement of the Fifth Symphony, as precedents for the treatment of two discrete themes as variations. Each of these movements also exhibits characteristics of rondo design.

25. The *Adagio* theme bears an uncanny resemblance to the slow movement of the "Pathétique" Sonata, op. 13. Another theme of this kind may be found in the second movement of the String Quartet in C Major, op. 59, no. 3.

26. See Charles Rosen, *The Classical Style* (New York: Viking, 1971), 387–388 to see how Beethoven performs a similar trick in the first movement of his Fourth Piano Concerto, op. 58.

27. Henry John Gauntlett, "Beethoven and the Philharmonic Society," *Musical World* 5 (April 28, 1837), 97–103.

28. This issue will be taken up again in chapter 7.

29.   Robert Winter, "A Close Reading," *Ludwig van Beethoven: Symphony No. 9,* computer software (The Voyager Company, Santa Monica, Calif., 1991), card 191.

30.   *Revue et Gazette musicale* 7 (1840): 177.

31.   The author wishes to thank Jeff Snedeker, Charles Waddell, and William Schaefer for information regarding this horn part.

32.   This passage poses a real problem for the conductor with respect to balance. The entrance of the second violins is marked *pianissimo.* Unless the rest of the orchestra starts its diminuendo immediately, the second violins—instruments that ought to occupy the foreground—simply cannot be heard. An auditorium with a long reverberation time exacerbates the problem. This probably is the reason why so many conductors change the dynamic marking in the second violins from *pianissimo* to *fortissimo.*

CHAPTER 4
The Ninth: The Choral Finale

1.   Donald Francis Tovey, *Essays in Musical Analysis* (Oxford: Oxford University Press, 1935), 2: 3–6.

2.   Maynard Solomon, "The Ninth Symphony: A Search for Order," *Beethoven Essays* (Cambridge, Mass.: Harvard University Press, 1988), 13.

3.   Further information about the concept of topics and semiotic codes may be found in V. Kofi Agawu, *Playing with Signs* (Princeton: Princeton University Press, 1991) and Leonard G. Ratner, *Classic Music: Expression, Form, and Style* (New York: Schirmer Books, 1980).

4.   Schiller's first version read "Beggars become the brothers of princes" (*Bettler werden Fürstenbrüder*). The German verb *werden* may be taken to express either the present or future tense.

5.   See chapter 2 for a more detailed examination of the Choral Fantasy and the final chorus from *Fidelio* as they relate to the finale of the Ninth Symphony.

6.   Heinrich Schenker, *Beethoven's Ninth Symphony,* trans. and ed. John Rothgeb (New Haven: Yale University Press, 1992).

7.   Otto Baensch, *Aufbau und Sinn des Chorfinales in Beethovens neunter Symphonie* (Berlin: W. de Gruyter, 1930).

8.   Ernest Sanders, "Form and Content in the Finale of Beethoven's Ninth Symphony," *Musical Quarterly* 50 (1964): 59–76 and Robert Winter, "A Close Reading," *Ludwig van Beethoven: Symphony No. 9,* computer software (The Voyager Company, Santa Monica, Calif., 1991).

9.   This table is a composite derived from Winter, "A Close Reading."

10.   James Webster, in "The Form of the Finale of Beethoven's Ninth Symphony," *Beethoven Forum* 1 (1992): 25–62, proposes a "multivalent" analysis that divides the movement into eleven sections and accounts for many layers of activity, each of which has the potential of generating points of formal articulation. His

analysis stresses the movement's "goal-directedness," maintaining at the same time its essentially through-composed nature.

11. Charles Rosen, *The Classical Style* (New York: Viking, 1972), 440. See also Leo Treitler, "History, Criticism, and Beethoven's Ninth Symphony," *Music and the Historical Imagination* (Cambridge, Mass.: Harvard University Press, 1989), 25, and Michael C. Tusa, "Noch einmal: Form and Content in the Finale of Beethoven's Ninth Symphony," *Beethoven Forum* 7 (Lincoln: University of Nebraska Press, 1999), 113–137.

12. A similar analysis was proposed by Ernest F. Livingstone, "Das Form-problem des 4. Satzes in Beethovens 9. Symphonie," *Bericht über den Internationalen Musikwissenschaftlichen Kongress Bonn 1970* (Kassel: Bärenreiter, 1971), 491–494.

13. Martin Cooper, *Beethoven: The Last Decade* (Oxford: Oxford University Press, 1985), 194. It is interesting to note that Beethoven revised the finale of this sonata in early 1822. The ultimate conflation of slow movement and finale, of course, are the slow finales to the Sonatas, opp. 109 and 111.

14. See Rosen, *The Classical Style*, 429–430 for a more detailed discussion of this passage in the context of his brilliant analysis of the entire sonata. Several other parallels have been drawn between the Ninth Symphony and the "Hammerklavier" Sonata. See chapter 2 for further observations on the relationship between op. 106 and the genesis of the Ninth Symphony.

15. Think, for example, of the transition from the development to the recapitulation in the first movement of the Second Symphony, op. 36 and the parallel passage in the String Quartet, op. 18, no. 3.

16. See chapter 5 regarding the problems Beethoven encountered in rehearsing the contrabasses prior to the first performance of the Ninth. Also see David B. Levy, "The Contrabass Recitative in Beethoven's Ninth Symphony Revisited," *Historical Performance* 5 (1992): 9–18.

17. Jurgen Thym, "The Instrumental Recitative in Beethoven's Compositions," in Jerald C. Graue, ed., *Essays on Music for Charles Warren Fox* (Rochester, N.Y.: Eastman School of Music Press, 1979), 230–240. Thym sensibly points out that the hermeneutic and structural interpretations of instrumental recitatives in Beethoven are not mutually exclusive.

18. Sanders, "Form and Content," 65, n. 16 suggests that this quotation "both points back to the beginning and points forward to the recapitulation" of the first movement.

19. The repetition of the final two phrases are justified later by the choral repetitions in the vocal presentation of the theme. Schenker, *Beethoven's Ninth Symphony*, 235 analyzes the tune as a three-part song form (a_1b-a_2) comprising $8 + 4 + 4$ measures.

20. Dénes Bartha, "On Beethoven's Thematic Structure," *The Creative World of Beethoven* (New York: Norton, 1970), 257–276. See also Robert Winter, "The

Sketches for the 'Ode to Joy,'" *Beethoven, Performers, and Critics* (Detroit: Wayne State University Press, 1980), 191–193 and Rosen, *The Classical Style*, 329–350 for further examinations of the place held by "popular" melodies in this repertory.

21.   The autograph score indicates that Beethoven wished to have the contrabass line in the first variation (beginning in m. 116) doubled by the second bassoon. See the Peters facsimile, 254, where the composer clearly has added in red crayon the marking, "2do fag[otto] col B[asso]." This same instruction may also be found in the British Library MS. source. There is no satisfactory explanation as to why this instruction never made it into the first, or any subsequent, edition. For further discussion of this point, see Igor Markevitch, *Die Sinfonien von Ludwig van Beethoven* (Leipzig: C. F. Peters, 1983), 538. Vaughan Williams, *Some Thoughts on Beethoven's Choral Symphony* (Oxford: Oxford University Press, 1953), 42–43, deemed the omission of the second bassoon to be fortuitous.

22.   The verse-chorus structure of "An die Freude" is given in chapter 1.

23.   Leopold Sonnleithner, "Ad vocem: Contrabass-Recitative der 9. Symphonie von Beethoven," *Allgemeine musikalische Zeitung*, n.s., 2 (1864): 245–246. I leave aside in this discussion the fact that Beethoven conceived the entire Ninth Symphony from the standpoint of the finale, discussed, among others, by Maynard Solomon, "Beethoven's Ninth Symphony: The Sense of an Ending," *Critical Inquiry* 17 (1991): 289–305. Beethoven's difficulties in arriving at a solution for the introduction of the human voice and the words in the finale, as discussed in chapter 2, are the province of his workshop as revealed by the extant sketches. The issue under examination here is an understanding of the end result of his struggle.

24.   Joseph Kerman, *The Beethoven Quartets* (New York Knopf, 1966), 191–196.

25.   For a different interpretation, see Stephen Hinton, "Not Which Tones? The Crux of Beethoven's Ninth," *19th Century Music* 22 (1998): 61–77.

26.   Much attention has been paid to Beethoven's precedents for this sudden drop of a third. See Rosen, *The Classical Style*, 407–433 to see how this harmonic movement is an essential feature of the "Hammerklavier" Sonata. One may further cite mm. 163–164 from the "Dona nobis pacem" of the *Missa solemnis* where the prayer for peace first yields to the noises of warfare. Indeed, the gesture is present throughout the first three movements of the Ninth Symphony, with the D♭ episode of the *Adagio* being the most striking instance.

27.   Hermann J. Weigand, "Schiller: Transfiguration of a Titan," *A Schiller Symposium* (Austin, Tex.: University of Texas, 1960), 101–102 also takes note of the connection between Psalm 19 and "An die Freude," reporting that the text in question was "Schiller's favorite verse" from this psalm. Weigand does not mention Beethoven's setting of the poem.

28.   William Kinderman, "Compositional Models for the Choral Finale of the Ninth Symphony," *Beethoven's Compositional Process* (Lincoln, Neb.: University of Nebraska Press, 1991), 174. See also Kinderman, "Beethoven's Symbol for the

Deity in the *Missa Solemnis* and the Ninth Symphony," *19th Century Music* 9 (1985): 102–118.

29. Winter, "A Close Reading," card 321.

30. Kerman, *The Beethoven Quartets,* 194–195.

CHAPTER 5
The Performances of 1824

1. See Joseph Kerman and Alan Tyson, *The New Grove Beethoven* (New York: Norton, 1983), 57.

2. "Musikzustand und musikalisches Leben in Wien," *Caecilia* 1 (1824), 193–194.

3. Alice M. Hanson, *Musical Life in Biedermeier Vienna* (Cambridge: Cambridge University Press, 1985), 82–83 cites a study by Hilde Fischbach-Stojan that accounts for seventy-five major concerts in Vienna in 1824, a statistic that supports the report in *Caecilia.*

4. The title of this organization was borrowed from its eighteenth-century French counterpart. Its name derives from the practice of holding purely instrumental concerts during the Lenten season, a period when the staging of operas and ballets was prohibited.

5. Adam Carse, *The Orchestra from Beethoven to Berlioz* (New York: Broude Brothers, 1949), 261–262. See also Hanson, *Musical Life,* 97–98. Otto Biba, "Concert Life in Beethoven's Vienna," *Beethoven, Performers, and Critics* (Detroit: Wayne State University Press, 1980), 77–93 offers further documentation regarding Viennese musical institutions and auditoriums.

6. Karl-Heinz Köhler, Grita Herre, and Peter Pötschner, eds., *Ludwig van Beethovens Konversationshefte,* vol. 5 (Leipzig: VEB Deutscher Verlag für Musik, 1970), 283. For further background on the role of private concert giving in Vienna, see Mary Sue Morrow, *Concert Life in Haydn's Vienna: Aspects of a Developing Musical and Social Institution* (New York: Pendragon, 1989), 1–33.

7. Thayer-Forbes, *Thayer's Life of Beethoven* (Princeton, N.J.: Princeton University Press, 1964; rev. 1967), 701 tells of Beethoven's reference to the institution as the Society for the *Enemies* of Music (Gesellschaft der Musik*feinde*). This was done, no doubt, only partly in jest since the composer could rarely pass up an opportunity for a good pun.

8. Thayer-Forbes, 883–886.

9. The details of Franz's policy have been outlined in various sources. Hanson, *Musical Life,* devotes an entire chapter to the relationship of Viennese censorship to musicians and other artists, 34–60. See also Robert A. Kann, *A Study in Austrian Intellectual History* (New York: Frederick A. Praeger, 1960) and C. A. Macartney, *The Hapsburg Empire: 1790–1918* (New York: Macmillan, 1969) for further information about the workings of the censorship system in Vienna during the *Vormärz.* Frida

Knight, *Beethoven and the Age of Revolution* (New York: International Publishers, 1974) also is useful as it examines the composer's career from a political perspective.

10.   Nothing suggests that Beethoven experienced difficulty with the censors with regard to "An die Freude" even though the composer and Count Lichnowsky were forced to intervene directly with Sedlnitzky, the head of the police, in order to get permission to perform the three movements from the *Missa solemnis* on the May 7 *Academie*. Permission was granted only after the title of the Mass was changed to "Hymns." Further confusion about "An die Freude" and its political implications stems from a cryptic footnote in Thayer's biography that suggests that the title of the poem once had been "An die Freiheit" (see Thayer-Forbes, 894). There is no evidence that such a version of the poem ever existed, although in 1838, Wolfgang Robert Griepenkerl's novella, *Das Musikfest oder die Beethovener,* implied that "Freude" and "Freiheit" were virtually synonymous. See chapter 6 for a closer discussion of the Griepenkerl work.

11.   *Wiener Allgemeine musikalische Zeitung* 8 (1824): 87–88 and *Wiener Theater-Zeitung* 53, (1824): 181–182.

12.   Thayer-Forbes, 899. A translation of the entire Petition may be found in Anton Felix Schindler, *Beethoven as I Knew Him,* trans. Constance S. Jolly, ed. Donald W. MacArdle (London: Faber and Faber, 1966), 273–275, Nef, *Die Neun Sinfonien Beethovens* (Leipzig: Breitkopf & Härtel, 1928), 302–303, and Thayer-Forbes, 897–899.

13.   Schindler-MacArdle, *Beethoven As I Knew Him,* 273–275.

14.   For a more detailed examination of the identity of the signatories, see the author's *Early Performances of Beethoven's Ninth Symphony: A Documentary Study of Five Cities* (Ann Arbor: University Microfilms, 1980), 40–42.

15.   *Wiener Theater-Zeitung* 53 (May 1, 1824): 212. For more information about the premiere of the Ninth and its context, see Thomas Forrest Kelly, *First Nights: Five Musical Premieres* (New Haven: Yale University Press, 2000), 108–179.

16.   *Wiener Allgemeine musikalische Zeitung* 28 (May 5, 1824): 112.

17.   Köhler, Herre, and Pötschner, eds., *Ludwig van Beethovens Konversationshefte,* vol. 5, p. 249. The "Krams" mentioned by Schindler was the contrabassist Anton Grams (1752–1823), formerly employed at the Kärnthnerthortheater. For additional discussion of the recitative and its execution, see chapters 4 and 7.

18.   Thayer-Forbes, 905. See also Daniel J. Koury, *Orchestral Performance Practices in the Nineteenth Century* (Ann Arbor: UMI Press, 1981), 118 and Shin Augustinus Kojima, "Die Uraufführung der Neunten Sinfonie Beethovens—einige neue Tatsachen," *Bericht über den Internationalen Musikwissenschaftlichen Kongress Bayreuth 1981* (Kassel: Bärenreiter 1984), 390–398. See Kelly, op. cit., 135–136.

19.   On 15 April, Bäuerle's *Allgemeine Theaterzeitung* announced that the concert would take place on April 22 or 23 at the Theater-an-der-Wien. Kanne's journal gave the same information on April 21. Bäuerle printed a correction of the site of the concert on May 1, but gave the date of the concert as May 4. Kanne's correction (this

time getting the date right) did not appear until May 5, only two days before the concert took place. As will be shown, the announcements for the second *Academie* were even more misleading.

20. *Wiener Allgemeine Theater-Zeitung* 58 (May 13, 1824): 230–231. Schindler-MacArdle, *Beethoven as I Knew Him*, 280, comments that only two full rehearsals took place. The next issue of the journal published a poem by Feska entitled "An Ludwig van Beethoven, nach seiner grossen musikalischen Akademie im k. k. Kärntnerthortheater in Wien."

21. *Wiener Allgemeine musikalische Zeitung* 30 (May 12, 1824): 120.

22. The expression "eyeglass basses" refers to a notational shorthand from the period in which two half notes are beamed together as if they were eighths, thus producing an image that resembles a pair of eyeglasses. Such notational signs appear frequently in Rossini's comic operas.

23. Leipzig *Allgemeine musikalische Zeitung* 26 (July 1, 1824), cols. 437–442.

24. *Caecilia* 1 (1824): B. Schott Söhne, 200.

25. See Thayer-Forbes, 908–910. The story about how Beethoven, oblivious to the audience, was prompted by Caroline Unger, the alto soloist, to turn around to face and acknowledge the cheering crowd is well known.

26. This was either Giacomo David or his son Giovanni. See *Beethovens Koversationshefte*, ed. Karl-Heinz Köhler & Grita Heere (Leipzig, VEB Deutscher Verlag für Musik, 1974) 6, p. 411, n. 387.

27. Thayer-Forbes, 912–913. According to a diary kept by Joseph Karl Rosenbaum, the weather was "trüb, kühl, und windig," contradicting the report in Thayer. See Hanson, *Musical Life*, 213–214.

28. Vienna *Allgemeine musikalische Zeitung* 8 (June 5 and 7, 1824): 149–151, 157–159.

29. *Wiener Theater-Zeitung* 67 (June 3, 1824): 266–267.

30. Leipzig *Allgemeine musikalische Zeitung* 26 (July 8, 1824): col. 422.

31. *Caecilia* 3 (1825): 242–243. Readers may recognize the Italian phrase at the end from the text of "Non più andrai" from Mozart's *Le nozze di Figaro*.

32. "Blicke auf die Literatur," *Caecilia* 1 (1824): 365–369.

CHAPTER 6
In the Shadow of the Ninth

1. Ernst Ortlepp, ed., *Großes Instrumental- und Vokal-Concert*, vol. 11 (Stuttgart: F. H. Kohler, 1841), 120.

2. Hector Berlioz, *Evenings with the Orchestra*, trans. and ed. Jacques Barzun (Chicago: University of Chicago Press, 1973), 322–323.

3. Adam Carse, *The Orchestra from Beethoven to Berlioz* (New York: Broude Brothers, 1949), is the seminal study on the size and nature of orchestras in the nineteenth century. Daniel J. Koury, *Orchestral Performance Practices in the Nine-*

teenth Century (Ann Arbor: UMI Press, 1986), also presents useful information based upon more recent research.

4.   See David Benjamin Levy, *Early Performances of Beethoven's Ninth Symphony: A Documentary Study of Five Cities* (Ann Arbor: University Microfilms, 1980) and Stefan Kunze, ed., *Ludwig van Beethoven. Die Werke im Spiegel seiner Zeit. Gesammelte Konzertberichte und Rezensionen bis 1830* (Laaber: Laaber-Verlag, 1987), 470–546, for the presentation of the complete texts of reviews between 1824 and 1852. See also Robin Wallace, *Beethoven's Critics* (Cambridge: Cambridge University Press, 1986).

5.   Adam Carse, "The Choral Symphony in London," *Music and Letters* 32 (1951): 47–48. The ledgers of the Philharmonic Society for 1825 (British Library Loan 48.9/1) show a payment of £31.4s. made to Hawes for the procurement of a chorus and singers.

6.   Minutes, Directors' Meeting of January 23, 1825, British Library, Loan 48 2/2.

7.   *Harmonicon* 3 (March 1825): 47–48.

8.   Beethoven's metronome indications for the work were not made available until 1827. Perhaps the experience in London served to convince him of the need for establishing and publishing them.

9.   Myles Birkett Foster, *The History of the Philharmonic Society: 1813–1912* (London: John Lane, The Bodley Head, 1912), 73. An advertisement for the concert called it a "New Grand Characteristic Sinfonia."

10.   See Carse, "The Choral Symphony in London," 52. Dragonetti's name is absent from the ledgers of the Philharmonic Society for 1825, raising a question as to whether or not he actually took part in the first performance. An entry in the Leipzig *Allgemeine musikalische Zeitung* 27 (March 9, 1825): 163, remarks that the Directors of the Society regretted that Dragonetti had quit the orchestra over financial disagreements, because "Beethoven has included in his newest (9th) Symphony a very difficult contrabass solo which is only playable by him and was written with him in mind." Foster recorded that Dragonetti, upon seeing his part in the Ninth Symphony, said that he "would have charged double!" had he seen this music in advance.

11.   *Beethovens Konversationshefte,* vol. 8, Karl-Heinz Köhler and Grita Heere, ed. (Leipzig, VEB Deutscher Verlag for Musik, 1981, p. 130). ("H.[err] *Smart* wünschte zu wissen, wie er den[n] eigentlich das *Recitativ* in der *Symphonie* gespielt haben will, er sagt, es hat ihnen sehr viele Mühe gekostet.") See David B. Levy, "The Contrabass Recitative in Beethoven's Ninth Symphony Revisited," *Historical Performance* 5 (Spring 1992): 9–18.

12.   *Harmonicon* 3 (April 1825): 69. The promised words were never published. As will be seen, the question of omitting repetitions became a lively issue in London in the 1840s.

13.   *Quarterly Musical Magazine and Review* 7 (1825): 80–84.

14.   *Quarterly Musical Magazine and Review* 7 (1825): 202.

218 NOTES TO PAGES 157–173

15. *Times* (London), June 22, 1835. Carse fails to mention that this performance was incomplete.

16. *Times* (London), April 16, 1836.

17. *Musical World* 5 (April 21, 1837): 93.

18. See *Harmonicon* 6 (March 1828): 55–56 and 110, and *Revue musicale* 3 (1828): 176–177.

19. Leipzig *Allgemeine musikalische Zeitung* 28 (December 27, 1826): col. 854.

20. Both reviews appeared in 1838.

21. See Robin Wallace, *Beethoven's Critics,* 73–92 for a more thorough investigation of these essays.

22. *Revue et Gazette musicale* 5 (1838): 33–37, 47–50, 64–66, 75–77, and 97–100.

23. Richard Wagner as quoted in Klaus Kropfinger, *Wagner and Beethoven,* trans. Peter Palmer (Cambridge: Cambridge University Press, 1991), 31.

24. *Richard Wagner's Prose Works,* ed. and trans. William Ashton Ellis, 7 (London: 1896. Rpt. NY: Broude Brothers, 1966), 247–248.

25. Griepenkerl, *Das Musikfest oder die Beethovener* (Leipzig: Otto Wigand, 1838), 89–90.

26. See Max Rudolf, "Beethoven's 'An die Freude' and Two Mysterious Footnotes," *The Beethoven Newsletter* 5 (1990): 29–33, and David B. Levy, "Wolfgang Robert Griepenkerl and Beethoven's Ninth Symphony," *Essays on Music for Charles Warren Fox* (Rochester, N.Y.: Eastman School of Music Press, 1979), 103–113.

27. Louis Spohr, *Autobiography* (Kassel: G. H. Wigand, 1861), trans. in Nicholas Slonimsky, *Lexicon of Musical Invective* (Seattle: University of Washington Press, 1969), 51.

28. Robert Schumann, "Florestan's Shrove Tuesday Address Delivered after a Performance of Beethoven's Last Symphony," in Strunk, *Source Readings in Music History: The Romantic Era* (New York: Norton, 1965), 93.

29. Friedrich Nietzsche, *Human, All-too-Human,* trans. Oscar Levy (New York: Macmillan, 1924), 158.

30. Friedrich Nietzsche, *The Birth of Tragedy,* trans. Walter Kaufmann (New York: Vintage Books, 1967), 37–38.

31. Carl Dahlhaus, *Nineteenth-Century Music,* trans. J. Bradford Robinson (Berkeley, Calif.: University of California Press, 1989), 78.

32. The thematic relationships also has been recognized by Antony Hopkins, *The Nine Symphonies of Beethoven* (Seattle: University of Washington Press, 1981), 253.

33. Richard Taruskin, "Resisting the Ninth," suggests that Brahms's hymn-like theme in the finale of his First Symphony was a "resistance" or "correction" to Beethoven's addition of voices and text in the finale of the Ninth Symphony. See also Mark Evan Bonds, *After Beethoven: Imperatives of Originality in the Symphony* (Cambridge, Mass.: Harvard University Press, 1996), 138–174.

34. Donald Francis Tovey, *Essays in Musical Analysis* (Oxford: Oxford University Press, 1935), 2:3.

CHAPTER 7

Performance Traditions

1. *The Letters of Beethoven,* ed. Emily Anderson (London: Macmillan, 1961), 3:1314–1315. See also Del Mar, *Symphonie Nr. 9 in d-moll, op. 125,* Critical Commentary.

2. Peter Stadlen, "Beethoven and the Metronome: I," *Music and Letters* 48 (1967): 330–349 concluded that the printed values are wrong. Unfortunately, Stadlen never published the second part of his study. Clive Brown, "Historical performance, metronome marks and tempo in Beethoven's symphonies," *Early Music* 19 (1991): 247–258 arrives at the same conclusion as Stadlen.

3. A faint marking at the bottom of the page of the manuscript reads *Prestissimo,* a tempo indication that was rejected. It is possible that Beethoven was thinking in terms of the quarter note, rather than the half or whole note.

4. See David B. Levy, "The Contrabass-Recitative in Beethoven's Ninth Symphony Revisited," *Historical Performance* 5 (1992): 9–18.

5. Leopold Sonnleithner, "Ad vocem: Contrabass-Recitative der 9. Symphonie von Beethoven," Leipzig *Allgemeine musikalische Zeitung,* n.s., 2 (April 6, 1864): col. 245, trans. Max Rudolf in *Beethoven Newsletter* 4 (1989): 57.

6. *The Letters of Beethoven,* ed. Emily Anderson, 3:1166–1167.

7. See Carse, *The Orchestra from Beethoven to Berlioz,* 46–63 on the sizes and proportions of orchestras throughout Europe in the first half of the nineteenth century.

8. Felix Weingartner, *Ratschläge für Aufführungen der Symphonien Beethovens* (Leipzig: Breitkopf und Härtel, 1907, rev. 1916). A second revision was issued as vol. 1 of *Ratschläge für Aufführungen klassischer Symphonien* (1928). For an English translation by Jessie Crosland based on the second revision, see *Weingartner on Music and Conducting* (New York: Dover, 1969), 177–234. Weingartner's 1926 recording of the Ninth Symphony was part of the first recording of all the Beethoven symphonies.

9. See Denis Stevens, "Why Conductors? Their Role and the Idea of Fidelity," in Joan Peyser, ed., *The Orchestra: Origins and Transformations* (New York: Scribner, 1986), 247.

10. Richard Taruskin, "Beethoven: The New Antiquity," *Opus* 3 (October 1987): 31–41.

11. David B. Levy, "*Urtext* or Performing Edition?" *Beethoven Forum* 9, no. 2 (Urbana-Champaign: University of Illinois Press, 2002), 223–232.

12. *The New Harvard Dictionary of Music,* ed. Don Randel (Cambridge, Mass.: Harvard University Press, 1986), 900.

13. Del Mar, Critical Commentary, 23.

14. See Del Mar, Critical Commentary, 14–23, and Rexroth, op. cit., 303–314.

15. Such an edition is in preparation by Dr. Beate Angelika Kraus under the auspices of the Beethoven-Haus Archiv in Bonn for eventual publication by G. Henle

Verlag as part of the *Neue Beethoven Ausgabe.* I am grateful to Dr. Kraus for her sharing of much useful information.

16.   Del Mar has communicated to me that he finds these shifted ties to be "interesting," and since they are "Ur," therefore belong in an *Urtext.*

17.   The other Beethoven symphonies, also edited by Del Mar, have been issued by Bärenreiter.

NINE NINTHS: A SELECT DISCOGRAPHY

1.   A recording made by Felix Weingartner for Columbia in 1926 is not available on CD.

2.   This recording also is available on Pearl GEMM CD 9407. The first track on this recording offers Beethoven's Eleven Viennese (Mödling) Dances, WoO 17, a set of pieces composed in 1819.

3.   The others recordings, in chronological order, were made on January 7, 1951 with the Vienna Philharmonic and Singakademie (Irmgard Seefried, Rosette Anday, Julius Patzak, Otto Edelmann, soloists), Bellaphon 689–22–005; July 29, 1951 with the Bayreuth Festival Orchestra and Chorus (Elisabeth Schwarzkopf, Elisabeth Höngen, Hans Hopf, and Otto Edelman, soloists), EMI CDH 7 69801 2; and May 30, 1953 with the Vienna Philharmonic and Singakademie (Bernadette Greevy, Rosette Anday, Anton Dermota, and Paul Schöffler, soloists), Hunt CD 532.

4.   As with Furtwängler's recordings of the Ninth, admirers of Toscanini have a choice. A live performance of February 6, 1938 is available (Vina Bovy, Kerstin Thorborg, Jan Peerce, and Ezio Pinza, soloists) on ATRA 3007. A studio recording with the NBC Symphony (RCA Gold Seal 60255–2–RG) also is available from the set of all nine Beethoven symphonies.

5.   Bernstein, in the booklet that accompanies the recording, implies that Friedrich Ludwig Jahn was the perpetrator of the story that Schiller had written a version of "An die Freude" called "An die Freiheit." Bernstein's attribution is unsubstantiated.

Bibliography

ARTICLES, BOOKS, AND SCORES

Agawu, V. Kofi. *Playing with Signs.* Princeton: Princeton University Press, 1991.

Baensch, Ono. "Die Aachener Abschrift der neunten Symphonie." *Neue Beethoven Jahrbuch* 5 (1933): 7–20.

——. *Aufbau und Sinn des Chorfinales in Beethovens neunter Symphonie.* Berlin: W. de Gruyter, 1930.

Bartha, Dénes. "On Beethoven's Thematic Structure." *The Creative World of Beethoven,* 257–276. New York: Norton, 1970.

The Letters of Beethoven. Ed. and trans. Emily Anderson. 3 vols. London: Macmillan, 1961.

Ludwig van Beethovens Konversationshefte. Vol. 1. Eds. Karl-Heinz Köhler and Grita Herre. Leipzig: VEB Deutscher Verlag für Musik, 1972.

Ludwig van Beethovens Konversationshefte. Vol. 5. Eds. Karl-Heinz Köhler, Grita Herre, and Peter Potschner. Leipzig: VEB Deutscher Verlag für Musik, 1970.

Ludwig van Beethovens Konversationshefte. Vol. 6. Eds. Karl-Heinz Köhler and Grita Herre. Leipzig: VEB Deutscher Verlag für Musik, 1974.

Ludwig van Beethovens Konversationshefte. Vol. 8. Eds. Karl-Heinz Köhler and Grita Herre. Leipzig: VEB Deutscher Verlag für Musik, 1981.

Beethoven, Ludwig van. *Sinfonie Nr. 9 d-Moll, op. 125.* Introduction and analysis by Dieter Rexroth. Mainz: Goldmann-Schott, 1979.

——. *Symphonie Nr. 9 in d-moll = Symphony No. 9 in D minor, op. 125.* Ed. and with Critical Commentary by Jonathan Del Mar. Kassel: Bärenreiter, 1996.

Berghahn, Klaus, ed. *Briefwechsel zwischen Schiller und Körner.* Munich: Winkler-Verlag, 1973.

Berlioz, Hector. *Evenings with the Orchestra.* Trans. and ed. Jacques Barzun. Chicago: University of Chicago Press, 1973.

——. *Memoirs.* Trans. and ed. David Cairns. New York: Knopf, 1975.

Biba, Otto. "Zur Uraufführung von Beethovens 9. Symphonie. *Münchener Beethoven-Studien,* 57–69. München-Salzburg: Katzbichler, 1992.

Bonds, Mark Evan. *After Beethoven: Imperatives of Originality in the Symphony.* Cambridge, Mass.: Harvard University Press, 1996.

Brandenburg, Sieghard. "Die Skizzen zur Neunten Symphonie." *Zu Beethoven.* Vol. 2, 88–129. Berlin, 1984.

Brown, Clive. "Historical performance, metronome marks and tempo in Beethoven's symphonies." *Early Music* 19 (1991): 247–258.

Buch, Esteban. *Beethoven's Ninth: A Political History.* Trans. Richard Miller. Chicago: University of Chicago Press, 2003.

Burgess, Anthony. *A Clockwork Orange.* New York: Norton, 1963.

Burnham, Scott. "Our Sublime Ninth." *Beethoven Forum* 5 (1996): 155–163.

Carse, Adam. *The Orchestra from Beethoven to Berlioz.* New York: Broude Brothers, 1949.

——. "The Choral Symphony in London." *Music and Letters* 32 (1951): 247–258.

Clark, Caryl. "Forging Identity: Beethoven's 'Ode' as European Anthem," *Critical Inquiry* 23 (1997), pp. 789–807.

Cohn, Richard L. "The Dramatization of Hypermetic Conflicts in the Scherzo of Beethoven's Ninth Symphony." *19th Century Music* 15 (1992): 188–206.

Comini, Alessandra. *The Changing Image of Beethoven.* New York: Rizzoli, 1987.

Cook, Nicholas. *Beethoven: Symphony No. 9.* Cambridge: Cambridge University Press, 1993.

Cooper, Barry. *World Premiere: Beethoven Symphony No. 10.* London Symphony Orchestra, Wyn Morris, conductor. MCA Classics, MCAD-6269 (1988).

——. "Newly Identified Sketches for Beethoven's Tenth Symphony." *Music and Letters* 66 (1985): 9–18.

——. "The First Movement of Beethoven's Tenth Symphony: A Realization." *Beethoven Newsletter* 3 (1988): 27.

Cooper, Martin. *Beethoven: The Last Decade.* Oxford: Oxford University Press, 1985.

Dalhaus, Carl. *Nineteenth-Century Music.* Trans. J. Bradford Robinson. Berkeley, Calif.: University of California Press, 1989.

Eichhorn, Andreas. *Beethovens Neunte Symphonie: die Geschichte ihrer Aufführung und Rezeption.* Kassel: Bärenreiter, 1993.

Foster, Myles Birkett. *The History of the Philharmonic Society: 1813–1912.* London: John Lane, The Bodley Head, 1912.

Gauntlett, Henry John. "Beethoven and the Philharmonic Society." *The Musical World* 5 (April 28, 1837): 97–103.

Griepenkerl, Wolfgang Robert. *Das Musikfest oder die Beethovener.* Leipzig: Otto Wigand, 1838.

Grove, George. *Beethoven and his Nine Symphonies.* 3rd ed. London: Novello, Ewer, and Co., 1898.

Hanson, Alice M. *Musical Life in Biedermeier Vienna.* Cambridge: Cambridge University Press, 1985.

Hinton, Stephen. "Not Which Tones? The Crux of Beethoven's Ninth." *19th Century Music* 22 (1998): 61–77.

Hopkins, Antony. *The Nine Symphonies of Beethoven.* Seattle: University of Washington Press, 1981.

Johnson, Douglas. "Beethoven Scholars and Beethoven Sketches." *19th Century Music* 2 (1978): 3–17.

Johnson, Douglas, Alan Tyson, and Robert Winter. *The Beethoven Sketchbooks.* Berkeley: University of California Press, 1985.

Kallick, Jenny L. *A Study of the Advanced Sketches and Full Score Autograph for the First Movement of Beethoven's Ninth Symphony, Opus 125.* Ann Arbor: UMI, 1987.

Kann, Robert A. *A Study in Austrian Intellectual History.* New York: Frederick A. Praeger, 1960.

Kelly, Thomas Forrest. *First Nights: Five Musical Premieres.* New Haven: Yale University Press, 2000.

Kerman, Joseph: "Viewpoint: Sketch Studies." *19th Century Music* 6 (1982): 174–180.

———. *The Beethoven Quartets.* New York: Knopf, 1966.

Kerman, Joseph and Alan Tyson. *The New Grove Beethoven.* New York: Norton, 1983.

Kinderman, William. *Beethoven's Compositional Process.* Lincoln, Neb.: University of Nebraska Press, 1991.

———. "Beethoven's Symbol for the Deity in the *Missa Solemnis* and the Ninth Symphony." *19th Century Music* 9 (1985): 102–118.

Kinsky, Georg. *Das Werk Beethovens. Thematisch-bibliographischen Verzeichnis seiner sämtlichen vollendeten Kompositionen.* Completed and ed. Hans Halm. Munich and Duisberg: G. Henle, 1955.

Kirby, Frank E. "Beethoven and the 'Geselliges Lied.'" *Music and Letters* 47 (1966): 116–125.

Knight, Frida. *Beethoven and the Age of Revolution.* New York: International Publishers, 1974.

Kojima, Shin Augustinus. "Die Uraufführung der Neunten Sinfonie Beethovens—einige neue Tatsachen." *Bericht über den Internationalen Musikwissenschaftlichen Kongress Bayreuth 1981,* 390–398. Kassel: Bärenreiter, 1984.

Koury, Daniel J. *Orchestral Performance Practices in the Nineteenth Century.* Ann Arbor, UMI, 1981.

Kramer, Lawrence. "The Harem Threshold: Turkish Music and Greek Lore in Beethoven's 'Ode to Joy.'" *19th Century Music* 22 (1998): 78–90.

Kropfinger, Klaus. *Wagner and Beethoven.* Trans. Peter Palmer. Cambridge: Cambridge University Press, 1991.

Kunze, Stefan, ed. *Ludwig van Beethoven. Die Werke im Spiegel seiner Zeit. Gesammelte Konzertberichte und Rezensionen bis 1830.* Laaber: Laaber-Verlag, 1987.

Levy, David B. "The Contrabass Recitative in Beethoven's Ninth Symphony Revisited." *Historical Performance* 5 (1992): 9–18.

———. *Early Performances of Beethoven's Ninth Symphony: A Documentary Study of Five Cities.* (Ph.D. diss. University of Rochester, 1980).

———. "Wolfgang Robert Griepenkerl and Beethoven's Ninth Symphony." In

Jerald C. Graue, ed., *Essays on Music for Charles Warren Fox*, 103–113. Rochester, N.Y.: Eastman School of Music Press, 1979.

Livingstone, Ernest F. "Das Formproblem des 4. Satzes in Beethovens 9. Symphonie." *Bericht über den Internationalen Musikwissenschaftlichen Kongress Bonn 1970.* Kassel: Bärenreiter, 1971: 491–494.

Longyear, Rey M. *Schiller and Music.* Chapel Hill, N.C.: University of North Carolina Press, n.d.

Markevitch, Igor. *Die Sinfonien von Ludwig van Beethoven.* Leipzig: C. F. Peters, 1983.

Macartney, C. A. *The Hapsburg Empire: 1790–1918.* New York: Macmillan, 1969.

McClary, Susan. *Feminine Endings: Music, Gender, and Sexuality.* Minneapolis: University of Minnesota Press, 1991.

Morrow, Mary Sue. *Concert Life in Haydn's Vienna: Aspects of a Developing Musical and Social Institution.* New York: Pendragon Press, 1989.

Nef, Karl. *Die Neun Sinfonien Beethovens.* Leipzig: Breitkopf und Härtel, 1928.

Nietzsche, Friedrich. *The Birth of Tragedy.* Trans. Walter Kaufmann. New York: Vintage Books, 1967.

——. *Human All-too-Human.* Trans. Oscar Levy. New York: Macmillan: 1924.

Nottebohm. *Ein Skizzenbuch von Beethoven.* Leipzig: Breitkopf und Härtel, 1865.

——. *Beethoveniana.* Leipzig and Winterthur: C. F. Peters. 1872.

——. *Ein Skizzenbuch von Beethoven aus dem Jahre 1803.* Leipzig: Breitkopf und Härtel, 1880.

——. *Zweite Beethoveniana.* Leipzig: C. F. Peters, 1887.

Ortlepp, Ernst, ed. *Großes Instrumental-und Vokal-Concert*, Vol. 11. Stuttgart: F. H. Kohler, 1841.

Parsons, James. *Ode to the Ninth: The Poetic and Musical Tradition Behind the Finale of Beethoven's "Choral Symphony."* Ph.D. diss., University of North Texas, 1992.

——. " 'Deine Zauber binden wieder': Beethoven, Schiller, and the Joyous Reconciliation of Opposites." *Beethoven Forum* 9, no. 1 (2002): 1–53.

Peyser, Joan, ed. *The Orchestra: Origins and Transformations.* New York: Scribner, 1986.

Ratner, Leonard G. *Classic Music: Expression, Form, and Style.* New York: Schirmer Books, 1980.

Rice, Eric. "Representations of Janissary Music (Mehter) as Musical Exoticism in Western Compositions, 1670–1824," *Journal of Musicological Research* 19 (1999), pp. 41–88.

Rosen, Charles. *The Classical Style.* New York: Viking, 1972.

Rochlitz, Friedrich. *Fur Freunde der Tonkunst.* Leipzig: Breitkopf und Härtel, 1824.

Rudolf, Max. "Beethoven's 'An die Freude' and Two Mysterious Footnotes." *Beethoven Newsletter* 5 (1990): 29–33.

Sanders, Ernest. "Form and Content in the Finale of Beethoven's Ninth Symphony." *Musical Quarterly* 50 (1964): 59–76.

Sanders, Ernest H. "The Sonata-Form Finale of Beethoven's Ninth Symphony. *19th Century Music* 22 (1998): 54–60.

Schenker, Heinrich. *Beethoven's Ninth Symphony.* Trans. and ed. John Rothgeb. New Haven: Yale University Press, 1992.

Schiller, Friedrich. *On the Aesthetic Education of Man.* Trans. Reginald Snell. London: Routledge and Kegan Paul, 1954.

Schindler, Anton Felix. *Beethoven as I Knew Him.* Trans. Constance S. Jolly. Ed. Donald W. MacArdle. London: Faber and Faber, 1966.

Shirakawa, Sam H. *The Devil's Music Master.* Oxford: Oxford University Press, 1992.

Slonimsky, Nicholas. *Lexicon of Musical Invective.* Seattle: University of Washington Press.

Solie, Ruth A. "Beethoven as Secular Humanist: Ideology and the Ninth Symphony in Nineteenth-Century Criticism." In *Explorations in Music, the Arts, and Ideas,* 1–42. Stuyvesant, N.Y., 1988.

——. "What Do Feminists Want? A Reply to Pieter van den Toorn." *Journal of Musicology* 9 (1991): 399–410.

Solomon, Maynard. *Beethoven.* New York: Schirmer Books, 1977.

——. *Beethoven Essays.* Cambridge, Mass.: Harvard University Press, 1988.

——. "Beethoven's Ninth Symphony: The Sense of an Ending." *Critical Inquiry* 17 (1991): 289–305.

——. "On Beethoven's Creative Process: A Two-part Invention." *Music and Letters* 61 (1980): 272–283.

Sonnleithner, Leopold. "Ad vocem: Contrabass-Recitative der 9. Symphonie von Beethoven." *Allgemeine musikalische Zeitung,* n.s. 2 (1864): 245–246.

Stadlen, Peter. "Beethoven and the Metronome: I." *Music and Letters* 48 (1967): 330–349.

Strunk, Oliver. *Source Readings in Music History: The Romantic Era.* New York: Norton, 1965.

Taruskin, Richard. "Resisting the Ninth." *19th Century Music* 12 (1989): 241–256.

——. "Beethoven: The New Antiquity." *Opus* (October 1987), 31–63.

Thayer, Alexander Wheelock. *Thayer's Life of Beethoven.* Rev. ed. Elliot Forbes. Princeton: Princeton University Press, 1967.

Thym, Jurgen. "The Instrumental Recitative in Beethoven's Compositions." In Jerald C. Graue, ed. *Essays on Music for Charles Warren Fox,* 230–240. Rochester, N.Y.: Eastman School of Music Press, 1979.

van den Toorn, Pieter C. "Politics, Feminism, and Contemporary Music Theory." *Journal of Musicology* 9 (1991): 275–299.

Tovey, Donald Francis, *Essays in Musical Analysis.* Vols. 1 and 2. Oxford: Oxford University Press, 1935.

Treitler, Leo. "History, Criticism, and Beethoven's Ninth Symphony." In *Music and the Historical Imagination,* 19–45. Cambridge, Mass.: Harvard University Press, 1989.

Tusa, Michael Charles. "Noch einmal: Form and Content in the Finale of Beethoven's Ninth Symphony." *Beethoven Forum* 7 (1999): 113–137.

Williams, Ralph Vaughan. *Some Thoughts on Beethoven's Choral Symphony.* Oxford: Oxford University Press, 1953.

Richard Wagner's Prose Works. Ed. and trans. William Ashton Ellis. London: Kegan Paul, 1892.

Wallace, Robin. *Beethoven's Critics.* Cambridge: Cambridge University Press, 1986.

Webster, James. "The Form of the Finale of Beethoven's Ninth Symphony." *Beethoven Forum* 1 (1991): 25–62.

Weigand, Hermann J. "Schiller: Transfiguration of a Titan." In A. Leslie Willson, ed. *A Schiller Symposium,* 101–102. Austin, Tex., 1960.

Weingartner, Felix. *Ratschläge für Aufführungen der Symphonien Beethovens.* Leipzig: Breitkopf und Härtel, 1907. Rev. ed. 1916.

Willetts, Pamela J. *Beethoven and England.* Edinburgh: T. & A. Constable, Ltd., 1970.

Winter, Robert. "The Sketches for the 'Ode to Joy.'" In Robert Winter and Bruce Carr eds. *Beethoven, Performers, and Critics,* 176–214. Detroit, 1977.

——. "Of Realizations, Completions, Restorations and Reconstructions: From Bach's *The Art of Fugue* to Beethoven's Tenth Symphony." *Journal of the Royal Musical Association* 116 (1991): 96–126.

——. "Noch einmal: Wo sind Beethovens Skizzen zur zehnten Symphonie?" *Beethoven Jahrbuch* 9 (1973/1977): 536–537.

——. *Ludwig van Beethoven: Symphony No. 9.* Computer software. The Voyager Company. Santa Monica, Calif. 1991.

NINETEENTH-CENTURY PERIODICALS AND NEWSPAPERS

Caecilia, eine Zeitschrift für die musikalische Welt. Mainz, 1824–1848.

Allgemeine musikalische Zeitung. Leipzig, 1798–1848.

The Harmonicon. London, 1823–1833.

The Quarterly Musical Magazine and Review. London, 1818–1828.

Revue musicale. Paris, 1827–1835.

Revue et Gazette musicale. Paris, 1827–1835.

The Times. London, 1785–.

The Musical World. London, 1836–1891.

Wiener Allgemeine musikalische Zeitung mit besonderer Rücksicht auf den österreichischen Kaiserstaat. Vienna, 1817–1824.

Wiener Theater-Zeitung. Vienna, 1806–1860.

Index